WITHDRAWN

SHIP OF FATE

INTERSECTIONS

Asian and Pacific American Transcultural Studies

RUSSELL C. LEONG
DAVID K. YOO
Series Editors

SHIP OF FATE

Memoir of a Vietnamese Repatriate

Trần Đình Trụ

Translated by Bac Hoai Tran and Jana K. Lipman

University of Hawai'i Press
Honolulu

In association with
UCLA Asian American Studies Center

22 21 20 19 18 17   6 5 4 3 2 1

Library of Congress Cataloging-in-Publication Data

Names: Trần, Đình Trụ, author. | Tran, Hoai Bac,
    translator. | Lipman, Jana K., translator.
Title: Ship of fate : memoir of a Vietnamese repatriate / Trần Đình Trụ ;
    translated by Bac Hoai Tran and Jana K. Lipman.
Other titles: Việt Nam Thương Tín: Con Tàu Định Mệnh. English |
    Intersections (Honolulu, Hawaii)
Description: Honolulu : University of Hawai'i Press in association with UCLA
    Asian American Studies Center, [2017] | Series: Intersections | Includes
    bibliographical references.
Identifiers: LCCN 2016046896| ISBN 9780824867171 (cloth ; alk. paper) | ISBN
    9780824872496 (pbk. ; alk. paper)
Subjects: LCSH: Vietnam War, 1961–1975—Personal narratives, Vietnamese. |
    Việt Nam Thương Tín (Ship) | Political refugees—Guam. | Political
    Prisoners—Vietnam. | Trần, Đình Trụ
Classification: LCC DS559.5 .T713 2017 | DDC 305.9/06914092 [B] —dc23 LC record available
at https://lccn.loc.gov/2016046896

CONTENTS

Map 1. This map illustrates Trụ's naval training and his early journeys between Vietnam, Japan, the Philippines, and Guam, and it shows the distance of his final trans-Pacific voyage from Guam to Vietnam. Map designed by Bill Nelson.

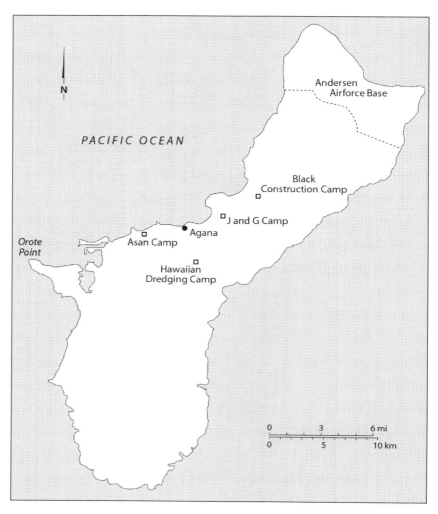

PACIFIC OCEAN

N

Andersen
Airforce Base

Black
Construction Camp

J and G Camp

Agana

Asan Camp

Orote
Point

Hawaiian
Dredging Camp

0   3   6 mi
0   5   10 km

Map 2. This map of Guam illustrates the Vietnamese refugee camps on the island in 1975.
Map designed by Bill Nelson.

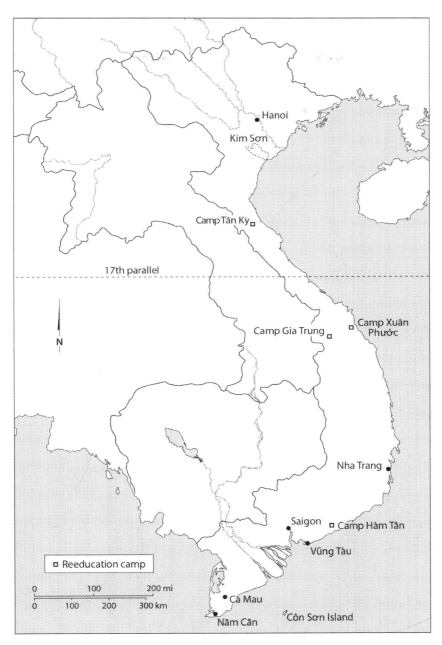

Map 3. This map of Vietnam includes both Trụ's hometown and his postings before 1975, and it also locates the position of the "reeducation camps" where he was interned after 1975. Map designed by Bill Nelson.

Introduction

JANA K. LIPMAN

In April 1975, Trần Đình Trụ, along with more than 120,000 Vietnamese, escaped Saigon during the last days of the U.S. war in Vietnam. In popular American memory, "the fall of Saigon" is punctuated by the scene of U.S. helicopters on rooftops, evacuating Americans and former Vietnamese allies.[1] What is less well-known is that the U.S. military brought these Vietnamese to refugee camps on Guam, a small U.S. island territory in the Pacific. After several weeks of "processing," the vast majority settled in the United States. However, unlike most of his compatriots, Trụ did not want to continue on to the United States. His wife and children had not been able to escape as he had. He wanted to return to his family in Vietnam.

Trụ's memoir is a remarkable testament to the ambiguities, uncertainties, contingencies, and chaos at the end of a war. And Trụ was not alone. On Guam, more than fifteen hundred Vietnamese repatriates decided that they did not want to relocate to the United States, and over the course of five months they protested, engaged in hunger strikes, and even burned down barracks to achieve the goal of repatriation. Their protests reached the U.S. government, Sadruddin Aga Khan, then serving as United Nations High Commissioner for Refugees (UNHCR), the Guamanian government, and the new revolutionary Vietnamese government—all which had to attend to this unexpected group of Vietnamese, who defied expectations on all sides.

When the United States eventually relented and offered the repatriates the *Việt Nam Thương Tín,* a large merchant ship on which they could return, the repatriates selected Trụ as their captain. He took on this responsibility with grace, bravery, and skill. Trụ prepared the ship and crew and steered them back to Vietnam, a country that viewed them all, and especially Trụ, with suspicion and distrust. After his return, Trụ suffered in "reeducation camps," better recognized as prison camps, for thirteen years. In 1991, Trụ migrated to the United States through the Humanitarian Operation (HO) program, which facilitated the immigration of former reeducation camp prisoners and their families directly to the United States.

1

This memoir joins a growing body of work by Vietnamese-American authors, who bring their stories of war and migration to a U.S. audience. After more than a generation of American authors and filmmakers defining the war in Vietnam as an American war and an American tragedy, Vietnamese-American writers challenge these U.S.-centric stories and reveal far more complicated political landscapes, and ones where American soldiers, politicians, and protesters remain in the background.[2] Early collections of oral histories, such as James M. Freeman's *Hearts of Sorrow: Vietnamese American Lives* and Mary Terrell Cargill and Jade Quang Huynh's *Voices of Vietnamese Boat People,* provided searing snapshots of South Vietnamese life before and after the war.[3] There is also a growing body of literature by 1.5-generation Vietnamese Americans, which deals with generational divides and coming of age in the United States.[4] Finally, fiction by Vietnamese-American authors allows for even more speculation about loyalties, trust, and betrayal in the aftermath of the U.S. war in Vietnam.[5]

Trụ's memoir complements these earlier works, and yet it provides a startling new story.[6] In Trụ's memoir, there are multiple reversals; we learn little about the war itself, Guam takes center stage, and Vietnamese return to Vietnam. Many of Trụ's memories illuminate the trajectory of thousands of Vietnamese men and women, including his childhood in northern Vietnam, his family's migration to Saigon after 1954, his experiences in the South Vietnamese military, the 1975 evacuation, and his imprisonment in Vietnam's postwar reeducation camps. However, Trụ's experiences were also decidedly singular: his steadfast desire to return to Vietnam, his focus on the refugee camp politics in Guam, and his leadership as the ship captain returning the repatriates to Vietnam in October 1975.

First, Trụ's memoir demonstrates the instability of a simplistic analysis of the Cold War. While Trụ is consistent in his anticommunism and narrates his decision to repatriate as an act of anticommunism, he also insists on returning to Vietnam, a choice many would see as unfathomable after 1975. Throughout the memoir, he freely criticizes the South Vietnamese government, and he is even able to recognize the humanity in his communist interrogators and prison guards. More than once, Trụ articulates that all Vietnamese are Vietnamese. As such, the memoir elicits a powerful sense of nationalism, but one that is not defined solely by ideology or geography. Instead, Trụ's memoir reveals moments of contingency, human encounter, and ambiguity in Cold War Vietnam.

Second, Trụ provides a unique account of Guam, a U.S. territory in the Pacific and a tangible legacy of U.S. empire. Trụ's naval training takes him to Guam multiple times before 1975, and these missions highlight Guam's role as a key U.S.

naval station, which, along with U.S. military bases in Japan, South Korea, and the Philippines, defined U.S. military power in the Pacific after World War II. And even though Trụ does not use the language of empire, his language implicitly recognizes Guam's nebulous, almost limbo status. At times, he refers to being in Guam as being in the United States, but at other times he distinguishes between Guam and the "mainland United States," and once he even refers to Guam as autonomous. The repatriates' decision to stay in Guam and *not* go on to the continental United States underscores Guam's existence as an island *in between* that is not quite part of the United States. The memoir therefore demonstrates the convergence of a longer history of U.S. empire in the Pacific and the end of the U.S. war in Vietnam.

Finally, Trụ's story reveals the brutality and hardships of postwar Vietnam, particularly for families tied to the South Vietnamese government and the United States. This testimony demonstrates the violence and arbitrary cruelty of postwar Vietnam and the history of reeducation camps, or forced labor camps, which remain relatively unknown outside Vietnamese diasporic communities.

Translation and Memoirs

Trụ began to write his memoir in 1991 following his arrival in the United States. He wrote in stolen hours between working the night shift in a convenience store and helping his children adjust to life in the United States. The memoir reflects his drive to document his story in his own words and get it down on paper as soon as he was able to do so. He then published two thousand copies in Vietnamese and distributed it to bookstores and readers in the overseas Vietnamese community. He also donated copies to the Library of Congress.

Almost twenty years later, I was researching the history of refugee camps in the United States, and I learned about the presence of the makeshift refugee camps constructed on Guam. I found documents about the Vietnamese repatriates, a cohort at its height of over two thousand individuals who had changed their minds and did not want to resettle in the United States. I was intrigued by the striking photos in the U.S. military reports, including images of hunger strikes, banners, and a portrait of Hồ Chí Minh, but I was skeptical that I would find enough material to write a full-fledged scholarly article.[7] Then, during my visit to the Library of Congress in Washington, DC, I came across Trụ's *Việt Nam Thương Tín: Con tàu định mệnh*. It was a four hundred-page memoir in Vietnamese by the Vietnamese ship captain of the *Việt Nam Thương Tín*, the ship that had returned to Vietnam with the repatriates. I had to know what it said.

That began the more-than-five-year process that led to this book, *The Ship of Fate: A Memoir of a Vietnamese Repatriate*. My co-translator, Bac Hoai Tran, and I spent countless hours translating Trần Đình Trụ's memoir and, in doing so, learned a great deal of Trụ's perseverance, philosophy, and unusual life trajectory. This project has been complicated by multiple methodological questions—the greatest being that I do not read or speak Vietnamese. Given my limited, elementary Vietnamese working on this memoir may have been an act of hubris; however, it has been a rewarding and time-intensive experience, driven by my dedication to make it available to a broader audience. Bac and I worked together in countless Skype conversations translating the memoir word for word, revising the English translation, reading it back against the original, and working with Trụ to ensure the authenticity of its tone and voice. As a result, English-language readers can gain access to this memoir for the first time.

This memoir has survived multiple iterations and, like most memoirs, reflects more than one moment in time. When Trụ began writing it, his purpose was to share his story with a Vietnamese community that only knew of the *Việt Nam Thương Tín* as an almost unknowable specter, lying in the shadows of the 1975 evacuation. His story defied the dominant narrative of Vietnamese passage and celebratory resettlement in the United States. In U.S. immigration history, Vietnamese migrants are generally portrayed as individuals who fled communism and unquestioningly came to the United States.[8] Trụ's decision to return to Vietnam turned this common wisdom on its head. Why would someone return to Vietnam after 1975? Perhaps recognizing the skepticism and even distrust within the Vietnamese-American community, as well as the singularity of his story, Trụ took his first opportunity to explain his motivations and tell his dramatic story himself.

However, readers should be aware that this was not the first time that Trụ had written his life experiences down on paper. In fact, a core activity of Vietnamese reeducation camps was forcing political prisoners to write their life histories over and over again in a rote manner. The aim was repetition and "confessions" of counterrevolutionary ideology. In this setting, Trụ's writing would have repeated what his interrogators wanted to hear. His testimonies would have been laced with omissions as well as truths and possibly lies. Yet these forced confessions linger in the background as an eerie, if violent precursor to this book. In this memoir, Trụ embraces the opportunity to tell his story the way he wants it to be remembered, and he does so with a zealous condemnation of the communist government in Vietnam. This anticommunism reflects his contemporary politics, and it also explains his decision to a diasporic Vietnamese a community that might have questioned his decision as ideologically suspect.

Almost two decades later, Bac and I translated this book from Vietnamese to English, and we worked with Trụ, now an elderly man just over eighty, who was eager for his legacy and experiences to reach a broader public. Trụ's memoir ends abruptly in 1991, when he arrived in California. Today, Trụ wants readers to know that he is thankful for the opportunities available to his children in the United States.

The memoir's multiple publications and permutations also underscore the instability of the memoir form itself. And one should also be wary of the objectivity of the historian, myself included. As an American born in the 1970s, I first learned of the U.S. war in Vietnam from my parents, who both opposed the U.S. military actions in Vietnam and participated in antiwar protests. Then in 1994, I took my first major overseas trip to Vietnam, studying Vietnamese and learning to navigate Saigon by bicycle, just as the United States and Vietnam were renewing their diplomatic relationship. It was in Saigon, and not Orange County or northern Virginia, where I first met Vietnamese Americans of multiple political perspectives; however, I have not been back to Vietnam in over twenty years. These memories and experiences also inform this introduction and my intellectual work at large. Like all memoirs, Tru's book includes silences, erasures, and elisions, but I am also attentive to the silences, erasures, and elisions in my own scholarship as well.

In this book, Trụ's voice remains calm, and almost gentle, throughout the memoir; he tells a story of great loss, great skill, and great decision at a time of unknowns. Throughout it all, his integrity and sense of dignity remain intact. His voice is even as he remembers a landscape defined by chaos and uncertainty. Trụ narrates his story in a matter-of-fact way, even the moments of greatest conflict such as the protests on Guam or his time in the prison camps. In some instances, this calm demeanor seems to glide over moments of pain and suffering or serves to smooth over memories he does not want to resurface. The tone also suggests that his experiences were logical, expected, and unsurprising, when, in fact, his decision to return and his time in Guam were anything but routine.

The memoir provides a window on Trụ's individual experiences, but he lets us in only so far. Clearly, some memories and experiences remain too painful or private for him to share. For example, his wife remains an almost ghostlike figure throughout the book. On one level, the memoir reads as a love story. Trụ repeatedly states that his great love for his wife was the burning reason he had to return to Vietnam. And we believe him. Yet at the same time, we learn little about this woman, not even her name, and Trụ keeps the contours and specificity of their relationship close to his heart and does not share it with us. At his core, he seems a private man.

His memoir pushes us as readers to consider how we might respond if we were suddenly separated from all our loved ones or thrust into the midst of a political crisis in which we imagined never seeing our families again. The answers are not simple or straightforward, and Trụ's memoir forces us to see the loss, ambiguities, and uncertainties that emerge at the end of war.

As in any translation, Bac and I had to make choices as we worked to make Trụ's memoir accessible to an English-reading audience. First, in the name of clarity for an English-language readership, we opted to use the Anglicized versions of common Vietnamese names and places, for example, Vietnam rather than Viet Nam, Hanoi, rather than Ha Noi, Saigon, rather than Sai Gon.

Second, in order to respect people's privacy, in most cases, we have used pseudonyms for the Vietnamese individuals mentioned in this memoir. Trụ is writing about events more than forty years in the past, and he has been in touch with relatively few of these men since then. Given the circulation of the English translation to a wider audience, Trụ, Bac, and I did not want to call attention to anyone who might not want their story to be publicized. Moreover, Trụ attributes long speeches and dialogue to a large number of people, and, with the passage of decades, the accuracy of these words reflects the accuracy of his memory, far from a verbatim transcript. The memoir represents Trụ's memory of the history of these events, and Trụ's alone.

Third, like most geopolitical names and encounters, the names here have political overtones and histories. Even the name "Vietnam" is contested, and before 1976 there was no single political nation-state called "Vietnam." During the French colonial era, the provinces of Tonkin (North), Annam (Central), and Cochin China (South) were the political names of distinct regions. During the French colonial war, the Democratic Republic of Vietnam (DRV) in the North and the Associated State of Vietnam (ASV) in the South were the key entities, and after 1954, the DRV continued to control the North, while the South was dubbed the Republic of Vietnam (RVN) in 1955. After the collapse of the RVN government in April 1975, the Provisional Revolutionary Government (PRG), which was the official state apparatus of the National Liberation Front (NLF), governed South Vietnam for just over a year. During this time, the country was effectively under the control of the DRV, and 1975 is the year that both Americans and Vietnamese cite as the point at which South Vietnam ceased to exist as an independent state. The two regions were formally reunified in 1976, and the country is now formally known as the Socialist Republic of Vietnam.[9]

Moreover, the terms "North Vietnam," "North Vietnamese," "South Vietnam," and "South Vietnamese" are also unstable and not as straightforward as they seem. In much of the literature, "South Vietnamese" is used as shorthand for individuals with an anticommunist ideology and a pro-American affiliation. In fact, the majority of the NLF supporters who fought against the RVN government and the U.S. military were also from towns and villages in South Vietnam. The historian Jessica Chapman has also detailed the extensive politico-religious groups in South Vietnam that challenged the RVN government but did not easily fit into a Cold War binary. Men and women who lived in South Vietnam had a range of political perspectives, from ardent anticommunists to militant communists, noncommunist nationalists, and individuals who vacillated, depending on the changing nature of the war.[10] As a result, the term "South Vietnamese" often too quickly elides a more complicated and contested political landscape, assuming an affiliation with the RVN, and thus erasing the very real political and military battle fought below the 17th parallel. Moreover, Trụ is originally from northern Vietnam, as many Catholic Southerners are, again upsetting the simplistic equation of region and ideology.

For the purposes of this memoir, Trụ (and Bac and I) generally refer to "North Vietnam" or the "North" and "South Vietnam" or the "South" as two separate governments and countries, but we also use the word "Vietnam" as a singular place when Trụ does so. We also refer to Trụ's childhood home in northern Vietnam (rather than the colonial term Tonkin). Trụ (and we) also consider the RVN to be synonymous with the South Vietnamese government and military, as is common usage. When we refer to northern Vietnam or southern Vietnam, it is to distinguish the regional identity from the government entities.

Finally, Trụ repeatedly uses the colloquial acronym VC or Việt Cộng (Vietnamese Communist). Coined by Ngô Đình Diệm in his 1955–1956 "Denounce the Communists Campaign," VC became an epithet aimed at Diệm's enemies in South Vietnam.[11] U.S. civilian and military personnel soon adopted VC, and, in American vocabulary, it came to encompass any Vietnamese who was fighting against the RVN government and the U.S. military. And sometimes American soldiers labeled all Vietnamese VC in a racist conflation that saw all Vietnamese as the enemy.[12] VC is almost always used pejoratively, and it ignores the coalition nature of the southern NLF, which initially included both communists and noncommunists. However, in the memoir, Trụ uses VC liberally; in particular, he uses it to label both suspected communists in South Vietnam and all the North Vietnamese interrogators and prison guards that he confronts. Trụ's usage of VC was representative of how anticommunist-identified Vietnamese would have deployed the term during and after the war.[13]

Trụ's Childhood: Catholic Vietnam, the Việt Minh, and the French War

Trụ was born in 1935 in a small provincial village in Ninh Bình Province, in northern Vietnam. He opens his story with idyllic memories of a pastoral childhood marked by the rhythms and architecture of the Catholic Church. Trụ records no memories of World War II, the Japanese occupation, or the 1944–1945 famine in northern Vietnam that resulted in the death of more than a million people. His mother dies when he is just ten years old, aligning it with the year of the famine, and yet Trụ does not record whether she died of starvation, childbirth, or another cause or illness. As a child, he is naturally more attuned to his loss and grief than he is to the historical circumstances of his mother's death.

The Red River Delta, where Trụ spent his childhood, was the center of Vietnamese Catholicism. Vietnamese Catholics always comprised a minority religious group, accounting for 6 to 7 percent of the population. According to the historian Charles Keith, by the late nineteenth century, Vietnam had approximately 700,000 Catholics, and by the 1930s, this population had surpassed one million. During this period, like Trụ and his family, 75 percent of Vietnamese Catholics lived in northern Vietnam.[14] Trụ notes the dominant presence of the Phát Diệm Cathedral, which was built in the nineteenth century and was a popular pilgrimage site.[15] Rooted in the Catholic tradition, Trụ's faith and spiritual commitment are introduced as core elements of his personhood and he repeatedly turned to this value system as he experienced traumatic events throughout his adult life.

Trụ's life coincided with the great upheavals in Vietnamese nationalism and civil war. France was the dominant European colonial power in the late nineteenth century, seeking access to wealth, trade, and commodities in Southeast Asia along with international prestige as a great power. In 1867, France governed southern Vietnam, or Cochin China, and it gained indirect control over northern Vietnam as the nineteenth century progressed. Anticolonial resistance emerged among the peasants and the intellectual classes at the turn of the century. The young man who became Hồ Chí Minh left Vietnam in 1911, worked at sea on French ships, traveling through multiple colonial and metropolitan ports. On his return to France, he became a cofounder of the French Communist Party and the Indochinese Communist Party, studying extensively in the Soviet Union and China; however, he remained relatively unknown within Vietnam. With the Japanese attack on Pearl Harbor and the outbreak of World War II in Southeast Asia, Hồ Chí Minh returned to the borderlands between China and northern Vietnam. There, he founded the Việt Minh, an anticolonial coalition and armed guerrilla force that fought against the Japanese occupation and the return of French colonialism.[16]

After the defeat of the Axis powers, Hồ Chí Minh seized the moment. On September 2, 1945, he declared Vietnam's independence. He embraced the soaring language of the Declaration of Independence and the French Revolution as he spoke to an audience of hundreds of thousands of Vietnamese in Hanoi. This was called the August Revolution.

Trụ's first political memory was of the Việt Minh and their romantic and heroic parades and revolutionary banners. Even if he did not know the history of the Việt Minh, Hồ Chí Minh, or French colonialism, he recognized that they were reshaping his village life. Trụ witnessed a local rally as a young boy, and his memories reflect both his boyhood wonder and his awe of military power as well as the optimism and nationalism the Việt Minh generated in the aftermath of the war.

The French did not recognize Vietnam's independence; instead, France reclaimed its colonial possessions, thus beginning the First Indochinese War or the "French War" in Vietnam.[17] Interestingly, the "French" soldiers that Trụ meets are not French but, rather, Vietnamese fighting for the French military. He discusses his attraction to their military uniforms and their gifts of candy, but he also acknowledges that as a young boy he saw both sides as Vietnamese and could not distinguish between their ideologies and political campaigns.

However, this is also when Trụ dates the beginnings of his anticommunist consciousness. Trụ writes about his nascent anticommunism through his memory of the bishop of Phát Diệm Father Lê Hữu Từ. He explains that Father Lê Hữu Từ respected Hồ Chí Minh's nationalism, but rejected any affiliation with communism. The historical record shows a fluid and initially prominent role for Vietnamese Catholics in the Việt Minh's nationalist coalition.[18] Charles Keith recounts that Catholic Vietnamese strongly supported Vietnamese independence and that they openly celebrated with mass rallies throughout northern Vietnam.[19] Later Vietnamese Catholic clergy broke away from the DRV, largely because the DRV government's Marxism interfered with Catholic schools and institutions and because of the Vatican's growing anticommunism in the global Cold War.

The Cold War now also intervened and redefined the anticolonial war in Vietnam. The Việt Minh acted as a nationalist coalition, which recruited many noncommunist forces, such as the Catholic leadership, as stated above, but it always had deep roots in the Communist Party. At the end of World War II, U.S. leaders began to view the world through the prism of the Cold War and feared that if one country "fell to communism," it would create a "domino effect," whereby all the bordering countries would fall under Soviet influence and communist ideology.

The United States followed a policy of "containment" and believed it was impera-
tive to contain communism to its current geography. This Cold War competition
between the Soviet Union and the United States manifested itself in the developing world during an era of decolonization and in a series of "proxy wars" in which
Vietnam would soon take center stage. The war's multipolarity, competing visions
for the future, and regional competition also made it a bloody civil war in Vietnam. And as many scholars have noted, the wars in Vietnam were both anticolonial wars and Cold War conflicts.[20]

Trụ does not write about the French War in any detail nor does that war seem
to have led to any upheaval in his early childhood. This was largely because Father
Lê Hữu Từ was able to create some autonomous space for the Catholic region of
Ninh Bình.[21] Trụ was fortunate in his relatively sheltered youth. However, the
war was traumatic for French and Việt Minh soldiers, and both sides suffered intense casualties. The French Union, including French metropole soldiers, French
colonial troops from North Africa, members of the Foreign Legion, and Vietnamese regulars, lost close to 112,000 men. The Việt Minh losses numbered approximately 300,000.[22]

The war between France and the Việt Minh ended in 1954, with the Việt
Minh's historic victory at Điện Biên Phủ. In this battle, the French General Henri
Navarre wished to bait the Việt Minh into a traditional military set piece, where
he believed his colonial forces would demonstrate their technical and military
superiority. Instead, General Võ Nguyên Giáp famously beat Navarre at his own
game, patiently sending Việt Minh into the mountains with supplies, military
hardware, and artillery, which enabled the Việt Minh to surprise the French colonial forces and soundly defeat them. The result was the first postwar military
victory of an insurgent guerrilla movement against a colonial power. Điện Biên
Phủ became a battle cry for anticolonial forces throughout the developing world.

In 1954, the Great Powers (the United States, the United Kingdom, France, the
Soviet Union, and China) met in Geneva and decided the future of Vietnam. Instead of acknowledging Vietnam's independence and unity under the leadership
of Hồ Chí Minh and the Communist Party, the conference divided Vietnam at
the 17th parallel, creating the Democratic Republic of Vietnam (DRV or North
Vietnam) and the Republic of Vietnam (RVN or South Vietnam) as two separate
countries. The DRV would continue to rule North Vietnam under the Communist
Party, while the RVN would be a noncommunist state with support from the United
States. In the North, Hồ Chí Minh was under great pressure from the Communist
Party to reject this agreement and continue the guerrilla war. However, he urged
compromise to allow DRV forces to regain strength and reunite the country under
a communist mantle later.

In the South, Bảo Đại, the former emperor, became the first leader of South Vietnam, but he was soon replaced by Ngô Đình Diệm, a Vietnamese Catholic from northern Vietnam. Diệm is a controversial figure in the scholarly literature on this period; however, it is inarguable that he was the most polarizing and powerful leader in the newly formed South Vietnam, along with his brother Ngô Đình Nhu and his wife, Madame Nhu.[23] At this juncture, the United States replaced the French as the primary financial and political backers of the South Vietnamese government. The Geneva Conference called for a national election in 1956 to put the future leadership of Vietnam to a vote, a vote that everyone, including U.S. President Dwight D. Eisenhower, believed Hồ Chí Minh would win. Given this electoral reality, Diệm refused to negotiate with Hanoi over election procedures, and the election guaranteed by the Geneva Conference failed to take place. Thus, communist North Vietnam and an anticommunist South Vietnam became geopolitical realities for the next twenty years.

In this rapidly changing political context, Trụ's family joined the approximately one million Vietnamese who migrated from the North to the South after the 1954 division of Vietnam. Nearly 100,000 Việt Minh militants and civilians also migrated from South Vietnam to North Vietnam. In his memoir, Trụ recounts how his father initially seemed reluctant to relocate, but the advice of a Catholic friend, who was also allied with the Việt Minh, spurred the family to leave their village and migrate to Saigon. Trụ's transition from North to South followed the pattern of hundreds of thousands of predominantly Catholic Vietnamese, and the U.S. military facilitated this migration by providing transportation and assistance for the massive migration.[24] The U.S. military's involvement in this operation would be repeated and mirrored in 1975, when it would again assist Vietnamese refugees leaving the then-communist-controlled nation.

Trụ's Young Adulthood and the American War

Trụ came of age in Saigon, where he enjoyed the city's social life, joined the South Vietnamese Navy, and fell in love with the woman who would become his wife. We learn about the war between the United States and the National Liberation Front (NLF) and North Vietnam, not through battle scenes but, rather, through Trụ's advancement in the South Vietnamese Navy.

This section of the memoir is valuable, because of the dearth of materials about the RVN military. Far too often in U.S. accounts of the war, the Vietnamese are presented as an undifferentiated "enemy," and, in the process, the experiences and participation of hundreds of thousands of Vietnamese as U.S. *allies* are either ignored entirely or these individuals are dismissed as untrustworthy double agents or incompetent. One of the few historical works to consider the experiences of the men in the RVN military seriously is Robert Brigham's *ARVN: Life and Death in the South Vietnamese Army*.[25] Trụ's memoir adds to the growing number of memoirs and accounts by South Vietnamese who have immigrated to the United States and reflected on their experiences as members of the RVN.

Through Trụ's memoir, we learn about his training and pride in his ability to advance in the South Vietnamese Navy. He is clear about his commitment to fighting communism, but he is also proud of the professionalism and training offered to him by the military. He recounts his numerous trips to the United States, and his opportunity to travel throughout the Pacific, namely to the Philippines, Guam, and Japan. Again, although Trụ does not characterize it as such, Trụ's journeys to California, Okinawa, Guam, and Subic Bay map the network of U.S. military power in the post–World War II Pacific. These chapters demonstrate the close professional relationships between the Americans and the South Vietnamese military personnel, the opportunity for travel and training available in the RVN, and Trụ's formative experiences in the United States. His trans-Pacific crossings also foreshadow his later evacuation route to Guam and his journey back to Vietnam under considerably changed circumstances.

Because Trụ served in the Navy, we learn little about the broader U.S. war in Vietnam. This is not a story of "search and destroy" campaigns or bombing raids or civilian casualties. The United States viewed the war in Vietnam as a Cold War conflict, and U.S. political leaders believed that keeping South Vietnam an anticommunist bulwark was essential to U.S. "credibility" on the world stage. However, opposition to Diệm's government persisted in both the South and the North, culminating in the formation of the NLF, another communist-led coalition, much like the Việt Minh. The growing guerrilla conflicts and popular unrest in South Vietnam led the United States to withdraw its support from Diệm and "greenlight" the 1963 coup which resulted in his assassination. After the 1964 Gulf of Tonkin incident, President Lyndon Johnson oversaw the escalation of a ground war in South Vietnam and a bombing campaign in North Vietnam. In the South, the U.S. military personnel fought against the southern-based NLF (or VC) and the North Vietnamese Army, which also sent troops South. From the U.S. point of view, the war was a pivotal fight against communism in Asia. From the point of view of the DRV and many southern Vietnamese, the war was about fighting imperialism, U.S. occupation, and, for many, but not all, communist revolution. Those in South Vietnam who supported the RVN government sought a stable, independent anticommunist government. Many Vietnamese saw the conflict as a civil war. Finally, still others in South Vietnam rejected the RVN government as illegitimate and also opposed communism.

The 1968 Tết Offensive was a turning point in the U.S. war in Vietnam. The North Vietnamese gambled on a southern offensive during the Vietnamese New Year, or Tết, in the coastal cities to launch a general uprising and defeat the U.S. military and South Vietnamese government.[26] However, Trụ's memoir portrays it mainly as an interruption in his military training. This shows how events that loom large in the historical narrative, in this case the Tết Offensive, are not necessarily the crucial moments in an individual's life. On the day of the Tết Offensive, Trụ is unable to get to the Saigon-based Tân Sơn Nhứt Airport, and he is diverted to join the general RVN response against the uprising. Thus, he mentions the Tết Offensive only in passing, and it is more of a detour on his way to further training in the United States. Although the Tết Offensive was a military disaster for the North Vietnamese, who overplayed their hand and needed another seven years to regroup, it was also a disaster for the U.S. military and President Johnson in particular, who had underestimated the strength and audacity of the northern strategy.

Elected president of the United States in 1968, Richard Nixon promised "peace with honor" and Vietnamization, whereby South Vietnamese troops would replace U.S. troops on the ground. The RVN always resented this coinage, arguing that from the start the war had always been fought with RVN Vietnamese soldiers. In 1969, Nixon began to withdraw U.S. troops even as he expanded the war into Laos and Cambodia and continued the punishing bombing raids against North Vietnam. In 1973, the United States agreed to withdraw its troops from South Vietnam, and North Vietnam agreed to return U.S. prisoners of war (POWs) to the United States. North Vietnam did not agree to withdraw its troops from South Vietnam. Recognizing the political weakness of South Vietnam, behind the scenes, U.S. secretary of state Henry Kissinger was hoping he could preserve a "decent interval" between U.S. withdrawal and what he anticipated to be the short-term life expectancy of the RVN state. The United States continued its economic and diplomatic support for the government of South Vietnam, but it withdrew all its troops in 1973.

The DRV bided its time and gained strength, and in the spring of 1975 began an offensive south. At this point, the South Vietnamese forces collapsed more quickly than even the North Vietnamese generals anticipated, and the RVN forces rapidly retreated farther South. In April 1975, the U.S. Congress debated sending further military aid to the South Vietnamese government, but by this point, Congress was unwilling to authorize any funds to shore up the faltering administration in the South. Instead, it approved $300 million for an evacuation effort.[27] The North Vietnamese Army marched into Saigon on April 30, 1975, ending the government of the Republic of Vietnam and triggering an exodus of tens of thousands of Vietnamese, the majority of whom identified and worked with the RVN and U.S. governments throughout the war.

This is where Trụ's story begins to diverge from the well-known story of Vietnamese migration to the United States.

The Evacuation: April 30, 1975

As the North Vietnamese Army marched South in March and April 1975, it set off fear and chaos throughout the military and civilian leadership in the RVN. Rumors began to circulate that men and women who had assisted the United States, from generals to secretaries, soldiers to sex workers, would be punished, potentially executed, and at best imprisoned and persecuted. The United States was reluctant to organize an evacuation, as it feared this would only generate greater uncertainty and fear.[28] For most Americans, the image of helicopters on Saigon rooftops with Vietnamese clamoring to get in them cemented images of U.S. loss and desperation and a failed war. For many South Vietnamese, the evacuation signaled the Americans' ultimate betrayal and broken promises to their RVN allies.

In this way, Trụ's story is not unique. Trụ, like many others, tried to make arrangements to secure an escape route for close family members. As a high-ranking member of the RVN Navy, Trụ was better positioned than most to do this; however, his story shows the interplay of chance, caution, and snap decisions that divided families and left people behind. Trụ was stationed on the southern tip of Vietnam, and his wife came to see him unexpectedly. She told him of the growing anxiety in Saigon and her desire to evacuate. Trụ traveled to Saigon to assess the situation. Then on April 29, with his wife still at the southern end of Vietnam, Trụ evacuated with other RVN naval officers and families. Although he tried to contact an officer to arrange his wife's evacuation, this attempt failed. Trụ was on a ship bound for another land; his wife remained with their children in Vietnam.

Over 120,000 Vietnamese fled between mid-April and the early days of May 1975.[29] Although the actual evacuation spanned more than two weeks—and Trụ personally escaped on April 29—April 30, 1975, is the date used to mark the evacuation and the "fall of Saigon." The U.S. military was a major actor in this operation, manning helicopters and ships at sea, and shuttling Vietnamese to larger U.S. military ships.[30] In addition, RVN naval ships and private vessels also joined the flotilla of escaping ships. In the end, the U.S. military directed the vast majority of Vietnamese to the island of Guam, although smaller contingents also went to Thailand, the Philippines, and Hawaiʻi.[31] This trajectory retraced the earlier naval missions Trụ had taken as an officer in the RVN Navy. However, he was no longer a captain or a sailor. On this journey, he was a refugee, alone and without his wife and family.

Refugee Camp: Guam

In May 1975, Guam, which measures just 50 kilometers by 19 kilometers at its widest points, became a temporary refugee camp for more than 100,000 Vietnamese. Most Vietnamese were on Guam for between two weeks and three months, before they traveled to the United States for resettlement. The U.S. military dubbed the overall mission Operation New Life.[32]

Guam is a pivotal place in Trụ's memoir. It is where he decides to repatriate. It is where he forms new friendships and relationships with both his Vietnamese compatriots and U.S. officers. It is also where the repatriates staged dramatic, and sometimes violent, protests in their quest for a ship. But why Guam? Where is Guam? And why did the United States have a refugee camp there?

Trụ's memoir tells us very little about Guam itself. We do not learn about its Chamorro, or indigenous, history or about the local population's ambivalent relationship with the U.S. military.[33] Like most Americans, Trụ seems to know little of Guam's history or politics and even less of its indigenous traditions and culture. Instead, Guam's importance lies in its military bases and its position as an island territory, under U.S. control, between the Pacific and the U.S. mainland.

The prominence of Guam in this memoir signals the need for readers to pay greater attention to histories of U.S. empire in the Pacific and the hidden value of "exceptional" spaces, such as Puerto Rico, Guam, and the U.S. naval base in Guantánamo Bay.[34] With the U.S. victory over Spain in the War of 1898, the United States gained control over Cuba, the Philippines, Puerto Rico, and Guam. While Cuba gained its formal, if limited, sovereignty in 1902, and the Philippines became independent in 1946, the United States continues to maintain large military bases and govern both Puerto Rico and Guam directly. Guam remains an unincorporated territory of the United States, without voting rights in Congress or in presidential elections. Guam's indigenous Chamorro population has been largely marginalized, and the island is dominated by U.S. military installations, which occupy more than 25 percent of Guam's territory. Notably, Andersen Air Force base in Guam was a significant launching pad for U.S. bombing raids during the U.S. war in Vietnam.[35] The militarization of Guam and the limited economic opportunities for Guamanians has led large numbers of young people in Guam to join the U.S. military, and Guamanians have suffered disproportionately high casualties in comparison to military personnel from U.S. states.[36]

The U.S. government selected Guam as the staging ground for the first refugee camps because of its geographic location and because of U.S. sovereignty over the island. In contrast, the Philippines would not allow the United States to establish refugee camps at their military installations in Subic Bay or at Clark Air Base. The locally elected Guamanian government cooperated with the refugee operation, but, as several members of the local council noted, they had little choice.

For Trụ, the refugee camps on Guam were oddly familiar. He had traveled to Guam multiple times as an RVN naval officer and had intimate experience with Guam's harbor and bases. After arriving in Guam, the repatriates recognized the ambivalence and limbo status of Guam, realizing that they had a much better chance of achieving their goal of returning to Vietnam from Guam than they would from the U.S. mainland. Some of the repatriates wrote letters to the editor to the *Pacific Daily News,* Guam's local newspaper, expressing their sincere desire to return and thanking the Guamanian public for its generosity. At the same time, others posted massive billboards near the refugee camp fence line, condemning Guam as a "Devil's Island."[37] Both acknowledged Guam's local dynamics and tried to take advantage of them as best they could, most forcefully by refusing to continue on to the United States. Instead, they held their ground on Guam.

The Repatriates

As early as May 3, 1975, men stepped forward and petitioned the UNHCR for the right to return to Vietnam. Over the next few weeks, more than two thousand men and women requested to be repatriated. They did not want to go to the United States, at least not at this point; they wanted to return to their families in Vietnam.

In this group, Trụ was a bit of an outlier. The majority of the repatriates were younger than Trụ by a generation. Although almost all had served in the RVN military, many of the repatriates were younger and had been enlisted men or drafted into the RVN Navy. For example, many had been sailors on RVN ships patrolling South Vietnamese waters, and as the NVA advanced south, the captains simply decided not to return their ships to port in Saigon. These men did not choose evacuation. RVN officers also ordered pilots to fly planes out of Saigon to Thailand, so that the NVA could not capture U.S. military hardware. Others feared the future in the United States or simply changed their minds. At age forty, Trụ was older than most and had more than a decade of experience in the RVN military.

Trụ's memoir captures many of the divisions within the repatriate camp, as the protests escalated in the summer of 1975. Trụ develops close friends and shares intimate conversations with other men of his generation who had also been separated from their families. Yet he also stands apart and observes. He positions himself as an outsider who does not participate directly in the growing number of militant repatriate protests, including hunger strikes, demonstrations, and even arson. Trụ's thoughts are somewhat ambivalent. He separates himself from the direct protests, but he is also careful not to condemn them. He sees all of this as a process that will enable him to reach his ultimate goal—his return to Vietnam and his family.

His memoir also demonstrates the distrust and factions within the camp leadership and worries about possible VC and Central Intelligence Agency (CIA) agents infiltrating the repatriate camps. The fear of espionage and lack of trust underscore the long-standing political reality of double agents and intrigue that defined South Vietnamese politics for two decades.[38] As author John Prados has written, the CIA was arguably equal to the U.S. Embassy in defining the U.S. government's relationship with the RVN leadership.[39] While I have not found any written evidence to this end, Trụ believes the CIA was operating covertly within the camp. Tru's memoir reflects the outsized role of the CIA and the culture of duplicity within Saigon and South Vietnamese politics at large. He looks on the camp agitators with suspicion and just a bit of disdain, and he clearly does not trust them. Ironically, Trụ has a more positive encounter with a VC agent, a man who claims that he was ordered to evacuate with the RVN elite, but who became lonely in the American refugee camps and decided to repatriate. Through these complex relationships and observations, Trụ's memoir captures the sense of anxiety, distrust, and doubleness that lingered in the camps.

Trụ also develops a strong relationship with Army Brigadier General James Herbert. General Herbert was the senior civil coordinator on Guam, and he was given responsibility for solving the repatriate crisis by the Interagency Task Force (IATF), a temporary U.S. agency responsible for the relocation and resettlement of Vietnamese refugees.[40] As a ship captain, Trụ was able to demonstrate his skill and expertise, gaining the respect of both the repatriates and the U.S. military personnel. Trụ presents the relationship as one of trust and mutual respect.

In the end, the U.S. government provided the repatriates with the *Việt Nam Thương Tín,* even though General Hebert repeatedly cautioned the repatriates that the North Vietnamese government would not welcome them. The North Vietnamese government had publicly and officially warned the repatriates against returning to Vietnam without its express permission. The Vietnamese government categorized the repatriates as potential spies, collaborators, and infiltrators. Many of the men discussed their fears of imprisonment on return, but Trụ decided that he would return, even if he was imprisoned or risked death. Along with more than 1,500 Vietnamese, Trụ captained the *Việt Nam Thương Tín,* which returned to Vietnam in October 1975.[41]

The Welcome: "Reeducation" Camps and Forced Labor

After landing in Vietnam, Trụ was imprisoned for thirteen years. Most Americans are unfamiliar with the reeducation camps in postwar Vietnam, where tens of thousands of Vietnamese suffered in the aftermath of the war because of their affiliation with the RVN government and military. The memoir reveals the grueling labor and the psychological trauma in these reeducation or, less euphemistically, prison camps, which were located throughout Vietnam after 1975.

In April 1975, members of the RVN military feared retribution and revenge, and they were correct to be afraid. Former RVN soldiers were asked to report to the authorities and bring a small bag of their belongings; most men were told they would be away for three to thirty days.[42] In fact, few were released after such a short time. Most were imprisoned for weeks and months on end, and more than 200,000 men were held in reeducation camps for more than three years; some, like Trụ, remained for more than a decade.[43] The camps were known for their brutality, forced labor, arbitrary violence, and even torture.[44] In many ways, Trụ's memoir downplays the more violent aspects of camp life, emphasizing the boredom, hunger, and routine more than the cruelty and punishment.[45] However, even in his account, Trụ's psychological and physical pain is palpable. He recounts only a single visit with his wife, in a difficult and stilted passage. After many years, their relationship seems strained, although, again, Trụ says relatively little. Ultimately, they are reunited, but this occurs only in the memoir's final chapters. He does not share all his pain with us, but he suffers for many years under an undefined sentence, always waiting for reunion with his family.

The scenes in the reeducation camps also contrast sharply with the camp scenes in Guam. Although the repatriates resented their confinement in Guam, they also organized politically and engaged in militant protests. They were in refugee camps, but they were not prevented from expressing their political will. In a tragic contrast, Trụ depicts the reeducation camps in Vietnam as places of violence, starvation, passivity, and despair. In the Vietnamese reeducation camps, there were no protests, no marches, and no hunger strikes. Instead, Trụ recounts his days of hunger and manual labor alongside ideological lessons and interrogations. Trụ, like many others, heartbreakingly regretted his decision to return to Vietnam.

By any measure, after its victory the new revolutionary Socialist Republic of Vietnam (SRV) faced severe economic problems and international isolation. The land itself was marked by more than 3.5 million land mines, which killed more than 38,000 people *after* the U.S. war had ended.[46] In addition, the economy was in shambles, and Agent Orange and other chemical agents destroyed vast acres of Vietnam's territory and made it unfit for agriculture. Vietnam requested U.S. aid and economic development as an act of both humanitarianism and compensation; however, the United States responded with an economic embargo and diplomatic isolation.

War in Vietnam also continued. Military attacks between the Khmer Rouge and Vietnam led to the Vietnamese invasion and occupation of Cambodia. The Vietnamese occupied Cambodia from 1979 through 1989, and their presence put a halt to the genocidal Khmer Rouge.[47] The Chinese also attacked northern Vietnam in 1979, which affected Trụ as RVN prisoners were moved away from the northern border.

While Trụ was in the reeducation camps, dreaming of reunion with his family and escape by boat, thousands of Vietnamese did take to the seas between 1978 and 1979. The Western media dubbed these Vietnamese "boat people," and they found themselves in refugee camps in Malaysia, Indonesia, Thailand, the Philippines, and Hong Kong. Vietnamese continued to leave both clandestinely via boat in the 1980s and early 1990s. However, over time, an increasing number of people applied for direct resettlement through the Orderly Departure Program (ODP), which, as its name implies, sought to halt the number of people risking their lives at sea. Again, Vietnamese men and women had multiple motivations. Many left because of political persecution, ethnic Chinese-Vietnamese were ousted because of the government's anti-Chinese measures, and others faced poverty because of the lack of economic development in the immediate postwar period. In addition, hundreds of thousands of people from Laos and Cambodia were displaced, leading to a massive crisis of "land people" on the Thai border.[48] As many as 500,000 Vietnamese drowned at sea in their attempt to seek refuge in Southeast Asia before resettling in the West.[49]

In the midst of the wars, mass migration, and stunning poverty, the Vietnamese government sought to normalize its relationship with the United States. The United States believed that the Vietnamese government was deliberating withholding information about American POWs and the remains of those missing in action (MIAs). This issue was particularly noxious for Vietnamese leaders, as they had more than 300,000 MIAs of their own.[50]

Change did not really come until 1986. Following the playbook of Mikhail Gorbachev and his economic policy of *perestroika* (openness) in the Soviet Union, the Vietnamese government began its policy of *đổi mới* (renovation) in 1986. This policy introduced market reforms and launched Vietnam's economic recovery. It also included greater rapprochement between the United States and Vietnam.

After many years in the reeducation camps, Trụ learned that John W. Vessey Jr. (ret.), the U.S. special envoy to Vietnam, was in the country. Beginning in the late 1980s, Vessey became a prominent U.S. official who traveled to Vietnam to secure the remains of deceased American soldiers and to help pave the way for diplomatic relations. Trụ recognizes Vessey's presence as a positive sign for the reeducation camp prisoners. They rightly believed that the United States was pressuring Vietnam to release the men who were still incarcerated because of their positions during the war. Trụ was released in 1988. In 1989, the United States and Vietnam concluded an agreement that expedited the release of the remaining reeducation camp prisoners. The United States lifted its embargo against Vietnam in 1994 and reestablished diplomatic relations in 1995.

After his release, Trụ initially contemplates another escape, this time illegally via boat with his family. However, he soon learns of a program for RVN officers released from reeducation camps, the HO program. It allowed individuals who had been in a reeducation camp for at least three years to gain expedited resettlement in the United States.

Trụ and his family apply to this program, and he recounts the government's confiscation of his property at the time of his departure. He concludes the memoir as he is en route to the airport. Marking a rupture and a final turning point in his life story, Trụ does not take a ship out of Vietnam. Instead, he leaves Vietnam via airplane, and the United States is his final destination.

The Captain

This memoir stands as a testament to the unknowability of the future and the precarious place in-between during a time of war and political change. It provides us with insights not only into the repatriates' lives but also into the ambivalence shared by many South Vietnamese military personnel in evacuating Saigon and relocating to the United States. Even when Trụ's memoir raises more questions than it answers, it reveals the challenge of finding coherence and meaning in one's life story. By writing this memoir, Trụ shows us the value of storytelling and how he sought to understand his journeys back and forth between Vietnam and Guam and the United States.

Throughout the memoir, Trụ insists that he did not want to return to Vietnam because he supported the communist government. In fact, he repeats his anticommunist credentials over and over again to clarify his political position. He explains his decision to return as a matter of love and commitment to his wife and family. He justifies his decision to return to Vietnam, because it will allow him to rescue his family and *then* leave *with* his wife and children. In this recounting, his eventual escape is in his mind from the earliest stages, and so each time he insists on his return, he tells the reader, he is also plotting his exit from Vietnam.

Of course, Trụ could not know the future. In 1975, he could not know that many Vietnamese would leave as "boat people" in the late 1970s and 1980s and relocate to the United States or that the ODP would facilitate Vietnamese migration after 1980. He had no way of knowing that one day he would have been able to sponsor his wife and children from the United States. Instead, his experience was based on his earlier migration from North Vietnam to South Vietnam in 1954. In his experience, this division was final. He had not seen his relatives in North Vietnam again nor had he been allowed to travel back and forth. In 1975, when Trụ was in Guam, he imagined that if he went on to the United States, he would suffer the same fate and never see his loved ones again.

Finally, Trụ's connection to the sea resonates throughout the memoir. In the early chapters, he looks out at the rivers and boats in northern Vietnam, and he is intimately involved with the water and the skills needed to navigate it. As he sails back to Vietnam, he has complete certainty and knowledge in his expertise and ability to safely steer the Việt Nam Thương Tín. The book ends with his boarding an airplane to the United States, where he has lived since 1991. In a way his final flight is bittersweet. The memoir is full of trans-Pacific crossings, from Saigon to San Diego, San Francisco, Subic Bay, Guam, and Okinawa, and back again to Saigon, his evacuation in April 1975, and his journey from Guam back to Vietnam. However, in all his previous journeys, he was at sea. There is something poignant about his final arrival by flight, marking the end of the major epoch in his life.

After Trụ arrives in the United States, he struggles to make a new life for himself, but this story is absent from his memoir. With the help of his sponsor, he was able to secure a job on the nightshift at a convenience store. In reflecting on those years, he told me he would have accepted any job to survive. He needed to pay his rent and support his children in the United States. At times, he worked two jobs, adding a shift on an assembly line at a medical supply factory, and his wife also juggled a variety of jobs and positions. He expressed his deep thanks to the United States and the opportunities it granted his children. However, his life in the United States has also been marked by silent sadness: after only five years in the country, his son, his middle child, died unexpectedly at the age of thirty. Trụ retired in 2005 and lives with his wife and daughter in Texas.

I last saw Trụ in Orange County at the fortieth reunion of members of the Việt Nam Thương Tín family. Several hundred men, now all between the ages of sixty and eighty, reconvened in a backyard in Southern California for Vietnamese food,

Trần Đình Trụ is reviewing the manuscript in Orange County, September 2015. Photograph from Lipman's personal collection.

beer, memories, and a reunion to recall a time and decisions they had shared. Trụ explained that he knew relatively few men there, maybe a dozen, but they all knew him. He had been their captain. Trụ then leaned over to tell Bac and me that these old men who were relaxing in the backyard were some of the same men who had set the camps in Guam on fire. Now, they were older, snapping pictures on their iPhones and animatedly talking with friends over a veritable feast.

It was an evening of joy and friendship but also one that resonated with sorrow, regret, and suffering. There was also an element of the surreal as we snapped pictures in front of a banner welcoming the "Family of the *Việt Nam Thương Tín*'s 40th Anniversary." Everyone I spoke to said they had made a mistake. They should not have returned to Vietnam, and, instead, should have continued on to the United States with the other evacuees. Many had suffered for years in reeducation camps, and few wished to share those experiences with me on such a festive occasion. After being released, some had escaped on small boats, taking advantage of their naval skills once again and hoping to be found by an international freighter or making their way to a refugee camp. Others stayed in Vietnam through

Jana K. Lipman, Trần Đình Trụ, and Bac Hoai Tran attend a reunion to mark the fortieth anniversary of the *Việt Nam Thương Tín*. The banner says, "The *Việt Nam Thương Tín Family*: Celebrating Our Reunion 'Looking Back after 40 Years.'" Photograph from Lipman's personal collection.

the 1990s and, like Trụ, came to the United States through the HO program. The dissonance in the celebration and their suffering created an intense and emotional atmosphere, at least for me, as an outsider.

In 1975, Trụ returned to Vietnam, defying the expectations of both Americans and Vietnamese. His bravery and perseverance remain palpable. Trụ was the captain of the *Việt Nam Thương Tín*.

Notes

1. For an important critique of this "rescue" narrative, see Yen Le Espiritu, *Body Counts: The Vietnam War and Militarized Refugees* (Berkeley: University of California Press, 2014); idem, "The 'We-Win-Even-When-We-Lose' Syndrome: U.S. Press Coverage of the Twenty-Fifth Anniversary of the 'Fall of Saigon,'" *American Quarterly* 58.2 (2006): 329–352; idem, "Toward a Critical Refugee Study: The Vietnamese Refugee Subject in U.S. Scholarship," *Journal of Vietnamese Studies* 1.1–2 (2006) 410–432.

2. For important new scholarly critiques, see Viet Thanh Nguyen, "Refugee Memories and Asian American Critique," *positions* 20.3 (Summer 2012): 911–942; and idem, *Nothing Ever Dies: Vietnam and the Memory of War* (Cambridge: Harvard University Press, 2016).

3. James M. Freeman, *Hearts of Sorrow: Vietnamese-American Lives* (Stanford: Stanford University Press, 1989); Mary Terrell Cargill and Jade Quang Huynh, *Voices of Vietnamese Boat People: Nineteen Narratives of Escape and Survival* (Jefferson: McFarland, 2000); James Freeman and Nguyen Dinh Huu, *Voices from the Camps: Vietnamese Children Seeking Asylum* (Seattle: University of Washington Press, 2003).

4. Sucheng Chan, ed. *The Vietnamese American 1.5 Generation: Stories of War, Revolution, Flight, and New Beginnings* (Philadelphia: Temple University Press, 2006); Andrew Lam, *Perfume Dreams: Reflections on the Vietnamese Diaspora* (New York: Heyday, 2005); Andrew X. Pham, *The Eaves of Heaven: A Life in Three Wars* (New York: Broadway Book, 2009).

5. For just a sampling see, Nam Le, *The Boat: Stories* (New York: Vintage, 2009); Viet Thanh Nguyen, *The Sympathizer* (New York: Grove Press, 2015); Lan Cao, *Monkey Bridge* (New York: Penguin, 1998). For a critique of Cao, see Andrew Friedman, *Covert Capital: Landscapes of Denial and the Making of U.S. Empire in Northern Virginia* (Berkeley: University of California Press, 2013), 163–219.

6. For a complementary memoir also now in translation, see Nha Ca and Olga Dror (translator), *Mourning Headband for Hue: An Account of the Battle of Hue 1968* (Bloomington: University of Indiana Press, 2014).

7. In fact, ample archival information was available, and I have published multiple articles on both the repatriates and the Vietnamese refugee camps in the United States. See Jana K. Lipman, "'A Precedent Worth Setting . . .': Military Humanitarianism: The U.S. Military and the 1975 Vietnamese Evacuation," *Journal of Military History* 79 (January 2015): 151–179; "A Refugee Camp in America: Fort Chaffee and Vietnamese and Cuban Refugees, 1975–1982," *Journal of American Ethnic History* 33 (Winter 2014): 57–87; "'Give Us a Ship': Vietnamese Repatriates on Guam, 1975," *American Quarterly* 64 (March 2012): 1–31. For another scholarly article on the repatriates, see Heather Stur, "Hiding behind the Humanitarian Label': Refugees, Repatriates, and the Rebuilding of America's Benevolent Image after the Vietnam War," *Diplomatic History* 39.2 (2015): 223–244.

8. For a critique of the discourse of gratitude, see Mimi Thi Nguyen, *The Gift of Freedom* (Durham: Duke University Press, 2012).

9. For an excellent analysis of the contested nature of nation, nationalism, and history in postwar Vietnam, see Patricia M. Pelley, *Postcolonial Vietnam: New Histories of the National Past* (Durham: Duke University Press, 2002).

10. For a book that examines the complexity of the South and the NLF, see David Hunt, *Vietnam's Southern Revolution: From Peasant Insurrection to Total War* (Amherst: University of Massachusetts Press, 2008); Jessica Chapman, *Cauldron of Resistance: Ngo Dinh Diem, the United States and the 1950s Southern Vietnam* (Ithaca: Cornell University Press, 2013).

11. For sensitive readings on the etymology of VC, see the work of Nu-Anh Tran, "South Vietnamese in the U.S. against U.S. Policy in Vietnam: Unintended Consequences of a U.S. Nation-State Building Initiative," SHAFR presentation, 2013; see also idem, *Cauldron of Resistance*, 118–120; Edward Miller, *Misalliance: Ngo Dinh Diem, the United States, and the Fate of South Vietnam* (Cambridge: Harvard University Press, 2013), 131–136.

12. For an analysis of American use of VC, see Christian Appy, *Working-Class War: American Combat Soldiers and Vietnam* (Chapel Hill: University of North Carolina Press, 1993), 103–107.

13. For a critical analysis of the politics and discourse of anticommunism in the Vietnamese diaspora community, see Thanh Thuy Vo Dang, "Anti-Communism as Cultural Praxis: South Vietnam, War, and Refugee Memories in the Vietnamese American Community" (PhD diss.,

University of California, San Diego, 2008); Tuan Hoang, "From Reeducation Camps to Little Saigons: Historicizing Vietnamese Diasporic Anticommunism," *Journal of Vietnamese Studies* 11 (2016): 43–95. These works provide excellent insights into the ways in which Vietnamese Americans have used and articulated the politics of anticommunism.

14. Charles Keith, *Catholic Vietnam: A Church from Empire to Nation* (Berkeley: University of California Press, 2012), 18–21.

15. Ibid., 165.

16. For a biography of Hồ Chí Minh, see William Duiker, *Ho Chi Minh: A Life* (New York: Hachette Books, 2000). For one of the earliest English-language works on Vietnamese intellectual history before World War II, see David Marr, *Vietnamese Tradition on Trial, 1920–1945* (Berkeley: University of California Press, 1984).

17. For one of the most recent books on the U.S. policies in Vietnam during the French War, see Frederik Logevall, *Embers of War: The Fall of an Empire and the Making of America's Vietnam* (New York: Random House, 2012).

18. Keith, "A National Church in Revolution and War," 208–241.

19. Ibid., 214–217.

20. For a sampling, see Logevall, *Embers of War;* Odd Arne Westad, *The Global Cold War: Third World Interventions and the Making of Our Times* (Cambridge: Cambridge University Press, 2007). For yet another critique of the bipolar framework of the Cold War, see Heonik Kwon, *The Other Cold War* (New York: Columbia University Press, 2010).

21. Keith, "A National Church in Revolution and War," 230.

22. The Indochina War 1945–1956, On-Line Resource Site of the Indochina War, University of Quebec in Montreal, http://indochine.uqam.ca/en/historical-dictionary/223-casualties-indochina-war.html (accessed September 11, 2015).

23. For a range of interpretations see Miller, *Misalliance;* Chapman, *Cauldron of Resistance;* Seth Jacobs, *America's Miracle Man in Vietnam: Ngo Dinh Diem, Religion, Race, and U.S. Intervention in Southeast Asia* (Durham: Duke University Press, 2004).

24. For accounts of the 1954–1956 migration of Northern Catholics to South Vietnam, see Nghia V. Vo, *The Vietnamese Boat People 1954 and 1975–92* (Jefferson, NC: McFarland, 2005), 9–41; Seth Jacobs, "'Christ Crucified in Indo-China': Tom Dooley and the North Vietnamese Refugees," in *America's Miracle Man in Vietnam* (Durham: Duke University Press, 2004), 127–171.

25. Robert Brigham, *ARVN: Life and Death in the South Vietnamese Army* (Lawrence: University of Kansas Press, 2006).

26. For a new interpretation of the Tết Offensive with an analysis of the DRV's strategy and decision making, see Lien-Hang Nguyen, *Hanoi's War: An International History of the War for Peace in Vietnam* (Chapel Hill: University of North Carolina Press, 2012).

27. Mark Atwood Lawrence, *The Vietnam War: A Concise International History* (New York: Oxford University Press, 2010), 166.

28. On the fortieth anniversary in 2015, numerous commemorations were held in the United States of this event, along with the release of Rory Kennedy's documentary *Last Days in Vietnam*.

29. The United States agreed to accept 130,000 Southeast Asians into the United States through the executive "parole" function. The United States exceeded this number of initial parolees, and 95 percent of this 1975 population was Vietnamese, with the remaining 5 percent being Cambodian. Sucheng Chan, *Asian Americans: An Interpretative History* (New York: Simon and Schuster, 1991), 155–156.

30. Lipman, "A Precedent Worth Setting."

31. Chan, *Asian Americans,* 155–156.

32. Espiritu argues that this nomenclature served to erase the failure and violence of the U.S. war in Vietnam, allowing the military to recast the operation in humanitarian terms. Espiritu, *Body Counts;* Asako Sahara, "Operations New Life/Arrivals: U.S. National Project to Forget the Vietnam War" (MA thesis, University of California, San Diego, 2009); Stur, "Hiding behind the Humanitarian Label"; Lipman, "A Precedent Worth Setting."

33. See Keith Camacho, *Cultures of Commemoration: The Politics of War, Memory, and History in the Mariana Islands* (Honolulu: Center for Pacific Island Studies, 2011); Michael Lujan Bevacqua, "The Exceptional Lie and Death of a Chamorro Soldier: Tracing the Militarization of Desire in Guam USA," and Keith L. Camacho and Laurel A. Monnig, "Uncomfortable Fatigues: Chamorro Soldiers, Gendered Identities, and the Question of Decolonization in Guam," in *Militarized Currents: Towards a Decolonized Future in Asia and the Pacific,* ed. Setsu Shigematsu and Keith Camacho (Minneapolis: University of Minnesota Press, 2010); *The Insular Empire: America in the Marianas,* dir. Vanessa Warheit, 2010. For a work seeking to remap academic inquiry into the Pacific, see also Janet Hoskins and Viet Thanh Nguyen, *Transpacific Studies: Framing an Emerging Field* (Honolulu: University of Hawai'i Press, 2014).

34. The literature on U.S. empire, particularly its Pacific and Caribbean outposts, is extensive. See Amy Kaplan, " 'Left Alone with America: The Absence of Empire in the Study of American Culture," in *Cultures of United States Imperialism,* ed. Amy Kaplan and Donald Pease, (Durham: Duke University Press, 1993); Louis Perez Jr., *The War of 1898: The United States and Cuba in History and Historiography* (Chapel Hill: University of North Carolina Press, 1998); Kristin Hoganson, *Fighting for American Manhood: How Gender Politics Provoked the Spanish-American and Philippine American Wars* (New Haven: Yale University Press, 2000); Paul Kramer, *Blood of Government: Race, Empire, the United States, and the Philippines* (Chapel Hill: University of North Carolina Press, 2006); Eileen Findlay, *Imposing Decency: The Politics of Sexuality and Race in Puerto Rico, 1870–1920* (Durham: Duke University Press, 2000); and Christina Duffy Burnett and Burke Marshall, eds., *Foreign in a Domestic Sense: Puerto Rico, American Expansion, and the Constitution* (Durham: Duke University Press, 2001); Jana K. Lipman, *Guantánamo: A Working-Class History between Empire and Revolution* (Berkeley: University of California Press, 2009); David Vine, *Island of Shame: The Secret History of the U.S. Military Base on Diego Garcia* (Princeton: Princeton University Press, 2011).

35. See Guam, Global Security.org, http://www.globalsecurity.org/military/facility/guam .htm (accessed September 22, 2015); Andersen AFB history, Fact Sheet, http://www.andersen .af.mil/library/factsheets/factsheet.asp?id=7063/ (accessed September 22, 2015).

36. Appy, *Working-Class War,* 15–16; Ali Meyer, "Maine Leads Nation in Patriots Killed in Afghanistan," cnsnews.com, November 11, 2014, http://cnsnews.com/news/article/ali-meyer /maine-leads-nation-patriots-killed-afghanistan (accessed September 11, 2015). This article notes that Maine has suffered the most casualties, with twenty-two casualties, equaling .0017 percent of the state's population. In contrast, Guam lost nine service members, equal to 0.0056 percent of its population, proportionately much higher than Maine.

37. Lipman, "Give Us a Ship."

38. For a fictional account of this doubleness, see Nguyen, *The Sympathizer.*

39. John Prados, The CIA's Vietnam Story, http://nsarchive.gwu.edu/NSAEBB/NSAEBB284/ (accessed January 27, 2016).

40. George R. Dunham and David A. Quinlan, *U.S. Marines in Vietnam: The Bitter End, 1973–1975* (Marine Corps Series, History and Museums Divisions, Marine Corps Headquarters, 1990), 225–227, http://www.marines.mil/Portals/59/Publications/U.S.%20Marines%20in%20Vietnam_The%20Bitter%20End%201973-1975%20%20PCN%201900310900_1.pdf (accessed September 22, 2016).

41. Throughout the memoir, Trụ states that there were 1,652 repatriates. The U.S. military's account puts the number at 1,546. In any case, the number was approximately 1,500–1,600 people.

42. Chan, *The Vietnamese 1.5 Generation,* 65.

43. Lawrence, *The Vietnam War,* 168.

44. Nghia M. Vo, *The Bamboo Gulag, Political Imprisonment in Communist Vietnam* (Jefferson: McFarland, 2004). Robert McKelvey, *A Gift of Barbed Wire: America's Allies Abandoned in South Vietnam* (Seattle: University of Washington Press, 2002).

45. For example, in other memoirs, authors emphasize the arbitrary brutality of the camps and the select murders of individuals, see Andrew Pham, *Catfish and Mandela: A Two-Wheeled Voyage Through the Landscape and Memory of Vietnam* (New York: Picador, 2000). For the best-known popular account of the reeducation camps, see the Vietnamese-American film *Journey from the Fall,* 2007 (director, Ham Tran, ImaginAsian Pictures).

46. Edward Martini, *Invisible Enemies: The American War on Vietnam, 1975–2000* (Amherst: University of Massachusetts Press, 2007), 41.

47. Sophie Quinn Judge, "Fraternal Aid, Self-Defense, or Self Interest? Vietnam's Intervention in Cambodia, 1978–1989," in *Humanitarian Intervention: A History* (Cambridge: Cambridge University Press, 2013), 343–362.

48. For the best synthesis of the refugee crisis that includes Cambodia and Laos as well as Vietnam, see W. Courtland Robinson, *Terms of Refuge: The Indochinese Exodus and the International Response* (London: Zed Books, 1998).

49. See Quan Tue Tran, "Remembering the Boat People Exodus: A Tale of Two Memorials," *Journal of Vietnamese Studies* 7.3 (2012): 80.

50. For the U.S. literature on MIAs and U.S. foreign relations, see H. Bruce Franklin, *MIA or Mythmaking in America* (New York: Lawrence Hill Books, 1992); Martini, *Invisible Enemies;* and Michael Allen, *Until the Last Man Comes Home: POWs, MIAs, and the Unending Vietnam War* (Chapel Hill: University of North Carolina Press). For a Vietnamese novel that excavates the memory of Vietnamese missing in action, see Bao Ninh, *The Sorrow of War* (New York: Riverhead Books, 1996). See also Heonik Kwon, *Ghosts of War in Vietnam* (Cambridge: Cambridge University Press, 2008).

SHIP OF FATE

CHAPTER ONE

My Early Life

The Boeing 747 airliner touched down at San Francisco International Airport. The plane had taken my family and me away from the most impoverished and backward land in the world and brought us to a civilized country, complete with modern science and technology. The airport was magnificent and majestic. Bright light spread across the sky.

Most people would probably think that I had traveled from hell and had landed in heaven.

However, I was in a unique position. This airport was not strange to me. Over twenty years earlier, I had had the opportunity to train in the United States with the South Vietnamese Navy. When I had stepped out of the airplane so many years earlier and walked through this same hall, I had wished that my wife and my children were by my side. Now, my wish had come true. My wife and my children stood by my side, and yet my heart tightened.

I was flooded with mixed feelings. I was about to confront many difficulties in this new land, and I would need strength to cope with the challenges I would face in the United States. All my energy and willpower had been taken by the communists in Vietnam. They had left me only this emaciated body. How would I manage in this new country?

Those thoughts went round and round in my mind. When I turned around, I saw my beautiful children following me. I thought about their future; they were innocent, but the communist world had dominated their youth for so many years. We had escaped from that bizarre world, where young people did not know what to do or where their lives were going. Today, we set foot in America. In time, they would go far. Thinking along these lines, I was elated. I wanted to forget what had happened in the past.

While we were living at my brother-in-law's house and completing the necessary paperwork, I had time to reminisce about the arc of my life and all the countless changes I had experienced, from childhood, to my career, and then to the time that turned my life upside down. Human beings can go from possessing nothing to possessing something and then return to having nothing again in a vicious circle with no escape. Thinking about the past made me recall so many emotions and memories. Whether bitter or sweet, all memories are worth remembering. I longed to relive my innocent years without the dust of life and remember the peaceful life, an honest life, led by rural people who worked hard all year round.

~

When I was young, I lived in a village located right next to a river in the outlying district of Kim Sơn in Ninh Bình Province in northern Vietnam. The river was the main transportation artery linking our village with the neighboring districts throughout the province. The boats plied back and forth, carrying merchandise, navigating the water traffic, carrying supplies for all the local residents, and enabling us to have a comfortable life, free of hunger and material want. My house was right next to the river. It was surrounded by a bamboo hedge, and we had a garden with betel nut trees, a fishpond, and many fruit trees, including guavas, longans, grapefruits, oranges, and plums. Almost all the villagers had houses like this, and each house was separated from the next one by a bamboo hedge. We lived near the water, both the river and the sea, and so the air was clear and healthy.

Each year, we experienced the four seasons: spring, summer, fall, and winter. The scenery was poetic, life was simple, and the people were gentle. Eighty percent of our community was Catholic, and the rest were Buddhists or ancestor worshipers. Each village had churches, temples, and shrines. The people in our village were devout and had faith in God. They worked long, hard hours, and the rest of their time was spent in religious pursuits. They offered their souls to God, and they prayed to God every day. They lived without competition, without jealousy, without concern about wealth and poverty; it was according to God's wishes.

The Phát Diệm Church was just three villages away from us. It was the biggest church in the district, and one of the greatest in all of Vietnam. It was a wonder of architecture, built with giant stones long before electricity. In order to erect this great church, each stone had to be moved entirely by human strength. Thousands of worshipers attended Mass every day. On major holidays, the district's entire population flocked to the church. The Vatican is the capital for Catholics worldwide, but before 1954 Phát Diệm was the capital for Vietnamese Catholics.

My father was a teacher, and he was born in the village of Thi Châu in Nam Định Province during the French colonial period. My father taught both French and Chinese, and he was assigned to the outlying district of Kim Sơn. This was a time when teachers were among the most revered men in the village, and everyone was taught the maxim: "A person who can teach you one word is your teacher; a person who can teach you half a word is also your teacher."

My childhood was marked by tranquility. I remember the clean air and the gentle people. At school, I learned about God, the Church, and my faith. Every day, the priest taught us about Christ and how to live a meaningful life driven by our love of God. As a child, I was shielded from all that is evil in the world.

My mother died in 1945, when I was ten years old. When I saw other children my age, I felt lonely. I watched their mothers caress and dote on them, and I longed for my mother's love. I became a dreamer. Every evening, I went to the dike and gazed at the sluggish river, contemplating the infinitely high skies. Floating clouds transformed themselves into multiple shapes, dissolving into one formation after another. Looking down at the river, I saw the lily pads flow downstream with the current, not knowing where they came from or where they were going. Sometimes, a few boats were sailing in the distance. Young men would handle the rudders and maneuver the boats down the river. In my childhood, everyone traveled by boat, traversing from one pier to the next. I noticed that even without modern machinery or oil, people could still achieve their purpose.

My district also had a motorized ferry that crossed this section of the river every day. I remembered its schedule. Every evening, I went to the dike to watch it carrying passengers and merchandise from the district up to town and back. The engine whirred, spewing black smoke and moving at a fast clip. I admired the pilot, and I dreamed that one day I would drive this motorized ferry. How could he control the boat so easily? How did it run so smoothly? These ferries were different from the ordinary boats that propelled themselves forward with cords and cables. I wished that I could control the ferry's rudder. If only I were a grown-up, I could be a riverboat captain. As a young boy, I looked out at the water and dreamed about things that were out of my reach.

In 1945, the August Revolution broke out, and I began to see soldiers in the streets. They wore khaki uniforms, rubber sandals, and pith helmets, with guns and knapsacks slung over their shoulders. People called them the Việt Minh. At that time, I didn't understand who the Việt Minh were. When they came to my village, they announced that they would parade in the district stadium, and I followed the crowd enthusiastically. I elbowed my way to the front to get a close look at the soldiers. They paraded in lockstep, wearing sharp uniforms, and displaying their force, with weapons and vehicles and a sea of flags and slogans. The red banners with the yellow star dazzled my eyes. The loudspeakers praised the Việt Minh soldiers and condemned the French colonialists: "Long Live Việt Nam,

Long Live Hồ Chí Minh." Men used microphones to call on the populace to join the so-called August Revolution, defeat the French colonialists, and fight for independence, the fatherland, freedom, and the Vietnamese people. Even though I had never met a French person, the emotion from the crowd overwhelmed me. Through the fervor of the rally, I felt hatred for the French enemies. We all supported the Việt Minh.

Then the rally ended. Independence, Freedom, Happiness and the Democratic Republic of Vietnam—all these slogans tapped into our subconscious, and the future seemed bright and hopeful. Who wouldn't feel a sense of national pride?

After the rally, the Việt Minh regularly sent out their armed propaganda units. These units became active even in remote villages, and their red flags with the yellow star flew everywhere. The Việt Minh idolized Hồ Chí Minh, the national leader who challenged the French colonialists and sought independence for the fatherland. The Việt Minh posted pictures of Hồ Chí Minh everywhere, in public offices, schools, and local buildings.

At first, Hồ Chí Minh's soldiers created a favorable impression among the population. They lived simply, and they helped the young and the old. However, the Việt Minh began to confuse their respect for Hồ Chí Minh with their respect for God. Hồ Chí Minh's soldiers revered him as a saint. They wanted the local people to believe that along with worshiping God, they should worship Hồ Chí Minh as well. The local people still attended Mass, and our whole family prayed together before going to bed. Life had always been this way, and no other saints could enter our spiritual world.

Notably, after the Việt Minh came to power, Hồ Chí Minh made an official visit to Phát Diệm and asked for an audience with Father Lê Hữu Từ, the archbishop of the diocese. Father Lê Hữu Từ was our spiritual leader; he was devout, ethical, a good organizer, and politically astute. Our community revered him and considered him a representative of God.

Hồ Chí Minh hoped to use Father Lê Hữu Từ's influence to win over the community and gain more trust for his revolution and the machinery of the state. In his meeting with Hồ Chí Minh, Father Lê Hữu Từ recognized Hồ Chí Minh's love of country, and Hồ Chí Minh tried to persuade him to be an adviser to the Việt Minh government. Father Lê Hữu Từ said he was willing to act as an adviser to the Việt Minh, on the condition that they would build an independent Vietnam based on the true meaning of freedom and happiness. He would *not* support a communist state, and he understood clearly that Catholicism could not coexist with a communist government.

⁓

In 1949, French paratroopers dropped down into Phát Diệm, and the Việt Minh soldiers retreated in silence. There were no gunshots or indication of any Việt Minh resistance.

The local people rushed to gaze at these brave men who had jumped out of planes and landed in our village. Out of curiosity, I approached the military station to see these new paratroopers. When I arrived, I was surprised. There was not a single French person. Instead, I only saw Vietnamese men who were also French soldiers. They wore beautiful uniforms with leather boots and red berets, and they were far more majestic and regal looking than the Việt Minh. They lounged about in groups, drinking coffee, eating cookies, and smoking together. Children, including me, approached the Vietnamese soldiers. The parachutists shared their cookies and candies with us, and they even shared their cigarettes with the older kids. Everyone was fond of the Vietnamese paratroopers, especially the youngest among us.

Even though the country was at war, the situation in our region was very quiet. We never saw any shelling or killing. At night, occasionally, cannons from the French station sounded, but where I lived we did not hear the explosions at all.

We called the paratroopers the Nationalist soldiers. I was too young, and, therefore, I was not able to separate the Nationalists from the communists or our friends from our enemies. I only knew that the French were the enemy. The Nationalist soldiers and the Việt Minh soldiers were both Vietnamese, and I saw both as Vietnamese and both as good.

At the end of 1949, my father was assigned to teach at an elementary school in the town of Vĩnh Yên, sixty kilometers north of Hanoi and about five hundred kilometers from our home. For us, five hundred kilometers was a vast distance, and we had only a few rickety old coaches and ferries. One would have to journey in stages over the course of several days. Rather than relocate us to Vĩnh Yên, my father found lodging for my older brother and me in Hanoi.

This was the first time I had left our quiet village, and in Hanoi, I felt as if I had stepped into paradise. Everything looked exotic to me. The houses were built close together, and there was constant traffic. The streets were paved with asphalt and had sidewalks with rows of tall trees on each side, creating a canopy of shade over the streets. At night, colored lights shone brightly, and people walked back and forth in droves, creating a lively, bustling atmosphere. Every day was like a festival day. I was fifteen years old—an innocent and most beautiful age. I soaked in the city. My friends and I explored the city, visiting the turtle shrine of the Lake of the Restored Word and walking along the Hồng Hà River. On summer evenings, we enjoyed *bánh tôm,* a shrimp dish, by the banks of the lake, picnicking and enjoying the night air.

The female students in Hanoi were very fashionable. They had new dresses for each season in bright, vivid colors. The flaps of their *áo dài* swayed gently in the wind as they rode their bikes downtown. A young boy would never forget these images. There were still skirmishes between the Việt Minh and the French, but those happened in the mountains or on the remote flatlands. As for Hanoi, all these elegant young men and women lived in peace until the July 1954 agreement.

～

In 1954, the Việt Minh defeated the French at Điện Biên Phủ. The Geneva Accords divided Vietnam into two regions at the 17th parallel, with the Việt Minh controlling the North and the Nationalists controlling the South. Vietnam became two countries, the Democratic Republic of Vietnam (DRV), meaning communist North Vietnam, and the Republic of Vietnam (RVN) in the South. The Geneva Accords allowed the Vietnamese people the right to choose where they wanted to live. The result was a wave of immigration, numbering millions of men and women leaving the North and moving South to look for freedom.

During the war against the French, my father had taught in a region under Việt Minh control. He found the Việt Minh to be good to the people, and therefore, he had no intention of leaving North Vietnam. I was still in school, and I did not have any understanding of communism, so I didn't think it mattered whether we stayed in the North or moved South.

At that time, I had a very close friend. He came to see me, and he advised me to go South. He told me that his older brother had taken part in the resistance against the French for many years, and he held a high-ranking position in the DRV government. Now, this brother had secretly come back home to tell his family that they had to go South immediately.

Hearing this, I was afraid, and I went home and persuaded my father to migrate South. Because our family was Catholic, my father agreed, and we followed the wave of immigrants southward. The majority of Catholics were afraid that the communists would forbid us to practice our religion, and a number of military and government officials who had worked for the French were afraid of retaliation.

Leaving was simple. All we needed to do was to go to the Ministry of Immigration and enter our names on a list and indicate whether we would be going by plane or by ship. In August 1954, my family and I climbed aboard a French cargo plane, leaving with only a few suitcases and personal items.

In 1954 Saigon was a commercial and industrial city. Compared to Hanoi, Saigon was bustling, and people and merchants overwhelmed the streets. In

Saigon, people had been far more influenced by French civilization, and numerous French people lived and worked in Saigon. The names of the streets and the big shops all carried signs in French, and Saigon people spoke and wrote French as a second language.

It was in Saigon where I became a young adult. Rather than visiting scenic parks or seeing wholesome movies, I began to relax in cafés, nightclubs, and coffee shops. The famous coffee shops became our central gathering places. On days that we didn't have to go to school, my friends and I went to Gió Bắc, Brodard, Givral, and La Pagode. In short, cafés replaced my books and studies.

CHAPTER TWO

Coming of Age

After the 1954 Geneva Accords, the South prepared for a war against communism, and Ngô Đình Diệm consolidated his position. He dethroned the emperor
Bảo Đại and eliminated the major religious sects, including the Bình Xuyên, Cao
Đài, and Hòa Hảo. He had the added support of close to a million migrants from
the North. With these forces, he succeeded in establishing the Republic of Vietnam (RVN) and became its first president.

Diệm understood the communist threat, and he quickly reorganized his administration and the RVN military. His administration established strategic
hamlets in the countryside, which aimed to isolate local communists. He also
modernized the RVN military, complete with a navy, an army, an air force, and a
police force. Each military branch organized its own schools and officer corps, and
the RVN recruited soldiers and officers from high schools and colleges from across
South Vietnam. We all volunteered to support this effort and trained to fight against
the North's communist military.

I volunteered for the Navy, and after two years of training I became an officer.
I was proud to serve the RVN flag and wear the Navy's white uniform. I was also
proud because my training sessions were the first to be taught entirely by Vietnamese officers. Before my class, we had still depended on the French for training and expertise. Most of the naval officers who guided me had graduated from
the French Naval Academy in Brest.

As a new officer, I was humbled by my new responsibilities and the ship's
power. I had mixed feelings of both happiness and worry. For sure, I could no
longer enjoy the innocent days of fun that I had experienced as a student. I felt
my youth slipping away, and I entered a new phase in my life. Now, I had adult
responsibilities as an officer. I had to be worthy of my position. How could I make
sure that my training did not go to waste? How would I measure up? More than
anything, I did not want to disappoint my father who had raised me since birth.

A year passed. Life on a warship was exciting, and I embraced the itinerant
life of a sailor. On the open seas, I experienced the waves and the winds, the immense sky and the sea. It made me realize that human beings were tiny and in-

significant. During the day, we would sail on the ocean, and we could see the horizon before our eyes. But as we sailed day after day, I realized that we would never reach the horizon—the sky and sea were grander than humans could comprehend. I loved the sailor's life. At sea, apart from when we had to carry out our training missions, life was tranquil. After my watch, I usually would stand at the railing and gaze out at the sky and sea. On nights when there was a bright moon and a cool breeze, I reveled in the moment. No painter could imagine the spectacular sights that I saw with my eyes and with my soul.

Looking out at the horizon, I would sometimes see a ship sailing in the opposite direction. I was awed that humans invented such machines and could transform iron into ships. The captain would chart the route, the mechanics cared for the engines, and the officers used a compass to keep the ship on course. Each person had his own task, and each task enabled this massive iron structure to move safely and arrive at its destination across the vast waters—it was truly miraculous.

~

In 1961, the United States began to intervene more directly in Vietnam. As part of this escalation and increased military aid, the United States offered to train South Vietnamese officers. I was in a group of junior officers chosen from the South Vietnamese Navy, and we all had a chance to go to the Philippines. That year, we flew from Tân Sơn Nhứt Airport to Clark Air Base in Luzon. After that, I was transferred to Subic Bay, the largest U.S. naval base in Southeast Asia.

I was excited to learn all about the United States. The country was so powerful that it even delivered all the conveniences and luxuries of the United States to Subic Bay. For the sailors there, it was just like living in America. Subic Bay was like a small city, with bustling traffic, broad, tree-lined streets, and spacious houses. This was my first time abroad, and it was my first experience seeing the world outside Vietnam.

Subic Bay was the home of the Seventh Fleet, and I was sent there to train on the U.S. warships. The ships needed constant maintenance and supplies so that they could stay at sea for days on end. There, I learned how to direct the ships' logistics. For example, if a ship needed supplies, an officer would send a telegram to the base, explaining its needs and providing us with an appointed time and place. Then, we would prepare the supplies and send another ship to that exact location at sea. While at sea, the two ships would sail parallel to each other at the same velocity. Next, one ship would shoot cables to the other, and the supplies were sent over the cables while the ships were still moving. This task was dangerous, and it required technology and expert training. We, in the South Vietnamese

Navy, were there to learn these skills so that we could accomplish these tasks in our own force.

We also sailed to Sasebo Harbor in Japan. After arriving, the crew was excited to go out on the town. Leave was essential for a sailor, because he needed to relax after long days of fighting against the sea.

As we approached the harbor, the U.S. captain went out to the ladder to greet and shake hands with the Japanese harbor pilot. The formal and courteous reception demonstrated that the Americans, the victors in World War II, still respected the Japanese. Even though Japan had surrendered unconditionally after the bombing of Hiroshima and Nagasaki, the Japanese never lost their national pride.

Sasebo is a small town located in southwestern Japan. Although it was a small city for Japan, I was impressed. The houses were five to ten stories high, and the commercial buildings had escalators and elevators; the traffic was dense, but the Japanese enforced all the regulations. Merchandise flooded the commercial centers, which had everything a customer would want to buy. I was overwhelmed by this abundance of goods, and I walked for a whole day in the business district without feeling tired. The Japanese lived and worked with discipline. When customers shopped or went to a movie theater, they all stood in line, first come, first served, and never jostled one another. The high school students, both boys and girls, all went to school in their clean, beautiful uniforms. Pedestrians walked quickly, almost as if they were running. They valued time, and they walked in the streets with purpose.

When I thought about my homeland and my people, I couldn't help feeling sad. Why was Vietnam lagging behind? Why couldn't we compete with Japan? Vietnam didn't lack intelligent or hardworking people, and we also had our own national pride. But Vietnam lacked talented leaders. There was no one to lead the Vietnamese people and keep up with the progress of humankind.

Almost all the U.S. and Vietnamese sailors had gone on leave and went out to the bars, cafés, and dance clubs, where they visited with the beautiful and attractive dancing girls. When it was time to return to the ship, they couldn't help feeling disappointed about having to say good-bye. This affected the crew's morale during the first few days back at sea.

After leaving Sasebo, the warship continued on its mission for three more weeks. Then we returned to Subic Bay. The majority of the sailors enjoyed their leave in Olongapo, filling up the whole town with the white color of the Navy. To get from the naval base to the city of Olongapo, we had to cross a small bridge over a river. The river smelled just like the rivers in Vietnam, and the scene reminded me of the Thị Nghè River, the Trương Minh Giảng Bridge, and the Ông

Lãnh Bridge. Even though we were in the Philippines, the scenery and smells seemed familiar to me.

While standing on the bridge, I saw several small boats, and in each boat was a small child holding an oar. Nearby were a few lovely young girls wearing tight, low-cut dresses that partly showed their ample breasts. They waited, glancing up at the bridge, and tried to seduce the sailors. The young girls laughed and sang, teasing us by saying "throw me a coin." Each sailor who crossed the bridge had to pause and fish for a few quarters to toss down to the girls. And, of course, many sailors found a way to become acquainted with these young girls. They went straight to a hotel, without even going to a café or a bar. The two worlds were separated only by a bridge—on one side was the U.S. naval base, with streets, houses, and vehicles and where everything was clean and tidy as in the United States. On the other side of the bridge was Olongapo, the Philippine city with dusty, bumpy streets, filled with trash and outdated vehicles. The city came alive at night, with dance clubs playing psychedelic music and many rows of bars. The young sailors hopped from one café to another, and the dancing girls stood in line near the door of each club waiting to greet new customers.

Soon it was time to return to Vietnam. My thoughts from the trip remained fresh in my mind. The emotional life of a sailor was like the ocean waves; the more tranquil life was at sea, the more fierce our love of life became on land. At sea, life is attached to the ship and the immensity of the sky and water. When we dock on land, we cannot help searching for strong emotions, for charming smiles, or for tender words. I loved the open seas, and I was fond of a sailor's life. On my return, I reported to the South Vietnamese naval headquarters with anticipation, and I received an order to transfer to a ship. I was pleased, because I would be able to apply all the new skills that I had learned from the Americans. Soon I was promoted to lieutenant junior grade. Compared with American sailors on the U.S. ships, Vietnamese sailors were less knowledgeable, their lives were harder, and they had to be prodded and controlled with frequent instructions from their commanding officer. I frequently had to remind them of their responsibilities.

I had many duties, and sometimes I felt like a housewife. A housewife is in charge of all the chores and household activities, just as I was, but at least in the evening, she could get a good night's sleep. I had all those responsibilities, but I also had to stay alert day and night, whether the warship was in the harbor or at sea. I always had to represent the captain and organize all the work: dividing up watches, providing sea training, and overseeing the material and spiritual life of the whole crew. I was very proud, because I was able to apply to the South Vietnamese Navy what I had learned from training with the Seventh Fleet.

Thanks to my youthful enthusiasm, my passion for work, and my love of the open seas, I always had the captain's trust. Now, I was no longer a young man, living a carefree and innocent life as before. I had matured in my work. I was aware of my responsibilities and duties, and I was acquainted with the outside world. I thought that it was time for me to get married and start a family, because a family would help me be more responsible. If I continued to live the bachelor's life, roaming from one dock to another, then my life would only drift from one place to the next. I intended to build a warm home for myself. I knew many young girls; however, I had love in my heart for only one.

~

No one can explain love. It was love at first sight. I loved her, and I didn't know why I loved her. I already knew her, but I had never had a chance to converse with her. I had no need to learn more about her before falling in love. That is my concept of love: love without a choice and love without thinking. I had silently been in love with her ever since the first day we met three years earlier. With my head in the clouds, I had never expressed my love for her. Now that I had been able to conquer the immense sea, I knew I could conquer love. I felt confident. Finally, I proposed to her, and we built a life together.

The wedding ceremonies were celebrated at the Notre Dame Cathedral in Saigon. I still remember the parish priest's holy words. We became husband and wife before God. I was moved to tears, and I prayed that we would be able to live forever in the love of God. I could never live far away from her, and my love became fiercer every day.

~

Right after our wedding, I was promoted to the rank of lieutenant. I was proud to have the star of leadership on my breast, but I was filled with sadness because I had just gotten married, and I would have to say good-bye to my bride. A sailor had to man his ship and was often away from his wife and children. How could I fulfill my duty as a citizen and my duty as a father and husband?

Almost two years later, I served on an even bigger warship. The war had become more ferocious, and the Việt Cộng (VC) increased their skirmishes throughout South Vietnam. Our ships operated very effectively on the rivers, and they were equipped with cannons that reinforced our military campaigns along the coast.

Four short years after I was promoted and married, I had frequent tours on the ships, and I always departed with tears and endless longing. Joy and sadness were mixed up together, and this pattern became familiar to a sailor like me. But my wife began to feel an emptiness in her heart during my missions, because the time I saved for the sea was always more than the time I saved for my family.

Because I was away so much, I asked to serve on land to be nearer to my family. My request was accepted, and I was allowed to work at the naval headquarters for almost a year. Then, once again, I was selected for a training course in the United States. To me, each opportunity to travel was an opportunity to learn more and to make progress. I would miss my wife, but my heart was filled with hope.

America. My superiors constantly praised America, and its people had created a modern civilization with a high level of technology and science. People in America could enjoy everything. I had to go there to see with my own eyes all the good things America had to offer.

Since 1965, the U.S. military had poured its troops into South Vietnam. American forces advised all the RVN military units and took part in the campaigns with the South Vietnamese units. We reported every single activity to our American advisers. The U.S. military was technologically skilled and modern, and its men gathered good intelligence. The American advisers aided us, and, for the most part, they made the RVN more effective and efficient. Some Americans played the role of adviser in the strict meaning of the word; if a Vietnamese officer asked for their opinions, then they helped and provided support. Other American advisers wanted to be in charge without considering the chain of command, even when they had lower rank and less experience than the Vietnamese unit chief.

It was 1968, and the Tết celebrations had just begun. Ironically, I was traveling to study in the United States, just as the VC invaded the South en masse. On the morning of the first day of Tết, a jeep picked me up to go to Tấn Sơn Nhứt Airport. We saw tanks, armed vehicles, and paratroopers along the way. I was shocked. I did not know what was going on. A military police officer stopped our jeep and asked, "Don't you know what's happening, Lieutenant? Where are you going?"

"We're going to the airport. I am going to study abroad," I answered while showing him my orders.

"I'm sorry, Lieutenant. We don't need to see your documents. Please go back and report to your unit right away. No airplanes can take off today. The VC have attacked the airport and even the headquarters. Many units are still fighting against them. The VC have attacked in great numbers, and they have mixed in with the general population. They are preparing new assaults, and we don't know when. Please turn around and go back right away."

We made a quick U-turn and went straight to the naval headquarters. There we learned the VC had launched attacks at midnight, at the most sacred time of the year. The VC had taken advantage of the fact that the sounds of their guns combined with the sounds of the firecrackers set off in celebration of the holiday. More than half of all RVN military personnel were home on leave for Tết. We did not expect the onslaught.

The VC flooded Saigon. The majority of VC fighters were still very young. They were from the North, and they had received orders to enter Saigon and take over, just as they had taken over Hanoi in 1954. They never suspected that in South Vietnam they would have to deal with a force much more powerful than their own. They were on enemy soil. They didn't know that they were only like mayflies—sacrificial soldiers for Hanoi to carry out its communist plan to conquer the South.

The VC also attacked the naval headquarters. The VC had sent eight commandos with a car and explosives, and presumably they intended to destroy our headquarters. Thankfully, we had accurate intelligence, and we had been prepared for battle. The result was that when the Simca drove up to the gate, we shot the VC fighters on the spot. The VC blitzkrieg caused insignificant damage to the ARVN, and in reality it was a fiasco for the North. Only a few weeks later, the VC were completely wiped out. Their campaign was destroyed, and the situation calmed down.

⁓

Activity in Saigon returned to normal. The airport began to function again, and, finally, I went to the United States. The 707 airliner left Tân Sơn Nhất Airport, taking off smoothly, and after seventeen hours in the air we landed in San Francisco. It was evening, and the San Franciscan sky shimmered with countless colored lights, spreading their beams across the city. It was majestic. Everything pulled me into this magical world.

I silently admired the people who had come from all over the world to start a new life in this country. Over the previous two hundred years, they had built the United States into a great and civilized country. For a moment, I felt depressed thinking about my beloved Vietnam, with its 4,000-year-old civilization, and I wondered why our country continued to be poor and backward even though we were also intelligent human beings.

A U.S. liaison officer picked us up at the airport, and we went to San Diego, where I would attend school. I enrolled in short courses, specializing in the study of military science in theory and practice. Apart from our studies, we were allowed to visit and sightsee throughout California: the San Diego Zoo, the Golden

Gate Bridge, Disneyland, and SeaWorld. We were even allowed to visit the office of then-governor Ronald Reagan, who later became president of the United States.

In America, I saw manicured grass along the streets, parks full of radiant flowers, and clean and well-kept neighborhoods. The shops were also pleasing to the eye, full of merchandise of all kinds at prices that were low, relative to American people's salaries. People needed to have only one job in order to be able to enjoy their lives. I needed to go abroad in order to appreciate the value of an old maxim that my ancestors had taught me: "Spend one day on the road, and you will gather a basketful of wisdom."

I was busy with my studies so the time passed quickly. When the training courses ended, I traveled back to my homeland, bringing with me my newfound expertise and knowledge about life in America. I had acquired new experience and knowledge from the U.S. Navy. Surely, I would be able to contribute to the RVN Navy. I wanted to be worthy of my superiors' decision to send me for this training. I was even more excited to be reunited with my beautiful wife and my children. Living far away from my family made me realize the value of the moments I spent by their side. I was lucky, because when I returned, I was finally stationed in Saigon. I would be close to my family after many years of constant absence.

During the following months, I enjoyed the happiness of having my family by my side. But my life as a sailor ultimately forced me back to the sea. The ship under my command went on a mission for two or three weeks, then returned to Saigon for a break before going out on the next mission. It was my responsibility to carry military supplies, equipment, and ammunition to the units stationed far away from Saigon. Under those circumstances, tears, longing, and farewells were part of my regular life.

Two years later, I was chosen to go abroad again to accept a new warship for the Vietnamese Navy. It was a coastal patrol ship, the first of its kind to be transferred to the RVN Navy. I received an order to fly to the Philippines. When I reported to the American captain, he introduced me to his deputy captain. This man trained me, and I gained a great deal of specialized knowledge. In addition, I had the opportunity to visit many places in Southeast Asia. We would sail out to sea for one month, and then we would go on shore leave for a week in a harbor. I stopped in the following harbors one by one: Bangkok, Thailand; Hong Kong; Singapore; Kaohsiung, Taiwan; and Manila, Philippines. Our leave time was exciting, and all our expenses were covered. We visited each city, and we toured all the scenic spots. I trained on the ship for almost a full year. That year was full of beautiful memories from all the spectacular visits in exotic lands. American officers were allowed to stay in hotels near the ship, and we also chartered whole nightclubs, so the crew could enjoy itself. The U.S. military took care of all the needs of its sailors, spiritually as well as physically. Everyone felt as if the ship was a second home.

By the end of our training period, our South Vietnamese crew had the ability to operate the ship on its own. Then the U.S. Navy formally transferred the ship to the South Vietnamese Navy. After loading the ship with adequate supplies and fuel, we returned to our country full of pride. Back in Vietnam, the warship patrolled the coastal waters, preventing the VC from infiltrating the South by sea and protecting the territorial waters of South Vietnam. This ship became a workhorse, and it logged many hours at sea. After only a few months with us, its machinery needed to be serviced, and unfortunately, we didn't have the skills or tools to provide this maintenance. Therefore, we had to bring the ship to Guam, and the U.S. Navy had to assist us.

Again, I packed my bags to leave. My life had become connected to rivers and oceans, and my emotional life was full of endless longing. In one place, I was a husband with a wife, and in the other, I was by myself with the water. This time, I was in Guam for five long months of repairs. Guam is a small island, isolated in the middle of the Pacific Ocean. I felt lost on foreign soil, and my soul always carried the burden of deep sadness.

After the repairs were done, I returned home and was assigned an even heavier responsibility. Now I was lieutenant of a landing ship tank, providing support for our amphibious operations in South Vietnam. I was able to spend an average of about a week with my family each month. In truth, for a sailor, I was lucky to have had even that much time with my family.

Then, I was again ordered to Subic Bay, and this time I was tapped to accept another coastal patrol ship. I was proud of this mission. I led a crew of two hundred sailors to Subic Bay to receive the ship. After receiving the ship, I made a list of all the needed repairs and services, and the United States paid for all the maintenance. Then, our crew trained at sea for a month under teams of experts from the U.S. Navy.

Even though most of the South Vietnamese sailors had not known anything about the ship, after only a month, everyone was familiar with the equipment. Adequately trained, prepared, and supplied, I brought the ship back to South Vietnam, and the South Vietnamese Navy formally received the ship when it anchored in Saigon.

I commanded this warship for two years. I had one mission after another, and it was not simple. I steered the ship along coastal Vietnam to remote islands. We even sailed to the Paracel Islands and Spratly Islands near the 17th parallel and then back again to the tip of Cà Mau, and then out to the Bay of Thailand. By this point, I was very experienced. I had been at sea for almost fourteen years, and I had captained ships large and small. After so many years at sea, I felt I had the right to ask for a transfer. I wanted to serve in a unit on land in order to rest and to have the opportunity to be with my family. Headquarters granted my request to work on land, but I could only do so outside Saigon. I was indignant. Why should those who worked at the headquarters be allowed to stay on, for five or ten years, without having to serve in another unit or at sea? Frankly speaking, serving as the captain of a coastal patrol ship, as I did, was quite an honor. But if I had asked anyone at the headquarters whether he wanted to volunteer to work as a captain, certainly no one would have volunteered. Living onboard a ship meant hardship and heavy responsibilities, plus having to be away from home regularly. Those of us who served at sea received no special privileges. Not one officer wanted my former position.

Unfairness could be seen everywhere at that time—not just in the navy, but in the entire Vietnamese military. Rampant favoritism, nepotism, and corruption were destroying Vietnamese society. In the end, I was transferred to the Fifth Zone with the rank of vice commander. The Fifth Zone was based in Năm Căn, an outlying district in Cà Mau Province at the southern tip of South Vietnam. Famous for its mosquitos, it was so remote that it could only be described as in the boondocks. Moreover, the unit was known for attracting thugs, deserters, and those who didn't obey discipline. It was full of outcasts.

I felt as if I was being exiled. Where were my willpower and fighting spirit? Where was my pride? Where was the hero? I didn't belong to the abovementioned elements, but every unit had to have a commanding officer. I accepted the sacrifices and the hardships, and I hoped that later I would be transferred to a more pleasant post. I said to myself, when you are in the military, you can't turn down an assignment. If everyone lived in a safe place, then we would leave the way open to the VC to take over. And so I accepted my new duties.

CHAPTER THREE

The Evacuation

I had already been in Năm Căn for four months when the war intensified. My unit was constantly at the ready for battle. However, many military personnel were absent or "on business," leaving our unit at only 80–90 percent readiness. Still, every day we had to prepare for campaigns along the coast or on the rivers in order to defend our territory. When night came, we gathered at the officers' club, and we listened to the radio broadcasts of the British Broadcasting Corporation (BBC) or the Voice of America (VOA) in order to keep abreast of the military situation. We often learned more from the radio broadcasts than we did from naval headquarters. Those who had experience with politics were disturbed by news about the increased intensity of the North Vietnamese communists' sabotage and infiltration in the South. But we were military men. We had to wait for orders and be ready to engage in the war under any circumstance.

My unit was located at the southernmost tip of the country. Our life was full of deprivation. We had no conveniences. The soil was acidic, and the waters were briny. Because we were military personnel, we forged ahead and were unafraid of hardship, but no one would bring their wives and children because the conditions were too harsh.

On the morning of April 23, 1975, my unit was still carrying out its normal activities. I lived in a Quonset hut, with a bedroom, a dining area, a bathroom, a kitchen in the back, and an office at the front. It was just like any other day, and I got up, showered, ate breakfast, and went to my office. I finished reading all the memos, reviewed the documents that needed to be signed, and went over the messages that needed to be relayed to other units. There was nothing special about the day. No news was conveyed regarding the tense situation and the advance of the VC units against our forces.

At exactly 10 a.m., the phone rang. I picked up the receiver and said, "Hello, I'm listening."

An officer answered, "I am the officer on duty from the base. Commander, your wife has come down from Saigon on a helicopter, and she is landing at the airfield."

It took a jeep only one minute to get me to the airstrip. I had a premonition there was bad news. I arrived at the airfield at the same time the chopper from Saigon landed. The helicopter pilot turned off the engine, and the crew and the passengers stepped out. My wife and children were the only civilians. The older children were age eight and eleven, and they each carried a bag. The baby was only ten months old.

I was afraid that something disastrous had happened and wondered nervously why my wife brought along the kids as if they were evacuating. Seeing me, my wife went pale. Tears streamed down her face, and she was in a state of panic. My two older children were usually playful and carefree, but now they sported dazed looks. The baby was, of course, too young to understand anything.

Immediately upon stepping into our living quarters, my wife explained that the situation in Saigon was unraveling. Every day, someone went to her, asking her for help in leaving the country. All the naval families were getting ready to leave, she told me. I had to go back to Saigon at once. I had to see what was going on.

I said angrily, "It may be like that, but headquarters hasn't said anything to us. They're only thinking of their own self-preservation in Saigon. We're dumped down here. They haven't thought about us at all."

"Every day, there are rumors that the VC will attack Saigon. There will be a bloodbath," my wife urged. "Our house is in a quiet neighborhood. I'm so scared, especially at night. The kids and I keep the door locked, and we stay inside. You need to go home and see for yourself."

The next morning, I took an airplane back to Cần Thơ, and from there I took a bus to Saigon. I hoped to get a handle on the situation and then, after a day or two, return to my family in Năm Căn.

I arrived in Saigon on April 24. I drove to our home, which felt cold and forlorn without my family there. I felt depressed. I didn't even want to enter the house, so, instead, I sat down on the porch and looked at our front garden. The ornamental trees and flowerbeds lacked attention. The weeds were sprouting here and there without anyone trimming or pruning them. My heart tightened, and my mind was in a void, not knowing what to think or what to plan. I sat like that for a long time, lighting one cigarette after another. I no longer wanted to enter my own home. I wanted to remember it as beautiful and warm and full of love. Now, the street in front of our gate was deserted. Not a soul passed by. Once in a while, a Honda zoomed by, but the atmosphere was desolate. It sent a shiver down my spine.

I waited until the sun was going down and, finally, opened the door to the house. I packed some clothes into a small suitcase and then jumped into the jeep and drove straight back to the naval headquarters. I ate at the club and stayed overnight to ensure my safety.

The next day, I visited a number of my relatives. Everyone was happy to see me, and they all hoped that I could help them leave Vietnam if the communists entered Saigon. Back on the base in Năm Căn, I had not heard any call to prepare for an evacuation. Why were so many civilians discussing abandoning the country and running away from the enemy? Rumors were spreading so quickly—even rumors that the VC had reached Saigon's perimeter. Wherever I went, people were discussing whether to go or to stay. Two days later, I went to the naval headquarters in order to return to my unit in the South. But it was too late. I no longer had any way to get back to Năm Căn. The road from Saigon to Cà Mau had been cut off completely, and the planes could no longer take off. The entire South Vietnamese Navy was in a panic. No warships were being sent out, and the only ships at sea were those already on missions.

I was distraught and confused. I did not know what to do next.

I waited, but to no avail. I was stuck at the naval headquarters in Saigon. The other officers had gathered together in small groups to plan their escape. No one felt inclined to work. The VC occupied the provinces in the second military zone, from Danang to Cam Ranh, and the northern zones had all fallen to the communists. The VC didn't even have to fight; our armed forces had already vacated the majority of the provinces before the VC even arrived.

Our national politics was also in crisis. One by one, battalions of RVN soldiers fled Danang and then the provinces of Ban Mê Thuột, Pleiku, and Kontum in the highlands. All this had caused terror in Saigon, and everyone was apprehensive that the communists would overrun the capital. People flocked into the streets, partly to fish for news and partly to spend money, fearful that after the VC entered the city, their money would become worthless. The price of gold and U.S. dollars increased by the minute, and no one could determine the rates, so the sellers could name any rate they wanted and still find buyers. Those with money jockeyed to buy gold and dollars, and the restaurants and sidewalk cafés were filled with patrons.

As of April 28, I still hadn't been able to secure the means to go back to my unit. Instead, the evacuation plan for RVN officers seemed to be in place, but no one had a firm grasp of where or when to go, including the highest-ranking officials. Everyone waited.

~

At the headquarters, only one officer had the authority to announce an evacuation—Rear Admiral Hoàng Cơ Minh. He was in touch with an American officer at the headquarters, and they spoke in secret. This officer had a Vietnamese name, "Phú." I had had the opportunity to meet "Lieutenant Commander

Phú" when he came down to Năm Căn once on a special mission. Apart from his duty as a naval adviser, he was also a member of the CIA, and therefore, he spoke Vietnamese very well. I still remember when I met him in Năm Căn. I was drinking coffee in the sailors' living quarters. He came up to me and spoke in a friendly manner. "Commander," he said, "you live here like a homeless person." He had used the Vietnamese term *bụi đời* (dust of life) for "homeless," demonstrating his language skills. I admired him, because he spoke Vietnamese more fluently than the playboys in Saigon. I had known quite a few American advisers, but I had never met anyone like him.

I asked him about his Vietnamese name, Phú. He explained to me, "My name is Richard, usually shortened to Rich. Rich in Vietnamese means *giàu,* but the name *Giàu* doesn't sound right. But in Chinese, *phú* [*fu*] means *giàu,* and I thought the name Phú sounded pretty good, and so I named myself Phú."

I admired him and remembered him. Taking advantage of this opportunity to speak with him again, I started a conversation by saying, "The situation seems so urgent. Can you tell me anything?"

"There is nothing yet, Commander. Do you still work at Năm Căn? Stay calm. When there is something more specific, I'll let you know."

He was calm while he was speaking to me; however, I sensed his nervousness. There seemed to be something secret he wasn't telling me. On April 28, the situation intensified, and yet he still continued to pretend that nothing was happening. In the meantime, Rear Admiral Hoàng Cơ Minh secretly told his relatives and a few officers, including me, that we all had to be ready to leave.

On the morning of April 29, officers readied themselves to evacuate, instead of readying themselves for battle. No one wanted to work; rather, everyone remained focused on his own private plans.

I was in a state of agitation. My wife and children were still in Năm Căn, and yet everyone was getting ready to leave Saigon. My unit of at least two thousand people had obviously been abandoned. No one was thinking about us anymore. The officers in Saigon were only taking care of their own families. The commanding officers no longer thought about their subordinates. Instead, everyone was only looking out for number one. With a crisis before us, we learned the true face of our leaders.

At exactly 3 p.m., on April 29, 1975, Rear Admiral Minh pulled his jeep up in front of the headquarters. Then he made the announcement: Evacuate!

Everyone boarded the ships as fast as they could. No one knew what else to do.

As for me, I was dazed. I went up to the campaign center and tried to contact Năm Căn. I had just enough time to speak to the captain of the zone: "I am the deputy commander. Let me talk with the lieutenant."

The lieutenant of the Fifth Coastal Zone was listening on the line.

"I am the deputy commander," I continued. "I am informing you that, as we speak, the officers in Saigon are moving their families onto ships in order to evacuate. All the ships are ready to depart from the pier very soon. No one knows where these ships will be going. Lieutenant, please order the retreat. Everyone should board the ships and go to the mouth of the river. Gather at Hòn Khoai Island, and please remember to stay in touch by radio. After we are finished talking, I will board my ship at once, and I will be in the radio room to stay in touch with you. Please tell my wife and children to stay calm and to go out to sea. I will contact them, and come and fetch them."

I was only able to say that much. It was brief, but adequate. I believed he would follow orders and retreat from Năm Căn right away. After our phone conversation, I got into my jeep and went back home. I grabbed a few personal belongings, locked up the house, and brought the key to a relative.

After leaving my house, I didn't know what to do . . . or, to be more precise, I could no longer think about anyone apart from my wife and children. I thought about rescuing my father and my father's family, but they were in the countryside, and all the roads were blocked. There was no way to help them. Then there was my wife's family. I hurriedly drove to pick them up and bring them down to the ship. When we reached the pier, we ran into a traffic jam. An officer was guarding the road, and because he knew me, he waved my jeep through, allowing me to bring my wife's relatives onto the ship safely.

There were people everywhere. I didn't know how many ships it would take to rescue them all. Furthermore, only relatives of Navy personnel and their acquaintances were allowed. For sure, some would manage to get on in all this commotion, but we had to take precautions to prevent any VC from boarding the ships. They could blend in with us and then sabotage the evacuation. We had to keep the ships secure.

After we were on the ship, I found a place for my wife's relatives to rest. Seeing that they had settled down, I went up to the radio room and tried to establish contact with the Fifth Coastal Zone.

At exactly 8 p.m., on April 29, a fleet consisting of about thirty ships departed, carrying about thirty thousand evacuees away from Saigon. Rear Admiral Minh commanded the fleet along with "Phú." Phú had his own radio in order to contact the U.S. Seventh Fleet, which was just outside Vietnamese waters and ready to guide us into the open sea.

In the process of evacuation the RVN naval officers had become passengers. We no longer possessed the capacity to command. I felt despondent. In one instant, the Army of the Republic of Vietnam had disintegrated without any announcement.

All our ships followed one another, sailing along the Saigon River by way of Nhà Bè, entering the Lòng Tào River in the direction of Vũng Tàu. I was familiar with this river. Only a few months earlier, I was still a warrior in charge of my ship. Now, I was only an evacuee, a passenger, walking back and forth on the deck. I felt lost and lonely, not knowing where I would be going. What if I never saw my wife and our children again? I had been unable to establish any contact with my unit, although I had kept sending messages.

I slowly gave myself up to fate, drifting along with the ship. What could I do now? I became entirely impotent. I was filled with indignation, depression, loathing, and exhaustion. I had no will left at all.

On the morning of April 30, the fleet neared Côn Sơn Island, which was a gathering point for others to evacuate. On the beach there were several barges, each of which carried many people, everyone jostling one another. A small tugboat was pulling a barge sailing toward our ship, and its captain asked us to let the passengers get on board. In the distance, Côn Sơn Island resembled a shark's fin. Two large American merchant ships were rescuing people fleeing the coast of Vietnam. I kept trying to contact the Fifth Coastal Zone, but failed. I didn't know what was happening to my unit or where my wife and children were.

Soon, General Dương Văn Minh announced Saigon's surrender. He had only been president for a few days, and he handed South Vietnam over to the communists. My wife and our children were now stuck in a communist country. I was in total despair.

I kept trying to reach the Fifth Coastal Zone to inform them about the evacuation and the gathering point. By then, twenty-four hours had gone by, and I still hadn't been able to establish contact. It was only twenty leagues from Côn Sơn Island to the tip of Cà Mau—why couldn't I establish communication? Unable to restrain myself, I picked up the radio to contact Rear Admiral Minh, and I urged that the two thousand sailors in the Fifth Coastal Zone be rescued. Rear Admiral Minh agreed and ordered the destroyer HQ17 to approach Hòn Khoai Island at Cà Mau to rescue the forces of the Fifth Coastal Zone. HQ17 sailed out of Côn Sơn Bay, but in reality, it sailed only a short way, just out of the sight of the other ships. Then, it stayed put, never approaching the tip of Cà Mau as it waited for the moment to leave Vietnamese waters. It never even tried to reach my men in the Fifth Coastal Zone or my family. Chaos ruled, and no one was in command anymore. No discipline was left in the ARVN, and it was risky for us to sail to shore, because we didn't know whether the communist forces were there waiting for us. In reality, they were not very strong in this region, but the rumors and propaganda were so exaggerated that everyone was terrified. I kept waiting for news from HQ17, but that evening it was announced that it had not been able to contact the Fifth Coastal Zone.

I only knew how to pray, and I asked Jesus to come to the rescue of my wife and our children and keep them safe from all the dangers at that moment. All I had was this last resort, my faith in God. As for me, I was resigned to my fate and continued on with this evacuation fleet, regardless of where it would take me. I would be all alone.

~

Only the day before, I had been a member of the South Vietnamese Navy, with countless achievements on the rivers as well as at sea. We were focused on destroying the communists. Now, our Navy had become an evacuation fleet, running away from chaos.

On May 1, 1975, our fleet received orders to sail in the direction of the Eastern Sea and proceed directly to the Philippines. Thanks to the favorable weather with calm seas, a few American merchant ships sailed alongside us to provide supplies. The journey lasted seven days and nights, and then the fleet safely entered Subic Bay. After that, the U.S. Navy transferred us onto large American merchant ships, which had been waiting for us.

Walking toward a merchant ship, I was a nervous wreck, as if still experiencing a nightmare. I had lost everything. I still had a military cap on my head and I was wearing a military uniform with a commander's insignia on the shoulders. But nothing was left of the South Vietnamese Navy. I removed the insignia and the cap and tossed them into the ocean before stepping onto the American merchant ship.

After we had boarded the new ship, everyone found a place to lie down and rest. Those who had all their family members with them gathered together, chatting merrily as they moved forward to a future filled with promise in America. Even though they had lost all their property and their homes, their land, and their gardens, thinking about their escape from the communists was enough to make them happy.

I had lost not only my house, my jeep, and my career, I had lost my wife and our children. I felt the absurdity of it, transferring from one ship to another, journeying to where? Voyages must have a purpose, but I had no purpose at all. Where am I going? What am I doing? And for whom? I felt so depressed thinking about my lot—how could my life be so lost, so lonely like this?

Our ship departed Subic Bay and sailed directly to Guam. The route was familiar to me—I had received a ship there not so long ago. The more beautiful that memory was, the sadder I felt now. Then I no longer dared to think about anything.

We voyaged for four days and nights across the Pacific. The weather was worse than in our initial evacuation, but thankfully, the merchant ships were so big that we suffered no adverse effects.

On May 13, in the morning, the merchant ships entered the harbor at Guam. A gigantic refugee camp was already waiting for us. It had been built to hold hundreds of thousands of people, and it was ready to receive us—the refugees.

CHAPTER FOUR

The Refugee Camp on Orote Point

One after another, men and women left the ship and stepped off the pier onto the shores of Guam. The Red Cross organized the reception stations very efficiently, and guides were ready to help each person. Thankfully, enough chairs were available for us all to sit down and rest. We had just experienced many days at sea, and so when we first stepped onto land, we were not completely ourselves. On arrival, we had a chance to rest and eat, and afterward, buses took us to a refugee camp on Orote Point, which was a five-minute drive from the wharf.

After the buses arrived at the gates of the camp, everyone had to go to the immigration office to complete the preliminary paperwork for entry to the United States, or if someone wanted to go to another country the Red Cross could help with that as well. Each person was provided with a canvas cot, bedding, a mattress, and blankets. Everyone was allowed to enjoy all the American conveniences as we waited and took care of the official paperwork to enter the United States. The camp had the capacity to hold about 100,000 people, with rows of tents close together, eight dining halls, and many medical stations. It had restrooms and showers, an entertainment area, a movie theater, and a Red Cross office, which helped everyone to find family members. In addition, trucks were selling food and cigarettes, and there was even an office where you could exchange your gold for dollars. All our material needs were addressed, and everyone felt reassured. After having escaped from the communists, most people were ready for a new life and a new future. Everyone had their own thoughts and their own plans.

But I was different. For me, each day brought with it a burden of sorrow.

I had been serving in the military at the rank of commander, and I had always been self-confident. Like millions of other soldiers, I was proud of being a brick in a solid wall against communism, defending my fatherland and protecting my family. In all my years in the South Vietnamese military, I had never seen a soldier afraid of the communists. Instead, I had only seen military units ready to engage in battle. But at the key moment when the communists came, all of us had run away. It was so absurd. After all the changes in the internal politics of

South Vietnam, we soldiers were supposed to stay together and remain disciplined. We had been trained and challenged together, and it seemed as if no force could destroy the army. But then the day came, as if there had been a hurricane, and it swept away everything in an instant. At the ultimate moment, we were ordered to throw down our weapons. We were completely stunned.

Certainly, this collapse had many political reasons. We were only soldiers, but, of course, we understood that a small nation like ours was dependent on the great powers. The Vietnamese politicians knew that Vietnam depended on the United States militarily, economically, and politically. Vietnam did not lack talented people, but where were our heroes? For example, the Chinese Nationalist leader Chiang Kai-shek fled to Taiwan after losing to the communist forces in China. Although Taiwan is a small island, located right next to communist China, Chiang Kai-shek still built Taiwan into a prosperous and powerful nation. He deserves to be remembered in history. When will Vietnam have such a leader?

The war had lasted twenty years, and it was a destructive war waged by Vietnamese against Vietnamese, between the South and the North. The Republic of Vietnam had only come into being in 1954, after the Geneva Accords, and it had to cope with an internal political situation that was always divisive and acrimonious. The political factions increased by the day, and the corruption became omnipresent. Only the RVN military had been able to show a spirit of discipline and keep up the fighting spirit. The RVN had been able to stop the communists' plans to invade South Vietnam, and it had defended South Vietnam until today. However, the situation in Vietnam had become so unstable that no country could help a nation lacking in organization, leadership, and with such pervasive corruption. As a result, South Vietnam had to constantly depend on America.

In many ways, the war had been controlled by America and the Soviet Union. All the weapons had originated from America, the Soviet Union, and communist China. If the great powers wanted to prolong the war, then the war continued, and if they wanted the war to end, then it would end. The Soviet Union and communist China had increased their military aid to the North, and, in the end, the United States had wanted to abandon South Vietnam. The United States and North Vietnam signed the Paris Peace Accords in 1973, and afterward, America collaborated with the communists, finding a way to withdraw and transfer South Vietnam to the communists.

Of course, Americans had their own plans, right or wrong. We had to criticize ourselves first. Americans always placed the interests of their country above all else, and so small and weak countries were only pawns in a larger game. America had taken part in the war in Vietnam for years, but not only did it *not* win the war in that country, it had also abandoned it. To the United States, the war had been a game.

~

After I arrived at Orote Point, I had the opportunity to meet with a local resident who worked for the Americans at the camp. Because I had taken a warship from Vietnam to Guam before, I had stood exactly where the refugee camp now stood only three years earlier. At that time, we had gone for many picnics on our rest days on this hill, which was covered with trees and located near Gab Gab Beach. Now, everything had been leveled, and a camp had been erected. Even with the sophisticated American building equipment, it would have required at least six months to complete such a massive project. I asked him how long this camp had been around, and he replied that the camp had been completed in March 1975. It was apparent that while the leaders of South Vietnam had been competing for power and forming sects, the Americans were developing a plan to transfer South Vietnam to communist North Vietnam. I thought that those of us with a fighting spirit could not gloss over this shame. I was only an inconsequential member of the South Vietnamese military, not worth mentioning; however, I could barely swallow the bitterness of my fate as I was swept along with the current all the way here to the camps.

Having lost all my property, my home, and my family, if I settled down in the United States, what meaning would my uprooted life have? In 1954, I had migrated from the North to the South, and in the twenty years since, no contact had been possible between North and South or between South and North. At this moment, I was half a world away from my wife and children. How would I have the opportunity to see them again?

Filled with longing and worry, I couldn't picture how my wife and children were living, whether they were still alive or dead or suffering or whether they had food to eat every day. With the communists entering Saigon, how would my wife and children live and what would they have to put up with? My family had been living in happiness and enjoying all the things that we desired. I had dedicated so much for so many years for the happiness of my family. I had established a beautiful house that I built myself, and it had a front yard and a garden in the back. My wife was a gentle woman, and my three children were always well-behaved. My family had always been solid, without a single crack. Our acquaintances, our relatives, and our friends all wished to have a family and a life like ours. And now, my beautiful family had fallen into the hands of the communists. My gentle wife and innocent children were all relying on me, and now, what would happen to them without me? How would they manage? How would they cope with a new life full of hardship, which would surely exceed my wife's strength? Would my position as a commander, with years of experience fighting the communists, put them at risk? Would the communists leave them alone? I didn't know whether I would ever have the chance to see my wife and children again. I had lost everything. All the work I had put into building such a family had gone up in smoke in a brief moment. Why? Why was this so?

What must I do now? It seemed like a math problem, and it was so difficult that I couldn't find the answer. Keep going, for what purpose? Living for whom? Only for myself? It was the only way. I was still in my prime. I was forty years old, an age that is often said to be a beautiful time in life—when a man is mature enough to begin building a career. If I moved to America alone, then it would be easy for me. I had the ability to build a new life, to start fresh, and in three or five years I was sure that I would have a stable career. I already had experience in living and working with Americans. I had studied abroad and received a warship on American soil. It would not be so difficult for me to build a career. But after I was living by myself in America, what would happen to me? Maybe I would meet someone new to console myself, and I could build a new family, and maybe even find more happiness than I had in Vietnam. Let's accept the fact that I loved my wife and my children more than ever before, but under these circumstances, what would happen? Only heaven knows. How can human beings foresee the terrible events that may happen in our lives? If I moved on and built a new family, perhaps this fresh start would go against my conscience.

⁓

Hundreds of questions filled my mind, but I had no answers. Although every math problem has an answer, this was not a math problem made up of numbers, which could be solved using a simple formula. This was a math problem that would need to be solved by my heart and my conscience. How could I move forward? The more I thought about my wife and children, the more agitated I became. I wept and wept during the days and nights lying alone in my tent. Each time I wept, I would be only somewhat relieved when I tried to calm myself through my faith and prayer. I was a Christian and believed in Christ wholeheartedly, but at the same time, I was weak and filled with doubt. Occasionally, I wondered whether my prayers would reach Christ. One day followed the next, and all I could do was pray that I would see my wife and children again. But despite my constant prayers, Christ did not respond. Christ, with his infinite mercy, infinite love, and understanding of every human action, did not answer my prayers. I only wanted to be with my family. My request was not excessive or out of reach. Then, why didn't Christ answer me? Instead, he let me plead like a beggar standing in front of a restaurant, quietly waiting until a patron doled out some money. Christ, who has performed miracles letting a mute person talk and allowing a deaf person to hear—why has Christ hesitated to help me? Pleading continuously without response, I became doubtful, filled with hatred, and then I lost my faith. If only Christ had allowed me to live an ordinary life as a bachelor, alone without a family, a wife, or children, then I could have lived a happy life. Why did Christ let me have such a beautiful family and then, in the blink of an eye, take it all away? What sin had I committed? At times, I lost my mind to the point that I doubted, and felt indignant toward Christ.

Thinking about my family, I lost my spirit.

At the camp, announcements of flights to the U.S. mainland were made throughout the day on the loudspeaker. I felt as if my soul was being torn apart. Day after day, groups of people followed one another, getting on the buses to be taken to the airport to travel to America for resettlement or to other countries, depending on each person's wishes.

Orote Point was a transit camp on Guam for evacuees to complete their entry paperwork. Four camps in America—in California, Florida, Arkansas, and Pennsylvania—were ready to receive the refugees. Each person would arrive at a mainland camp for a short period, until a sponsor was identified to help them adapt to life in the United States. After arriving in the United States, they only needed to wait for Americans to sponsor them, and then they would officially be assimilated into their new life. Naturally, they would have to cope with many difficulties during the initial stage of resettlement in the United States, but in time, everyone would adjust easily. American history is only two hundred years long. The ancestors of contemporary Americans had come from all over the world to build their lives. The founding fathers of America initially met with difficulties, which were a hundredfold more difficult than those facing the Vietnamese evacuees. Then they had built the land into a country, which had become the most civilized, wealthiest, and strongest country in the whole world. The first Americans looked for gold with a gun on their hips, rode horses, and protected themselves when America was still barren. In comparison to these cowboys and pioneers, the Vietnamese evacuees could only be considered lucky; present-day America was so civilized, and every modern convenience was available. The Vietnamese refugees only needed to know how to accept their new American reality, how to adjust to their new circumstances, and learn to work hard. After that, every difficulty would vanish, and the future would be bright.

But for those of us who waited for our families, it was a different story. The Red Cross office had lists of the evacuees who had arrived on Guam, and each day they added the names of those who had just arrived, including those who came via Wake Island and Subic Bay. I still had one last hope that my wife and our children had been rescued by an American ship during those final days in South Vietnam. Every day messages from those looking for lost relatives were broadcast on the Red Cross loudspeaker, and each day ships carrying the new refugees docked. I constantly waited at the Red Cross office, hoping that my wife and our children would be among those new arrivals, but one day followed another, and I still had no news of my wife and our children.

~

A few weeks later, the United Nations High Commissioner for Refugees (UNHCR) opened an office to help those of us who wanted to go back to Vietnam. If someone wanted to return they could just go to the office and sign up.

This news came to me like a flash of lightning, and I didn't hesitate. Instead of applying to go to America, I went directly to this office to inquire about the procedures and processes needed to go back to Vietnam. Not all of us who had been taken to Guam wanted to go to America. There were still some people who didn't want to abandon our homeland and who considered their families, their wives, and children even more precious than America.

The day I went to the UNHCR office, I saw a large crowd gathering there. Like me, they had all fled in a panic and had lost contact with their families. In shock, they had come to Guam by themselves. Now they all wished to return, and they had the same state of mind as I did. After talking with a number of people, many of whom were my friends and acquaintances, I stepped into the office without hesitation. The UNHCR officials informed me that if I wanted to go back, I could go ahead and sign up. I only needed to fill in some details, and they would process the form. The UNHCR was the only intermediary organization between America and Vietnam, and so it would negotiate between the two countries. We hoped that the new Vietnamese government would agree to accept whoever wanted to return.

After I was photographed and fingerprinted, I returned to my tent with a sigh of relief, thinking about the day that I would see my wife and children again. At the same time, I could not avoid imagining the consequences of my return. I knew there would be many surprises, but I was ready to accept my fate, including the fact that I might be sent to jail. Even though I knew I could even die in the process, I still wanted to return. So as long as I didn't die, even if the North Vietnamese put me in prison for a few years, upon my release, I could still find a way to escape from Vietnam and bring my wife and children out by boat. I didn't think it would be too difficult. By sea, we could go from the Vietnamese coast to Singapore, Malaysia, Thailand, or the Philippines; for me, it was very routine. I would risk everything to get my wife and our children out of communist Vietnam.

After having made the decision to return I felt the agitation and anxiety diminish in my soul. Instead, a ray of hope shone in me. Whether good or bad, what had to happen would happen—every event takes place in its own time. I would wait calmly, believing in the future. Someone had once said that "the traveling road is not difficult because of all of the rivers and mountains blocking it; it is difficult because our hearts are hesitant when facing obstacles."

Those of us who wanted to return to Vietnam knew that we would have to cope with more difficulties than those who went to the United States. In the short run, the future would be dark, not to mention that we would have to live in fear for our lives. We had left in a panic, afraid of the communists, and now we would return, risking our lives and spiritual values. Many Vietnamese moved to the United States because of the possibility of making money and having a house and cars and all the material things that America promised. However, this future could not bring me any happiness if my wife and our children were not by my side. My conscience would not allow me to live selfishly and think only of myself, while my wife and children were experiencing deprivation in Vietnam. I would rather share the same fate as my wife and children. Hopefully then, my conscience would no longer be tormented, my soul would know peace, and life would still be sweet for me even if I went hungry. I no longer had any other choice.

~

Everyone advised me against going back to Vietnam. My friends argued that I wouldn't be of any help to my wife and children and that I would just bring hardship upon myself. When my younger sister from Australia learned that I would be returning, she hurriedly wrote me a letter to dissuade me. She included letters just written from Saigon, describing life there as hellish. She wrote that everyone was trying to find a way to escape Vietnam, and every day people were fleeing the country by boat, despite danger of the sea and storms.

Many families advised me to join them in going to America and starting a new life. They knew that I had some previous experience in America and that I would be able to guide them during their initial days on American soil. A close family friend who had been living in America for many years also wrote me a letter, trying to convince me not to return to Vietnam. Both she and her husband were now university professors in Virginia, and she also had parents and siblings stuck in Vietnam. She told me that because she and her husband taught at the university, they were able to interact with several high-ranking U.S. officials and politicians. They told her that there would be a program for families to be re-united one day, and so I should go to the United States and calmly wait. She was confident that one day there would be a way to bring my wife and children over, just as she would be able to bring her relatives over.

My friends and relatives offered so many priceless words of advice and so much help. They all worried about my going back and risking my life, but regret-tably my mind wasn't clear enough to think or plan anymore. I had lost my faith. I no longer wanted to believe in anyone. I couldn't even believe in myself. My emotions had caused me to lose my mind. I only knew how to make decisions based on my feelings, and I knew that anything could happen to me, even death. But I no longer wanted anything. My stubbornness and my embrace of danger had made me decide once and for all to return, and nothing could make me change my plans.

CHAPTER FIVE

The Repatriates

After several weeks, fewer and fewer flights carried Vietnamese to the mainland United States. By this point, only five thousand or so people were still waiting at Orote Point, and almost three thousand of us had registered to return to Vietnam. The military scaled back activities in the camp. At first, eight kitchens served over 100,000 people, but now only two were still operating. The Red Cross, the medical stations, and the immigration office were consolidated, and the base was no longer a bustling hub. Instead of having ten families packed into a tent, rows and rows of tents were deserted. It was a dilapidated scene.

Those of us who wanted to return to Vietnam felt agitated. Every day we lined up to receive our meals, and when we were done, we would return to our tents and lie down, waiting, but not knowing what to wait for. What would the future bring? No one wanted to think about it anymore. One day followed another. Time passed slowly in the camp. Those who remained lived silently, and a few people almost went mad because of the meaningless waiting. Sometimes, an individual who had been living in one tent suddenly moved to another tent, without any purpose, because each tent resembled the next. Life lived in a tent was just temporary. We were all waiting to go elsewhere.

Some repatriates were women, and some were elderly, but the majority were young men who had been officers and military personnel in the South Vietnamese military. Until quite recently we had been heroically fighting the communists, but after April 30 we had been forced to lay down our arms. Here, we were just the remnants of an army, running everywhere with no direction, dejected, exhausted, and despondent. In the end, we preferred to return to Vietnam and put our fate in the hands of the VC. More than a million members of the RVN military were still stuck in Vietnam. It didn't stand to reason that the VC would take them all out before a firing squad and execute everyone. But even if we had to face a firing squad, we, the future repatriates, accepted that possibility without fear.

At the end of August 1975, Camp Orote Point closed down. The UNHCR announced that everyone should prepare their luggage in order to transfer to another camp in Guam, where we would continue to wait. The next morning, we all

A military photographer captures a scene of the repatriate refugee camp at Orote Point. Courtesy of the National Archives and Records Administration, Record Group 319, Box 19, declassification number 984082, Records Relating to Operations New Life and New Arrivals, 1975–1976.

lined up and boarded the buses, knowing only that we were leaving Orote Point. We didn't care if we were going to another camp, because it would all be the same. We would continue to wait.

As I sat on the bus and gazed out into the distance, my heart tightened. This was the first time I had stepped outside the camp since arriving on the island of Guam. The camp had organized buses to take people downtown before this, but I had never left the confines of the camp.

It was so different from the last time I had been in Guam. I remembered that when I had first stopped here to receive a warship, my heart had been filled with life. Those memories came to life, and I was unable to hold back my tears. I longed for my wife and children. Here was the same street, the same scenery that I had seen before, but now I was here under entirely different circumstances. It was as if I had two separate states of mind and two separate lives. Filled with sorrow, I no longer had enough self-control to make my own decisions. I knew only to give in to my fate, whatever it turned out to be.

I was taken to Camp Black Construction along with five hundred other people. This camp was surrounded by a fence. It looked like a residential complex, and it had five rows of long houses with a cafeteria, latrines, a movie theater, a ball field, and offices. This camp had been built for the Filipinos who had worked for the U.S. Navy and Air Force units stationed in Guam. It felt too comfortable. I feared that the waiting would only continue. We did not know when we would be allowed to go back to Vietnam or even whether that day would ever come.

Stepping into a room, I picked a bed in a corner in order to enjoy the illusion that I had found a remote place, far away from everyone. I wanted to live my days in peace while waiting. I placed my luggage in my individual locker and took a shower. I returned to my bed and heaved a sigh. A few of my close friends lay nearby, but none of us cared to speak with one another. Each of us was thinking about the day when we would be able to return to Vietnam. We were all spiritually exhausted.

The next morning the Civilian Affairs officers gathered everyone together in the auditorium to introduce us to the new camp. The office staff were all Americans, and they represented the U.S. government. They would be responsible for every aspect of our camp life, from our meals to our aspirations. In fact, the food was fresher and better than it had been at Orote Point. Every week, we would each receive five packs of cigarettes. If we were ill, we would receive adequate medical attention, and the Red Cross would provide clothing, footwear, and daily necessities. In sum, camp life was full of conveniences. We could stay here comfortably until we were permitted to go back to Vietnam. Also, if any of us changed our minds and asked to go to America, the office staff was willing to assist us. We could reverse our decision whenever we wanted.

Almost all the camp members were RVN officers and military personnel. For example, there were three lieutenant colonels, over twenty majors, and many captains, as well as doctors, dentists, and lawyers. The other repatriates came from all walks of life, including petty officers, enlisted men, and police. We gathered together to organize a leadership structure. We selected a committee of representatives through a voting process. The men we elected were respected thanks to their experience and their rank. I became a member of this committee. We became liaisons to the U.S. military's Civilian Affairs officers and represented the repatriates.

We also regularly contacted the UNHCR in order to expedite our return to Vietnam, the sooner the better. The UNHCR representative let us know that he was in a position to negotiate with the Vietnamese government. While we waited for the Vietnamese government to approve our requests for repatriation, we would have to be patient. At least, at this point, we felt somewhat reassured that the process was in motion, and we took part in camp activities in an orderly manner.

Our planned repatriation was a source of worry for many people, but the majority of us had made up our minds to return, regardless of the danger. During this time, we received news from Vietnamese friends and family in France, England, Australia, and Canada. Everyone shared their letters with everyone else in order to gauge the current situation in Vietnam. Good news and bad news spread very quickly throughout the camp. Every day, after we had received our letters, we all gathered together to discuss and interpret any news related to our eventual return. Most of our news came from France. Our relatives in France sent us the communist Vietnamese newspapers, but there wasn't much actual news about those of us waiting in Guam.

There was also a good deal of gossip and word of mouth. This kind of news always travels faster, and most of it seemed favorable to our return. We received news about Vietnamese evacuees in Singapore who had been able to return safely to Vietnam by ship. We also learned that the communists were showing some mercy in the name of national reconciliation and not punishing those who had returned.

Whenever some fresh information arrived, we would discuss, interpret, and analyze every iota of it. Apart from sending letters, we were also permitted to send telegrams straight to Vietnam. Almost all our telegrams announced that we would be returning, so that our relatives would feel heartened. We also received telegrams that read: "Having received news of your impending return, the whole family is happy and look forward to it." Other telegrams had more ambiguous content. There was always a lot of confusion. Though some camp members believed they'd return to a favorable situation, others were worried. Would our return bring revenge upon us?

One day, a former RVN petty officer came to see me, and he showed me a telegram from Saigon. The message was brief: "Stay on and go on with your studies." My friend and I tried to analyze the content of this telegram. This officer's uncle was Huỳnh Tấn Phát, who had been one of the top leaders in the NLF and who had been working for the communists for many years. Because of this connection, the telegram seemed important. This young man asked me, "Commander, please take a look at this telegram, and try to interpret it for me. Why is my family advising me to go to school? Should I return or not?"

"You and I are in two different circumstances, so how can I answer you?" I responded.

"My uncle is Huỳnh Tấn Phát. Perhaps you know him?"

"I do. But what is your family situation? What are your wife and children's circumstances?"

"I'm still single and homesick," the young man said. "I miss my older sister and all her children. They are closer to me than their own parents. And I don't know what I will be doing in America. I am afraid of being by myself in a foreign land. Advising me to continue to go to school? What does it mean? I don't understand."

I tried to offer the young man some advice: "Since you have asked me, I will share my ideas with you. The content of this telegram is obvious. You were in the military, so you didn't even go to school; then why is your family telling you to continue your schooling? It means that if you go back, things will not be good for you. You are young, so move on. Going back will only mean facing a lot of unexpected difficulties. Life in America will be free and easy and you will have a future. If you return to live with the communists, you don't know what will happen. I'm different from you, because my wife and children still live there. I don't have the heart to go on, so I have decided to go back. Even if I have to die, I still need to go back. I'm sure your family asked for Huỳnh Tấn Phát's opinion before sending you this message. If I were single like you, then I would think that this is the best opportunity to travel around the world. You are a young person with no worries, no responsibilities. What are you waiting for? I advise you to go on."

"Despite all that, I still want to go back," he replied. "Commander, you are not afraid, so what should I be afraid of?" He remained determined to go back with me.

~

Days passed in anticipation, slowly, like a languid river. Every day, similar news still came to the camps. Many of us were regularly in touch with individuals in other camps, and so we knew about their lives and activities. Like us, they gathered news, but all the news was similar. There was nothing new, nothing special. Day after day, everyone ate three meals and then waited for more news. Sometimes, a UNHCR staff member came to the camp, and then we all gathered around him, hoping for some fresh information, but the response was always the same. "Keep waiting." We lived in idleness and waiting. There was no way to mark the time. It was a kind of torment.

~

The majority of camp members were young men, single and full of enthusiasm. Those of us who were older could wait, but the younger people couldn't sustain this kind of life of waiting without hope, without action. Some of the younger men began organizing to demand to return. All at once, it seemed, groups of young people began to agitate within the camps. They hung slogans along the fences and participated in demonstrations. They demanded that the Americans release us and send us back to Vietnam as soon as possible. In their view, America was responsible for returning us to Vietnam.

The Civilian Affairs officers did not stop these protests; however, they increased security and the police presence at the camps. The representative committee of each camp began to meet with the protesters in order to coordinate their activities. The UNHCR staff came to the camps more regularly, and they urged us to wait and be calm.

Despite these calls for patience, the protests escalated. Men in all four camps simultaneously began to fight for their return. First, they gathered all the camp members in the yard. Then they painted slogans on banners, protested on the camp grounds, and waited to see the U.S. response. With all the passion of youth, the young men kept on protesting. Once they had decided that they wanted to return to the land controlled by the communists, they no longer had anything to fear, including death. Being in America, this free land, made their struggle even fiercer.

The majority of representative committee members, by contrast, were middle aged and at least forty years old. We had had some leadership experience, and so we were calmer and more mature. All of us, however, still had the same purpose, and therefore, the two generations were united. Every individual opinion was respected, and every act was put up for discussion and analysis, in order to arrive at a consensus before we carried it out. Of course, this was an entirely democratic organization, or, to be more precise, everyone was everyone else's equal. No one could command anyone else. Moreover, we were a community and lived together in the same painful circumstances. We valued feeling above all else. We had meetings to discuss everything, and these meetings were smooth and harmonious.

The UNHCR responded by sending a Swiss man of Vietnamese descent named Cảnh, who had worked for the UNHCR for many years. He had regular contact with high-ranking government officials in Hanoi, so he had a lot of news about Vietnam. Every time he got in touch with us, he gave us favorable news about the Vietnamese government's willingness to process our request. Therefore, we camp members were fond of him.

After a week of peaceful demonstrations, complete with banners and slogans, there was still no reaction from the U.S. side. As a result, we escalated our protests and began a series of hunger strikes. Hunger strikers in every camp would sit in the middle of the campground and refuse to eat or drink for one or two days. Each camp raised banners with slogans such as "We Go on a Hunger Strike to

Demand the American Government Return Us to Vietnam," "We Are Determined Not to Go to America," and "We Are Vietnamese, We Are Determined to Go Back to Vietnam, Even Though the Country Has Been Occupied by the Communists." At the time, there was a lot of media attention on the camps. The local newspapers had begun to print news about our protests. High-ranking U.S. officials were forced to pay attention. General James Herbert was the commander of the Civilian Affairs division, and he was directly responsible for supervising all activities at the four camps. During the hunger strikes, he decided to come to the camps and speak with us to learn more about our goals and aspirations.

First, he requested that we disperse and return to our normal activities. Then, he promised to get in touch with officials in Washington, DC, to resolve the issue. The hunger strikers didn't budge, and they continued their hunger strike despite his requests. A few of them had become exhausted, ready to collapse in the yard, but they still refused to leave. Those of us on the representative committee removed those who were so exhausted that they were no longer alert, and we carried them back to their rooms in order to take care of their health.

A few days later, General Herbert and his entourage entered each camp again and requested a meeting with the representative committee and the UNHCR.

"We represent the U.S. government, and we have direct responsibility for taking care of all of you," he addressed our group. "We want to provide you with material and spiritual resources while you are waiting to return to Vietnam. Our purpose is to satisfy your aspirations. We praise your fighting spirit and your non-violent protests. The hunger strike shows your courage and your noble conscience. We always respect the freedom of choice for each person. We have already helped many Vietnamese men and women escape communism and resettle in the United States. If you wish to go to the United States or a third country like France, you can. We do all the paperwork so that you can go wherever you want to. However, your return cannot be simple. Currently the United States and Vietnam do not have any diplomatic ties, and we have to rely on the role of the UNHCR as an intermediary."

"I now yield the floor to Cảnh, who is the UNHCR representative."

Cảnh took the floor after General Herbert, and he, too, introduced himself:

"I am a Vietnamese with Swiss citizenship, and I work for the UNHCR. Although I have lived and worked overseas for many years, I'm still Vietnamese, and, more than anyone else, I understand and sympathize with you in this current situation. I understand your innermost state, your sentiments, your conscience, your duties, and your responsibilities toward your families, wives, and children, as well as toward your homeland. That is exactly why you want to return, and if I were in your situation, perhaps I also would make the same choice.

"I am assigned by the UNHCR to work here on the island of Guam, and I am responsible for helping you return to Vietnam as soon as possible. You should not forget that you are victims of the times. First of all, I would like to tell you that, as General Herbert has said, the United States and communist Vietnam do not have diplomatic relations with each other, but both of these countries are critical to solving your problem. This is a complicated and difficult issue, and of course, it requires time. The UNHCR has contacted the Hanoi government, and, in principle, it has agreed to let you return safely but you will have to wait.

"I know that your protests and hunger strikes are legitimate. I promise that I will do my best to help you. However, I must also offer a piece of advice from the bottom of my heart. You must wait patiently and take care of your health. The hunger strikes will not help protect your health, and once you are back in Vietnam, you will see that you need your strength. You will not be free like before. You must ready your spirits for your return. I would like to stop here. I wish you all good health."

General Herbert sought the opinions of our representative committee. Our chair stood up and responded: "This kind of waiting is impossible. How long will we have to wait? One more month, two more months, or how many more years? We cannot keep on idling and waiting like this. We have to fight in order for the U.S. government to find a solution. We only have this question—tell us how long we must wait for our return. That is all."

General Herbert said to us, "I am a representative of the U.S. government. However, I am not the person who can decide what will happen next. I hope you will understand this. Of course, we hope to be able to resolve this issue as soon as possible, but we also would like to demand a proper response from the Vietnamese. We can't afford to be irresponsible and let you return without any protection. We will make a note of everything, and I will bring it up to my superiors in Washington, DC."

One of our representatives responded: "We know we will have to continue to wait. We also want to inform you that any kind of waiting has a time limit. Please present our aspirations to Washington, DC."

No one said anything else, and the meeting ended. The representative committees agreed that General Herbert and the UNHCR's positions were legitimate, and we would need to be calmer; however, some of the young people still felt restless. They doubted General Herbert's words, and they feared he and Cảnh had only made their speeches to calm us down. Would they keep their promises?

Personally, I believed that each side had its own logic. General Herbert and Cảnh sounded quite sensible, and they needed more time to negotiate and plan.

As for the opinions of those of us in the camps, our doubts were also quite reasonable. The young people were restless. They had engaged in hunger strikes and sacrificed for a common purpose, and I had to admire them. They had acted courageously without thinking about harm to themselves. I was close to these young men and had given my advice, and they, in turn, respected my judgment. Although we had different opinions about our actions, peaceful or forceful, we were always unanimous in our decisions and united in our goal. We met with camp members to tell everyone about our meeting with General Herbert and the UN-HCR. Afterward, the hunger strikers paused their protests, and activities in the camp returned to normal.

This calm did not mean that we had stopped fighting. Rather, we had decided to suspend our protests and wait for more news from General Herbert and Cảnh.

The next morning, my close friends gathered together for a cup of coffee and some cigarettes to exchange confidences. Our small group consisted of four people: me; Nguyễn Thy Tấn, a lieutenant colonel in the Air Force; Lý Duy Trọng, a major in the Air Force; and Dr. Huỳnh Nhã Phù. We were very close and shared the same sentiments. We had all studied abroad in America during the war, but we believed that life in America without our wives and children would have no meaning.

Tấn confided in us: "When we were studying in America during the war, even then we wanted to go back to our wives and children. Now we have nothing, and our careers have collapsed, and our property is destroyed. Why should we go to America?"

Trọng answered: "I used to work with Americans in Vietnam. I never got along with them, and now I have to drag this empty shell to America to find employment with the sole purpose of making a living? I would rather return to Vietnam to my wife and children."

Then Tấn jumped back in: "What about you, Phù? You spent so many years in school to earn your medical degree. You were making bundles of money in Vietnam, now if you go to America, you will have to go back to school in order to be accredited. This would take at least a few years, and you would be homesick for your wife and children every day. How could you go on studying?"

Phù didn't bother to say anything. Fishing a photo out of his pocket, he looked at it closely and then passed it on to us. His face turned pale, and he flung himself onto his bed, heaving a sigh, "My wife and children are still in Vietnam, so how can I help but go back? I am determined to go back with you."

Then it was my turn to share my thoughts, "I am no different from you all. We share the same state of mind. I also have lived in America. I went there to receive ships for the RVN Navy. For years I lived on American ships and with Americans, but we still belonged to two different worlds. We could never empathize with one another. During my time in America, I had financial support, and I could afford to bring gifts home. Even then, I would sit and count off each day until I could go back to Vietnam. America is truly beautiful, but there's nothing there that can tempt me.

"If my wife and children were by my side, then it would make sense for me to go to America and start a new life—but all by myself? It does not make sense for me to go. I'm going back at all costs. I must return. Going back, of course, will mean hardship, but my life in the military has at least trained me to be able to survive obstacles and overcome life's struggles. I will march onward to Vietnam, and then afterward I will just leave my life to fate."

~

Our conversations continued to revolve around our wives and children and the day of our return. A few days later, while we were chatting over some morning coffee, Trần Khoa Mạc and Lê Bá Khúc, leaders of the young hunger strikers, approached us. They had decided to remain militant. Khúc said to me: "Commander, have you heard? A group of ten Vietnamese who had originally evacuated and resettled in America have just returned to Guam. They were fighting to return to Vietnam like us, and America has allowed them to come to Guam and join us.

"Võ Quỳnh Thiện has flown here from France. He used to be a representative in the National Assembly in Saigon. He fled to France, but now he wants to return to Vietnam. Another leader is Trương Ngọc Khoa. It seems that he was very active in leading a group of Vietnamese repatriates in Fort Chaffee, Arkansas. The U.S. government got spooked and sent them all here."

"Do you know anything about Trương Ngọc Khoa's background?" I asked.

"It seems he worked in an American office in Saigon for seven or eight years."

Soon, a group of young people led by Mạc and Khúc began to display banners and support the hunger strikes at Camp Hawaiian and Camp Barrigada more publicly. The U.S. officials increased the number of U.S. employees in the camps in case any violence broke out. The atmosphere in the camps became tense. The number of people participating in the direct struggle increased every day; however, the majority of us were still outsiders. We all wanted to go home, but when it came to joining the protests, we were afraid that it would cause trouble. We were weak and depressed, and so most of us were too exhausted to take part in such volatile and controversial activities.

~

Soon, the demonstrations at Camp Barrigada and Camp Hawaiian led by Trương Ngọc Khoa and Võ Quỳnh Thiện became more violent. These two men had just set foot on Guam, but it seemed as if they had come with plans. Led by Khoa, the group carried banners, climbed over the camp fence, and marched in the direction of the capital of Guam. The demonstrators flocked into the street demanding that America return us to Vietnam. After they reached downtown, they planned to demolish some houses and cause chaos for the local population. They believed that if they only demonstrated at the camps, they would never be heard. If they disrupted the local community outside the base, they hoped it would force the United States to come up with a solution. However, before the young men could destroy anything, the U.S. marshals forced all of them onto trucks and drove them back to the camps.

The news spread very quickly to the other camps. Their militant spirit inspired everyone, and many of the repatriates became ready to support the next protests. The young people were especially elated, and they were quick to participate if it would help us return to Vietnam quickly.

The capital of Guam was small, with a population of only around 100,000 people, 30 percent of whom were Americans. These protests naturally shocked the local people. The people here lived in peace and had never experienced anything that upset their lives. Of course, the U.S. government responded.

Early the next morning, the Civilian Affairs officers announced that the governor of Guam would pay a visit to each camp. Those of us on the representative committees had a meeting to prepare ourselves for the governor and voice our desire to return to Vietnam. A number of the people who had protested hurriedly painted a few banners with strong words: "We Demand the U.S. Return Us to Vietnam as Soon as Possible." "We Are Not Responsible If We Have to Continue to Wait Any Longer on the Island of Guam." Of course, when the governor of Guam saw the banners, he would see them as threats to Guam. He couldn't risk such disruptions to his own community, so he would have to speak up and pressure the U.S. government to meet our demands.

At exactly 10 a.m., Governor Ricardo Bordallo and General Herbert arrived together with their entourages, followed by a squad of local police and some police dogs. They wanted to warn the camp members not to cause trouble. Outside the fence, a special police squad equipped with weapons and armor was at the ready in case of any violence. The heavy security, together with the police dogs, caused some indignation among camp members, but nonetheless we gathered calmly in order to listen to the delegation. Governor Bordallo spoke to us directly:

"Perhaps you all know, we have come here with the purpose of asking you to stay calm. We understand your aspirations, and we want you to be as comfortable as possible in these camps while you wait to return to Vietnam. Last night you disrupted the peace and order downtown simply because you felt impatient for your return. While we are sympathetic to your desires, I would like to ask all of you to understand that our local people do not expect any disruptions in their daily lives. When they are provoked, they must react, and I'm sure that you would do the same. I honestly call upon you all to wait calmly. The day of your return will surely happen, I can guarantee that. I hope that you will understand and sympathize with me like I have sympathized with you. I promise that I will do everything possible in order to satisfy your goals."

There was no applause and no discussion, but everyone seemed to understand that there would be more waiting, without knowing how long we would have to wait.

Phạm Văn Luyện broke the silence: "Governor Bordallo, I would like to represent all the camp members who are present here. As you well know, we have one single wish, which is to return to Vietnam and be reunited with our families, our wives, and children as soon as possible. We have waited for several months already, and we haven't had a ray of hope. We cannot wait in hopelessness. Worries have been weighing down our souls every minute, every hour, every day during the past few months. How can we not be impatient? Our demand is legitimate. Our protests have not caused destruction. We protest in a spirit of righteousness, and not in hatred. We believe that you also recognize that our aspirations are legitimate. Most of the men in the camps are younger, and so they are enthusiastic, but a bit inconsiderate. When they act, they bring with them all their spirit and zeal. Occasionally, they forget to weigh the pros and cons of their actions. The acts committed by the young people from Camp Barrigada last night were just like that. We would like to ask you to keep your promise and let us know how much longer we'll have to wait to return to Vietnam."

The camp members applauded in approval for a long time.

General Herbert responded: "I have a few brief words for you. First of all, I would like to let you know that right after your demonstration, I made a phone call to Washington and reported the situation. DC ordered me to immediately contact you and announce that the day of your return is a sure thing. It is being processed. It cannot be much longer, so you must stay calm. I would like to also add that the United States is responsible for your presence on Guam. We have had to rely on the help of Governor Bordallo and the people of this autonomous land. I also would like to add that the United States has done everything possible to help the Vietnamese escape from communism. We have helped the Vietnamese evacuees build new lives and new careers, for surely it will be better than staying in Vietnam. We're even helping you in your desire to go back to Vietnam and live with communists. You cannot deny our good will. The events that happened last night are regrettable, and we have apologized to Governor Bordallo on your behalf. Today, I call upon you and hope that you will sympathize with me and my position. Until you return to Vietnam, I also cannot go back to the United States. My office is always open, and your representatives can meet with us anytime. I would like to ask you to go back, rest, and take care of your health."

The speeches by Governor Bordallo as well as General Herbert partly calmed our spirits. Everyone had to think. As for me, I made a mental note of the logic of waiting patiently and calmly, but a number of young people still were not satisfied. A promise is just a promise. The prospect of more waiting still seemed to make everyone exhausted and depressed. We didn't know what to do. At least, the continuous protests had forced the United States to take us seriously and try to find a solution.

⁓

Two days later, Cảnh, the UNHCR representative, entered the camp to visit us again. We all surrounded him to learn more about the diplomatic situation. He told us that life in the North was desolate, and the streets were empty. Food was in short supply, and everyone could only hope to have two meals per day. In the South, the situation was a bit more lively. Northerners, especially government officials, had rushed to the South in waves to have a better life. Flea markets were springing up everywhere in the South, because Southern families were selling off their household furniture and foreign goods in order to have enough money to survive. Plus, many new foreigners, mostly Russians, Poles, and Czechs, had arrived, and they, too, thirsted for these sales, because in their own countries they didn't have these valuable French, Italian, Japanese, and American products. How could these western goods be imported to communist countries? Even if they could have been imported, the people wouldn't have the money to buy them.

In fact, Cảnh could see only a façade of Vietnam. He could not see the depths of the communists' policies, the ways they governed, or their plot to revenge themselves against the RVN. How could Cảnh understand? He was only a foreigner in Vietnam on business. Every time he took a step, he would find it difficult to avoid the owlish eyes of the police, let alone the opportunity to observe everything objectively. Cảnh almost always brought us favorable news. We knew the reality would be much harder for us. We wondered if we would be killed when we returned or if we would be imprisoned. Cảnh only let us know that Vietnam had agreed in principle that we could go back. That was all.

This time, however, Cảnh also let us know that the Aga Khan, the UNHCR's special envoy, would visit our camp the next day. Hearing this news, everyone was elated.

At exactly 9 a.m. the next day, General Herbert and the Aga Khan came to the camp. Everyone clapped their hands in approval. The Aga Khan said to us: "Only two days ago, I was working at UN headquarters. Unexpectedly, I received an order to abandon my work and prioritize a new mission—finding a solution for your repatriation. Please understand that it is a complicated issue. Your return is not simple. In principle, Vietnam has agreed to let you go back, the United States is always ready, and we at the United Nations have the means to take you back anytime. However, Hanoi still has many internal issues and is not ready yet. Tomorrow, I will be going to Hanoi to move the process forward. While waiting for the results of our trip, I hope that you will keep a civil attitude and avoid any actions that might cause disruption in Guam. We ask for your understanding. Please help us to find an effective solution. That is all I have to say."

General Herbert added that the trip would cost the United States more than a million dollars, and so we should recognize the U.S. commitment to our cause.

Phạm Văn Luyện stepped forward: "Your Highness, the Aga Khan, we would like to thank you for your consideration. We ask you to pass along our words to the Hanoi government that we want to return entirely because of our families and our homeland. We also want Hanoi to know that we will report to the new government. We recognize our responsibility. Our only goal is to go back. That is our sole aspiration."

The Aga Khan took note of his words and promised to do his best. Everyone responded to him enthusiastically and waited, with hope overflowing.

After the delegation left, we felt as if a burden had been lifted. In the camps, we were always exhausted. Each time a U.S. or UN officer came to the camps, we would try to grasp their words and promises. Our discussions now had an element of optimism. We didn't forget General Herbert's words that the United States had spent close to a million dollars on the Aga Khan's trip. It couldn't just come to nothing. We understood very well the power of the dollar. The United States could do anything. If the United States wanted to do it, then it could be done. Our return was a trivial thing, so if the United States wanted it, then it would be easy.

The situation at the camps returned to calm and normalcy. We all looked forward to the Aga Khan's return, and we were optimistic that the date of our return would soon be revealed.

Exactly one week later, the Aga Khan returned from Hanoi. Everyone was nervous, waiting for this meeting.

He had a cold expression on his face, and he stood next to General Herbert, unsmiling. He greeted us and went straight to the point. Looking at his face, I already realized that the news was not favorable. He was tense and nervous as he spoke: "I went to both Hanoi and Saigon, and I was able to speak with top-ranking leaders, and your return was the main point of my discussion."

"Today, as I promised," he continued, "I will give you a full and detailed report on my trip to Vietnam. In general, Vietnam appeared very desolate, and the remnants of the destructive war were still apparent, especially in the North. From the 17th parallel on up through central Vietnam, there hasn't been any rebuilding to the houses, streets, or bridges. The scene was bleak beyond my imagination. I don't know if Hanoi will have the ability to rebuild. Even if they have the will, it will take countless years for Hanoi to carry it out. For now, they are content to wait for scientific and technological aid from abroad before they begin work on the reconstruction. Peace has been restored in Vietnam, but Hanoi does not have any concrete plans to improve the country. The North does not have enough competent people to run the Southern factories and industries, and the South seems empty. In other words, the situation in Vietnam right now is extremely difficult.

"The Vietnamese leaders took me out to observe all the remnants of the war, and it was only after touring the countryside that they sat down to speak with me about your repatriation. I would like to repeat to you what the prime minister said to me in this discussion. He said, the Aga Khan, representative of the UN, we will fight those who ran away, but we won't fight those who return. We offered mercy to all of the RVN government officials and army officers who came out and reported to us. There was no bloodbath. However, before we entered the South, there had been many rumors that we would take revenge, and so those who were fighting against us ran away. Now some of them want to return. We welcome them and are willing to receive them, but, Mr. UNHCR Representative, we also want to emphasize the devastation caused by the American War. We took over the South with countless insurmountable problems, and we haven't been able to solve them yet. We still have many internal affairs that must be prioritized. As for those who want to return, in principle, we agree, but we cannot let them come back at this time. Please tell them that they have to wait. We will let them come back when there is a place for them to stay and proper employment for them. Only then can they come back. Currently, we don't even have enough jobs for the millions of people who stayed in the South. We hope that they will understand and keep on waiting there."

When we heard these words, we all held our breath in despair. He went on, "That is what they said. I explained that the UNHCR would be willing to help resettle everyone if Hanoi agreed to let you come back right away. However, Hanoi rejected our proposal. They did not want a foreign office to monitor you or be involved in their internal affairs. In truth, what they said makes sense, and they are determined to advise you to keep waiting in Guam.

"That said, there is nothing else to do but wait. I hope you understand the problem clearly and calmly wait here. We hope to continue supporting you until the mission is completed. Do you have anything to say?"

The Aga Khan's declaration was like a gourd of cold water splashed into our faces. Everyone seemed stunned. We had invested so much hope in the Aga Khan's trip to Hanoi, and, now in an instant, it had gone up in smoke. We were impotent. Our disappointment weighed down upon us, and we didn't know what to say. We only knew that we had to wait, there was no other way. We had no power—we had to wait for a miracle, wait until the VC agreed to let us return.

Deep in my heart, I felt confused and despondent. I wondered what would happen if I just went on to America. I could find a job on a merchant ship, and then one day when the ship stopped over in Saigon, I could jump ship and stay. However, I didn't even know whether the ship I would be working on would ever stop in Saigon or whether it would sail to other continents or other seas. I would keep traveling in endless loneliness. While I pondered this alternative, the image of my wife and children came back to me. At all costs, I had to return to them. I had to see them in the flesh.

I was deep in thought and forgot that I was in a room in with the Aga Khan and General Herbert. Suddenly, General Herbert spoke up, and his words startled me, bringing me back to reality. He said: "You have to stay calm, to have faith. You must wait calmly and avoid causing disturbances or staging demonstrations. They won't bring the results that you wish, and they may even have an adverse impact on your return. I will go back to Washington and discuss your desires with the authorities. Then, I will come back here, and I hope that I will have fresh ideas that will help you."

We went back to our rooms feeling dispirited and dejected. The day of return had receded into the distance. No one wanted to talk to anyone else. What was to be done now? Everyone posed this question to themselves, but no one had an answer.

Two days later, there was another violent demonstration inside Camps Hawaii and Barrigada. The repatriates there had damaged or destroyed a number of barracks. At Camp Barrigada, a group of young people was very passionate about the fight for repatriation. Approximately twenty of them had gone to America, but they did not want to stay. They felt as if they had been treated like slaves, and they were depressed and indignant about their lives in the United States. Therefore, they had returned to the camps and fought fiercely. Trương Ngọc Khoa attracted everyone's attention, because he dared to do things so forcefully, openly fighting America in order to achieve repatriation. A lot of people admired him. He usually acted unilaterally without consulting anyone. He was ready to do whatever he wanted to, and all the young people supported him. At Camp Hawaiian, the demonstrations were led by Võ Quỳnh Thiện who also fought actively and forcefully.

Many of us were suspicious of Khoa and Thiện. These two men obviously worked for the CIA. In many ways, this was nothing new, because the CIA always had a hand in foreign affairs. These two men—one who had come from America and the other from France—now returned to Guam at the same time, and, before arriving at the camps, they had stayed together at the Hotel Tokyo in Guam. Then, the moment they entered, they had called for violent protests, assumed leadership roles, and synchronized their activities. It was apparent that they had made plans while they were staying at the hotel, and, of course, the United States was guiding them as they prepared for violent demonstrations. We could see this very clearly, but we couldn't understand America's goal. There were so many questions.

I no longer wanted to listen to everyone constantly discussing these two men. I said, "Keep calm, everyone. There's nothing to be afraid of—just let them act. Violent or not, in the final analysis, it is all planned out by the Americans. We only need to know that we want to go home, that's all. At the Paris Accords, the Americans arranged the transfer of South Vietnam to the VC, and on April 30, the VC overran the South. So now, the Americans are using these two guys to play games. It is not worth talking about."

My friend Tấn responded: "Or maybe they planned to make things ugly. America might want to use it as a pretext to take us to a deserted place where we would just lie and wait. Then if we protest, nobody will ever hear even an echo of our struggle."

In fact, the protests, organized by Khoa and Thiện, caused a great deal of commotion among camp members. All of us who had stepped into these camps truly intended to go back to Vietnam, but if going back became too difficult, the majority wouldn't want to struggle. A few had begun to change their minds, and they chose to go to the U.S. mainland and seek a new life. Among the four of us, Trọng and Phủ had a change of heart. Trọng told us: "Phủ and I have decided to move on. We no longer want to go back. We don't know how much larger the next protests will be. We have run away from our enemy. If we keep waiting here, will we be left alone? I see these violent demonstrations, and I feel scared."

Tấn cut in: "I will be the last one to return. If all of you change your minds and go, the last one to remain here in Guam will be me."

I quickly added, "You should remember that there will be a second person with you—me. I have thought so much about this. There is nothing anyone can do to change my resolve."

Soon thereafter, Trọng and Phủ left Guam. Tấn and I were left behind, and we got along well because we had the same philosophy. One day he said to me, "I am determined to go back to Vietnam, but, deep in my heart, I occasionally wonder: if I go back, will I be of any help to my wife and children?"

I answered him: "Tấn, you and I have a very similar state of mind and very similar thoughts. We live by noble sentiments, and we are true to our hearts. I understand you, and, therefore, I want to confide in you. I have thought a lot about going and staying, considering the pros and cons of both. Like you, I cannot abandon my wife and children. Therefore, I must go back. If we choose to move on by ourselves, how can we avoid the birth of new feelings? Thinking about the future is like that, but what about thinking backward? How can we enjoy happiness while our wives and children are suffering and living in poverty in Vietnam? How could we have the heart to do it? We will suffer when we go back, but our consciences will find peace. We will share the sadness with our families, and this will give our lives some meaning. I am content to accept it."

Tấn replied, "But with communism, we don't know whether we will even be able to help our wives and children."

Tấn usually conjured up the worst-case scenario, and he seemed deeply worried. He was not as tranquil as I was. As for me, I no longer wanted to make any plans; I only wanted to go back and let fate decide my life. I was ready to accept anything.

I continued: "Tấn, we won't be able to help our families at first, but afterward, we can help them, because life is long. Even if the communists throw us into jail, it will probably be for only five years. We can accept five years in prison, and then, after that, we will be able to find a way to get our wives and children out. In five years, we will still be young. We will still have the strength to prepare for a new life. It will not be too late. Our children are still small, and their future is still very long. Five years, and then we will be out of prison, and you and I will find a boat to escape to Thailand, Malaysia, or the Philippines. The sea routes are so familiar to me. I tell you all this in confidence. Please remember to keep my thoughts secret and do not reveal them to anyone. Many people will return to Vietnam, and if they hear of my plans, they will report them to the communists and try to curry favor with them. If that happened, there will be trouble for us."

Tấn said: "You think so far ahead. I agree with you. In five years, we will still be full of energy. But from now until then, our sentiments and our conscience will drive us crazy. The Aga Khan's trip has failed. Let's just wait to see how this group

led by Trương Ngọc Khoa and Võ Quỳnh Thiện reacts. Each time they take action, some of us get frightened, give up, and move on to America. In our camp,
scores of people have given up. I'm afraid that if too many people change their
minds, then the United States will not try to find a solution for us."

I answered him, "You must stay calm and ignore other people's decisions. We
only know that we are determined to go back, and we are not changing our minds.
As for Khoa and Thiện, it is so obvious that America has given them orders, which
means that everything is out of our control. We can only wait calmly. There is no
other way. Not many people have gone to the United States, and there are still
more than two thousand people to repatriate in the camps. Even if half these people
go on, there will still be one thousand people left. This will force America to find a
solution. Wait and see. These two protest the loudest, but when it is time to return
to Vietnam, they will not be present among the returnees."

Tấn continued, "Why don't Khoa and Thiện ask our opinions? We are on the
representative committee."

"I agree," I said. "However, our organization isn't bound by any legal rules.
Everyone is like everyone else. No one can command anyone else, and we are no
different. That is obvious. If they truly want to collaborate and reach a common
consensus, that would be good. But if not, then we just have to put up with it.
Again, I suspect that those two work for U.S. salaries. They don't need our opinions.
Let's just ignore them and allow things to take their own course. I am already so
depressed."

CHAPTER SIX

Give Us a Ship

After his failed trip to Hanoi, the Aga Khan returned to UN headquarters, and General Herbert flew back to Washington, DC. While General Herbert was in the capital, numerous demonstrations broke out again at Camp Barrigada and Camp Hawaii. These protests caused great damage to the camps and alarmed the U.S. government.

General Herbert urgently returned to Guam. He quickly convened a meeting with the representative committee. This time, he came to the camp with two new men accompanying him. They both appeared to outrank General Herbert. As he spoke with our representative committee, he did not introduce either of these individuals. The two of them flanked General Herbert on either side and observed the situation without any expression on their faces.

Next, General Herbert said to us: "I am meeting with you for the sole purpose of informing you that Washington wants a solution for your return. I want to emphasize that the United States cannot make this decision unilaterally. Instead, we must have an agreement with the communist government in Vietnam.

"I have urged you to wait calmly, but when I was in Washington, there was a series of riots in Camps Barrigada and Hawaii, causing considerable destruction to the camps. Violence will not solve anything. Today, we sit together with one another. I expect you to be straightforward with me and help find a solution, rather than cause more damage. Let me have your opinions and your thoughts."

Phan Tụy Trang, the deputy leader of the representative committee, stood up and said: "General Herbert, when the Aga Khan went to Hanoi, all of us had great hopes for his trip, but when he returned, we all became despondent. What must we do now? After someone has lost hope, he will do anything, with no concern for the consequences. The fact that there have been riots in Camps Barrigada and Hawaii attests to that frame of mind. We would like you to understand that we cannot wait any longer. Washington must find a solution for us to go home as soon as possible."

Trần Khoa Mạc, a leader of the young people, continued: "General, the Vietnamese who came here in April brought forty, even fifty South Vietnamese ships

83

with them. They are all still anchored in the Port of Guam. We would like the United States to give us one of the ships. Then we could return by ourselves without Hanoi's permission."

It should be noted that he had been an interpreter in the RVN Army. He spoke English fluently and expressed himself very eloquently and forcefully. He had been a leader at the camps, egging on and leading the hunger strikes and the riots. Over the past few days, he frequently went to Camps Barrigada and Hawaii to work with Trương Ngọc Khoa and Võ Quỳnh Thiện. Today was the first time that he expressed himself so clearly. Perhaps, these were the words that Khoa had fed him.

Even though I was a member of the representative committee, I was just an observer. I no longer wanted to say anything.

General Herbert replied, "This is an idea. There are many ships and planes. The key concern is that we must have Vietnam's permission for you to return. Furthermore, sailing a ship back to Vietnam is not easy. How can we let you go back on your own? Acting like that would prove that we are irresponsible, because there would be no guarantee for your safety."

Mạc argued, "General, there are many among us here who were naval officers with experience at sea. Go ahead and give us a ship. We guarantee that we can go back on our own."

General Herbert answered back, "I respect your opinion, but can you guarantee that you are skilled enough to sail the ship and get back to Vietnam? This distance is not as easy as you say. Who has the ability to perform this task?"

Mạc had an answer: "Here in Guam, there is a naval commander, Trần Đình Trụ. He was a captain for many years, and he sailed ships from America back to Vietnam."

～

Hearing my name mentioned I startled. I did not understand why this man had mentioned my name without consulting me. I had never spoken with him at all about my experiences at sea.

～

General Herbert continued, "I would like to meet with Mr. Trần Đình Trụ."

I stood up and introduced myself.

General Herbert asked me, "Please let me know whether you can perform this task."

I answered slowly: "Is there a ship for us? I was in the Navy, and I am a professional sailor, but, General, please let me know whether there is a ship or not, before asking about my ability."

General Herbert prodded: "I would like to know more about you. Please tell me about your activities in the Navy."

"General, I would prefer not to answer this question. I don't want to talk about the past; I have lost everything."

General Herbert answered: "I would like to point out that providing you with a ship is just a proposal, but it is an innovative idea. If I am to present it to Washington, then I must know whether there are enough people trained to sail the ship. Only then would Washington consider it. I apologize for having mentioned your past, but this is critical if we want to find a solution."

"If that is the case, then I will answer you. I was a deputy commander in the Navy, and I have thirteen years of experience at sea. I held the position of lieutenant for over ten years, and I studied abroad in the United States at the Center for Naval Training in San Diego. I went abroad many times to receive ships that the U.S. Navy had transferred to the RVN Navy. If there is a ship for our return, I am ready to accept this mission, because it would allow me to return to my family. With experience and confidence, I tell you, I can do it."

General Herbert responded, "I have one more request. Can you give me a list of potential crew members? This will make it easier for me to propose this 'ship solution' to Washington. And who knows? This might be a solution that Washington can accept."

"General, once I have said that I can do something, I can do it," I replied. "There are many naval officers in this camp who also want to return. I can promise you that if there is a ship, I will need only one day to organize a crew."

General Herbert appeared to trust me, and glancing at the two men who had accompanied him, I noticed that they seemed to approve as well. One of them spoke up for the first time: "Go ahead and give us a list of crew members and provide details about their experiences, their specializations, and their individual duties. When Washington looks at your list, they will recognize your ability. That way the ship will materialize."

I understood right away that this man was an important person who could make a decision on behalf of the U.S. government, so I replied: "As I've just said, I don't believe you will give us a ship, because the United States has so many airplanes. Wouldn't it be easier just to fly us back to Vietnam?"

General Herbert answered: "The United States has always been ready to take you back to Vietnam whenever Hanoi agrees. Right now, this ship is only hypothetical. But if we do propose it to Washington, we need evidence and plans that it could work."

Huddling around me, many camp members encouraged me to accept the proposal and give a list to the Americans.

General Herbert spoke to me directly: "I would like to tell you this story, Trụ, so that you will understand. Not long ago, who would have thought human beings would be able to travel to the moon—but now there are Americans landing on the moon and walking up there. There is nothing we cannot do. You should believe in us. Let us have the list of crew members. It will make it easier to explain our plan to Washington."

General Herbert's confident voice caused me to have more hope. It was true that the United States can do whatever it wants to do. Therefore, I felt I had no choice but to tell him that I would carry out his request. I told him I would make a list of all the crew members.

General Herbert continued, "The sooner you can give me the list, the better. Can you do it within three days? When the roster is in my hand, I will immediately fly back to Washington."

I agreed to have a list ready for General Herbert within two days. He appeared to be satisfied, and the meeting came to an end. When we said good-bye, General Herbert grasped my hand tightly. He seemed to have great confidence in me.

~

As they left the meeting, the camp members surrounded me joyfully. They appeared to trust me. I became like a life preserver in the midst of the open seas for our group of drowning people.

As I returned to my room, I was deep in thought. Again, it seemed as if there had been an arrangement in advance. Trần Khoa Mạc had clearly known about my background before he stood up to present his proposal for a ship. In truth, this solution was logical, and I also hoped that it would materialize. Vietnam did not seem interested in granting us permission, and America was afraid that if we stayed in the camps there would be further protests and violent developments. The governor of Guam was ready to kick the refugees out of Guam as soon as possible. All this being the case, a ship would enable us to go back according to our wishes, and it would mean that the United States could wash its hands of us. It would no longer be responsible.

However, the United States needed for us, the future repatriates, to request the ship ourselves. Obviously, it was an American plan, and the Americans had planted the idea with Mạc and the other protest leaders. They couldn't let us stay in this situation forever. If I accepted this mission, I would rescue myself and help all the other people who shared my state of mind.

~

After lunch, I gathered together all the former naval officers and sailors and told them about the possible ship solution. I created a roster of the men and asked them to sign up, noting their name, date of birth, rank and expertise, and years of service in the RVN Navy: "There are more men here with experience than we need," I explained, "and so I will have to select the men with the greatest expertise. Our list must look logical and defensible to the Americans, and so if I don't choose you, please don't feel disappointed or angry with me. I also would like to stress that this is volunteer work. If there is a ship for us, then our work is a form of sacrifice, and our participation comes out of our goodwill. Just like those of you who have been on hunger strikes, this will be our sacrifice for the group, for all of us who want to return. Those who are chosen will have to work hard throughout the voyage, without the freedom of the others. I have to tell the truth in advance: think before putting your name down on this list."

Everyone was happy and supported the plan enthusiastically. They placed their trust in me, because all the officers and sailors had known me before, and because I had been a captain on one of the largest cruisers in the South Vietnamese Navy. The camp members took turns writing down their names with all the required details.

By that night, more than two hundred men had volunteered to join the crew. I thought to myself, even if they gave us five ships, we would still have enough trained manpower.

The next morning, I woke up very early. After washing myself, I went out onto the porch to sit and drink a cup of coffee and smoke a cigarette by myself. Smoking one cigarette after another and gazing at earth and sky, I looked out at the thousands upon thousands of heavenly bodies and planets in the vast universe. Human beings were so tiny. Our hopes and wishes couldn't compete in the vast universe, but our feelings still seemed so potent. I pictured my wife and children on the other side of the horizon.

While I was still in a reverie, blowing cigarette smoke, and letting my soul drift toward the horizon, Tấn had woken up and approached me. He asked, "Why did you wake up so early? Were you too happy to sleep?"

"Heaven loves me, so heaven lets me fall asleep easily and wake up early. Tấn, do you know what is in that direction?" I pointed in front of me, and Tấn looked ahead without seeing anything.

"What is it? I don't know what you are trying to say."

I explained, "That is the West. Far in the distance on the other side of the horizon is where our wives and children are living and waiting for us. I am sure that we will be reunited with them."

Tấn smiled happily. "Are you done with the list of crew members?"

"I have it," I said. "I can complete the whole thing today with time to spare. Tomorrow morning, I will go to the office and contact General Herbert and give it to him. You can rest assured that if we have a ship, then the direction I just pointed out to you will be the direction that we will be taking shortly to go home to Vietnam."

Tấn fell silent as if he were thinking about something else: "Even if there is a day of return, I don't know if we will be able to do anything useful for our wives and children. Will the VC leave us alone? Reality still presents us with so many obstacles—I can't picture our return. Do you think it could become a pretext for them to torture our wives and children?"

"I used to think like that, too, but what can we do? We only know that we are acting according to our conscience and our ethics. I always believe in that principle. There are often hardships, even when we do the right thing. Life is still long, and we will surely meet adversity, but in time, everything will pass by. Heaven has eyes, don't you see?"

"I know," Tấn responded. "But sometimes we have to think about the worst-case scenario, so that if it comes to pass, we won't be shocked. That's all. I suppose that if they kill us, I am ready. There is nothing to be afraid of."

"I completely agree with you, you and I always think alike. We are two souls together in pain. Our sentiments are deeper and more profound than Trọng's and Phủ's. As for choosing wisely, we cannot know yet who is right and who is wrong. It's best that we let heaven plan for us."

I continued to think about the hard days ahead and my need for a healthy breakfast. I said to Tấn, "I am luckier than you right now. I am about to have work to do, and working will help me forget my sorrows. If America truly gives us a ship, I will be busy until the day of our return, so I won't have so much time just to think by myself day after day."

In the end, more than three hundred former RVN sailors volunteered to help sail the ship. The majority of these naval members had been manning their ships at sea, when on April 29, they received an order to reroute their ships to the Philippines or Guam without ever having chosen to leave Vietnam themselves. They weren't informed that the evacuation was final. After they arrived here, they were shocked. In Guam, they saw this RVN "Big Shot" and that RVN "Big Shot" in the camps. These men had brought their wives, children, and other relatives with them, while the young sailors had just been tools, helping these big shots leave. The young men became indignant and fed up with the RVN officers' lack of respect for their lives. There was a great deal of irony in their situation, but to be fair, in April, everyone was confused—no one knew what was going to happen. No one had the ability to think about or take care of those who were below them.

For our crew, I selected those with the highest seniority at sea and the necessary expertise. As for the chiefs of staff, I needed a deputy captain, a voyage officer, an information officer, a mechanical officer, a transportation officer, a medical officer, and a disaster officer who would be in charge of all the fire-fighting equipment, life preservers, and life rafts. I would also need a logistics officer, who could organize the kitchen, the mess hall, and meals for two thousand people each day. Finally, I would need four voyage shift officers who could take turns on watch. In total, we would need twelve officers.

Everyone on the crew had over five years of experience at sea, and we had the expertise to sail the ship anywhere in the world, so going back to Vietnam would be easy. Of course, we would need at least a month to train and familiarize ourselves with the new ship. Then, the journey could begin.

The next day, I met with General Herbert again. He shook my hand, thanked me, and smiled. Next, he raised two fingers to form the letter V, for victory. He said, "I hope you will advise camp members that they shouldn't cause any more disturbances during this waiting period."

"General, just go ahead and give us the ship, then I can guarantee that there will be no more riots. As for advising camp members, I am in no position to do it. For myself, I don't approve of violence. I just want to be left alone. However, I don't control the camps. General, I hope that you will make an extra effort to help us return to Vietnam."

After our conversation, the camp members gathered around me to ask about our conversation. Soon, everyone began paying attention to me and placing their hopes in me. The news that I had handed the list to General Herbert spread to the other three camps very rapidly. Everyone seemed to feel buoyed up.

The next day, there were no protests, but a few young people were still restless. They believed that the Americans were just lulling us to sleep and making empty promises. We had hoped that the Aga Khan would be able to persuade Hanoi, but that had come to nothing, and now there was this proposal for a ship. We had no way of knowing whether this promise would be real. This ship might be a ship of paper. This time, if there was no ship, the young people threatened they wouldn't let things rest.

CHAPTER SEVEN

Camp Asan, Guam

When General Herbert returned from Washington, he ordered that all the repatriates be transferred to a single camp, Camp Asan. Over two thousand people were still waiting to return, and we believed that the move meant progress. Everyone was eager to pack their bags and get on the buses. I still had only the small suitcase that I had brought from Saigon, with just enough clothes to wear every day. I had been so depressed that I hadn't ever waited in the Red Cross line for anything other than essential items such as soap, toothpaste, and toothbrushes.

Within a week, we were all relocated to Camp Asan. Originally, this camp had been built as a barracks for U.S. Marines waiting to embark on their tour of duty in Vietnam. Now, ironically, this same camp had become a temporary shelter for us, the Vietnamese repatriates.

The camp faced the water, and in another context, it might have been quite romantic. Every evening, I went out to the beach. Looking out at the sky and the sea and listening to the waves as they lapped against the shore helped my soul calm down. I could finally jettison all my sorrows.

The camp had plenty of activities, and all our basic needs were met. We had sufficient food and drink. It had reading rooms, newspapers, and televisions on twenty-four hours a day. It also had a movie theater, which showed a new film every night. A health clinic provided medical exams, and a Red Cross station provided all the essentials for camp members. For our spiritual needs, there was a church, where Catholics could attend Mass and read the Bible together. One of the repatriates was a priest, and he agreed to lead the church and hold daily Mass for camp members. Later, we also established a place of worship for Buddhists, because the majority of our camp members were Buddhists.

Life was comfortable and free, and the officials even arranged our transport when we needed to leave the camp. We were mostly idle, because all our necessities were provided for us. We could live like this for many years without ever having to worry about anything.

Still, the camp was surrounded by barbed wire and had a gate. On the one hand, the base could be seen as an apartment complex, but on the other hand, it could also be seen as a detention camp. It was all the same.

~

After everyone had settled in at the camp, we gathered into groups, hunting for news, following developments, and discussing every possible angle.

I had nothing to talk about. I always just wanted to be left alone. I had a few trusted friends who would go outside to listen to any new developments, and then whatever happened, I would know right away. There was no need for me to go anywhere.

The first important piece of news concerned the agitators Trương Ngọc Khoa and Võ Quỳnh Thiện. We learned that instead of being transferred to Camp Asan with the rest of us, they had been taken by the Americans to the Hotel Tokyo downtown. Now, it was even clearer that these two men had been prepped and trained by the Americans. In the coming days, would there be any new developments? We would have to wait and see.

We almost all believed that the Americans had gathered us together in preparation for sending us back to Vietnam on a ship. As a result, I became the center of attention. A lot of people loitered in front of my door every day, curious about what I looked like. They didn't realize that I was an emaciated body, just like them. There was no difference between us. Most of the men did not know me. While most people came to know my name, they couldn't even pick me out by sight. Soon, my bunk became extremely crowded. People kept coming by to greet me and to get acquainted with me. A number of naval officers expressed their affection for me, and they took very good care of me, including bringing me my meals. I had lost my insignia and my uniform, but I still ran into people who respected my rank, and this brought me some solace. The men treated me as their superior.

I felt joy in this enduring sense of camaraderie, living in the camp, getting meals for one another, and sitting down together to eat. This brotherhood was priceless. I recognized our common humanity.

Vũ Lê Hân entered my room and introduced himself as someone representing Camp J & G. Hân had been a lieutenant colonel in the army. At the end of April 1975, he had been working at Vice President Trần Văn Hương's mansion. In a panic, he had climbed onto a helicopter and escaped to Thailand by himself. Now he was here in Guam. His wife and children were stuck in Saigon, and so he had decided to go back just as I had. We shared the same state of mind. People who share the same circumstances can easily become close to each other. He had heard that I had created a crew list and had handed it over to the Americans. He had become hopeful and wanted to come and meet me. After a few social pleasantries, he went straight to the point. "Do you know why America has gathered all of us into this camp? I have been following all the developments very closely, and I think that the day of our return will soon come."

I responded, "To tell you the truth, I am so sick of it, I don't pay any attention anymore. As you know, General Herbert asked me to organize a crew. I didn't believe it would happen, and so I didn't want to do it, but because he kept insisting, and because people kept urging me, I had no alternative but to do it. Making the list is one thing, but believing that there will be a ship is another. If there is a ship, then we can go home; if not, then we can only keep waiting. What else can we do? Everything is beyond our control. I also have heard a lot of rumors, but I don't want to pay attention to any of it."

Hân continued to push the subject, and he said, "As you know, I still have close friends in Vietnam, and I also have relatives living in France who are in touch with the Vietnamese embassy. They have told me that Hanoi has agreed to let us go home. Publicly, they had to reject us, but in truth, they haven't. The Aga Khan's report from Hanoi was incorrect. You can believe me, there will be no retaliation from the communists. We will be able to go back in safety. We are not the only people with high rank who are returning."

"Whether they will retaliate against me or not, I have decided to go back," I replied. "I'm tired of seeing Americans. We have lost our country because of them. What do we follow them for? I would much rather return to Vietnam and my family regardless of the consequences. It will have more meaning, and my soul will feel more at peace."

"I'm not that different from you," Hân answered. "Still, we need to keep our eyes open. When we moved into this camp, I did some investigating and found favorable news."

"Have you met Trương Ngọc Khoa and Võ Quỳnh Thiện yet?"

"These two men are currently staying at the Hotel Tokyo, but I hear that they will be transferred here soon," Hân answered. "Those two have been very feisty and very effective. America only found a solution for us because they were so forceful. I think we should consolidate the four camp committees and vote for one single representative committee so that we can speak with America more easily. What do you think of that?"

I said, "Of course, I agree we must be organized. We must have representatives in order to speak with one voice. I'm willing to participate, but I will only be a member of the committee. I want to avoid any trouble. Please allow me to stand outside the protests. If we receive a ship, then I will be responsible for it. You can do whatever you want, but I feel too tired already."

"The most important thing is whether we will get a ship or not," Hân concluded. "Everyone trusts you. The reason I wanted to meet you was that I wanted to see whether you were determined to go home or not. Right now, we have a great deal of hope that the United States will give us a ship, but some of us are afraid that you will change your mind about captaining the ship. As you have seen, the number of people who have changed their minds increases every day, partly because of the long wait and partly because the protests have scared them. The sailors and naval officers have a great deal of faith in you, but we want to make sure."

"You can believe it," I answered. "I have made up my mind. Nothing can make me change my intentions. I also would like to suggest that you become the camp representative. Many of us do not want Trương Ngọc Khoa or Võ Quỳnh Thiện to have this responsibility. These two men are involved in a lot of secret activities that are very difficult to comprehend. Have you seen that? I am afraid if these two are in charge, they will not fight for us to return to Vietnam but will instead guide us in another direction. They always act unilaterally, and it's not clear whether it's according to their own ideas or whether they're acting on behalf of the U.S. government. In any case, I'm afraid that our plan will come to nothing if they're in charge. Hân, you should be our representative, and I will support you. Everyone knows that you are a straightforward person and that you always act ethically."

Hân did not agree right away. Instead, he said, "I understand your concerns, but we cannot isolate those two completely. Whether we want it or not, they have a lot of credibility in the camps. The young people are very enthusiastic about them, and they are ready to lead riots to force the Americans to make a decision. We cannot completely break off from them—we need to understand why the young people want to be so aggressive."

"I sympathize with them, too, but I have become extremely anxious from all this tension, and I am afraid that my brains will explode. I don't oppose the riots in any way. However, deep in my heart, I only want to find a place where I will be left alone. I am so afraid of having to witness disturbances."

Hân understood my concerns. He comforted me a bit, but he also explained that Trương Ngọc Khoa and Võ Quỳnh Thiện were going to enter Camp Asan the next day.

Three days later, Hân invited all the representatives from all the camp committees to come together, a total of over twenty participants, including me. As we entered the meeting room, we all shook each other's hands and exchanged greetings. It was a friendly atmosphere, and everyone was introducing the new faces to everyone else. Trương Ngọc Khoa came toward me, shook my hand, introduced himself, and expressed his admiration for me.

"It is an honor to know you," Khoa began. "We have been talking so much about you, and finally I have the honor of meeting you. You can rest assured that once we have fought together, there will be a ship for you to sail back."

I answered back just as formally, "You are even more famous than I am. I have heard much about you, and you are always talking about our 'struggle.' Perhaps you have never been in the military and really had to fight. As for me, I have been in the military for almost twenty years, and all that time I was fighting against the communists, so I know what it means to fight. Right now, we are all exhausted, but still we have to fight against the Americans as well. Do you find that funny? We are returning to our wives and children, not returning to the communists. Isn't that true?"

"Of course, that is true, but let me tell you this," Khoa answered. "This time, we have to fight until we go back. Today, we are voting for the chair of the representative committee. I suggest that you become a candidate, because you have a lot of credibility among us here. I see that everyone has mentioned you."

"Please let me enjoy my peace of mind. I am no different from a dead chicken. Don't you see? I just want to be left on the outside until there is a ship. Then, I will climb on it and sail it back for you. That is good enough, isn't it? Please understand, and don't nominate me. You can do whatever you want."

However, I also wanted to advocate for Hân—I did not want Khoa to lead the group. I continued, "I would suggest that Vũ Lê Hân would be an excellent representative. He has a great deal of credibility among us, and he is an honest person with a lot of experience. We should let him have this position of representative; it will be best."

In reality, many of us had been networking and jockeying for Hân to win the election. I was quite sure that he would win, because we couldn't let Khoa or Thiện represent us. We all cast our ballots, and just as we had prepared for and predicted, Hân received the most votes.

Hân had a lot of goodwill within the camp leadership, and he also formed an active advisory committee, with individuals responsible for security, logistics, and continuing our protests. The logistics committee was in charge of daily routines, such as ensuring sufficient supplies of clothing, toothpaste, toothbrushes, bath towels, washcloths, soap, cigarettes, sports equipment, entertainment, and so on. Each row of houses also elected a representative and a few assistants who could submit requests to the U.S. Office of Civilian Affairs. Every request submitted was fulfilled by the United States 100 percent. They even exceeded the requests.

The law and order committee was responsible for maintaining internal security and ensuring that all camp members could live in peace. Many of these representatives were well-versed in martial arts, and they had experience as body guards for elite officials in Saigon. They also were asked to suppress any violence within the camp. The health-care committee organized requests for medicine. Finally, the protest committee continued to organize demonstrations in order to expedite our demands. Although I was a member of the advisory committee, I was not allowed to take part in plans for any protests, because they knew that I would advocate for peace.

After the committees were formed, life in the camp stabilized, and activities took on a normal rhythm. Every day, we had our meals, and we had time to relax, swim in the sea, play sports, and read newspapers. If we wanted to leave the camp, we could take a bus to town. As far as our material life was concerned, we had nothing to worry about. However, regarding our spiritual life, every day was fraught with our longing and anticipation for our return.

Trương Ngọc Khoa and Võ Quỳnh Thiện were still very active, and they collaborated with the logistics committee, asking for fabric, paint brushes, and wooden planks in order to make banners and a stage for the hunger strikers. In particular, a number of people came up with the novel idea of painting a flag with Hồ Chí Minh's portrait on it.

At the camp was an artist named Bình who used to be rather famous in Saigon. In Camp Asan, he organized an exhibition of his paintings, and most of them depicted fairly typical scenes, landscapes, farmers harvesting rice, and mothers rocking their children in hammocks and feeding their babies. His artwork had drawn the attention of the U.S. authorities in Guam, and he had also received many valuable gifts. A few Americans had even offered him a few hundred dollars for his paintings, but he didn't care about the money. Instead, he painted for art's sake, and he would give the paintings away for free. If he had chosen to go to America, he would have been able to make a lot of money because of his artistic talents; nonetheless, he valued his wife and children still living in Vietnam more than future wealth.

When Bình had lived in Saigon, all his friends had been artists, and he had never taken active part in the fight against the communists. He did not have to fear the communists—but still, he chose to fight for our return through his paintings.

To aid in our struggle, he drew a huge portrait of Hồ Chí Minh and the flag of the National Liberation Front. I don't know whether these paintings represented his own opinion or the opinion of those standing behind him, pulling the strings. Nonetheless, he was able to weigh the pros and cons for himself, and he must have thought that if he produced this procommunist artwork, he would not meet with the same vicissitudes back in Vietnam as the rest of us.

Some people are just opportunists. Any given society always has people who wait for an opportunity and seize it. Even here, among souls tormented by their longing to return, one could see that a number of people worked to score points with the communists even before they returned. No one dared to criticize them, even when they engaged in excessive and loathsome acts, because they ultimately had reasons of their own.

In reality, even great statesmen are opportunists. The only difference is that their loathsome acts are usually concealed. Knowing this, we shouldn't criticize the few people who try to take advantage of trivial opportunities. We are all just like water lilies, carried by the current without ever knowing where the river flowed. We had lost our country, and our families had been dispersed. Who should we follow? Who was still worthy of being followed? The Americans had abandoned us, and now we had to run after the Americans—in order to get what? In order to have the life of an exiled beggar?

To be free, there must at least be honor. There must be self-esteem. The majority of us who had left Saigon left because of our families and the future of our own children. Those who had gone on to the United States had sacrificed everything. They had left in shame and humiliation, leaving everything behind.

Those of us who wanted to return would have to carry our own shame as well.

CHAPTER EIGHT

The Struggle

The protesters erected a stage made of planks with enough space for fifty people to sit together. The stage was built close to the camp's fence, and it looked out onto the road so passersby could see the demonstration. Many anti-American banners framed the stage, along with a portrait of Hồ Chí Minh.

Early the next morning, many men and women mounted the stage and began a hunger strike. Dozens more people were ready to join the demonstration, but there was only so much space on the stage.

I was still in my room. I waited with my cup of coffee and my cigarettes and observed the events and watched what developed together with a few friends. A few journalists came to the camp and began taking pictures and filming the hunger strikers. The camp office bustled with commotion, and the camp security increased, as if to warn us that if any violence broke out, they would be ready to put it down.

The hunger strikers stayed together steadfast and seated on the stage even after nightfall, and the rest of us attempted to lead a normal life. As the hours grew late, a few of them collapsed, because they were so tired. Our law and order committee carried them back to their rooms, so they could rest. However, other people were always ready to replace them. The stage remained crowded with hunger strikers on the first day, the second day, and then the third day, but still there were no new developments. The U.S. authorities came to the camp to meet with our representatives and to request that the hunger strikers disperse, but Hân, our chief representative, didn't respond. He informed the U.S. authorities that a number of camp members wanted to protest until we could return, and no one could prevent that. Furthermore, he argued that the hunger strikers weren't causing any disturbances or damage to the camp, and the only risk was to their own health. The U.S. authorities gave up. In reality, the demonstrations were well organized, planned, and directed by the representative committee. This was our time of struggle. However, Hân had given the Americans evasive answers so that no one would be held responsible for the demonstrations.

The hunger strikers entered their fourth day without any sign that their demands would be met. Trương Ngọc Khoa then clandestinely organized even more militant actions. At exactly 8 p.m. a fire broke out in the barracks. In addition, some of the young men vandalized the houses nearby. Hân and those on the representative committee did not know that Khoa's group had set fire to the buildings. Everyone rushed out into the campground, and many people carried their possessions out of their rooms as a precaution. They were afraid that the fire would spread to the barracks where they lived. In fact, the agitators had chosen the empty houses at the back of the camp, far from the inhabited barracks. Therefore, none of the camp members were injured, and no damage was done to the camp members' belongings.

Ten minutes after the fire broke out, fire engines, ambulances, and trucks carrying soldiers gathered in front of the camp gate. A squadron of special police armed with guns and wearing armor and masks entered through the gate. The loudspeakers broadcast announcements calling upon everyone to stay where they were, so that the firefighters could put out the blaze.

This is an exterior shot of one of the buildings that was destroyed by the repatriate protesters at Camp Asan. Courtesy of the National Archives and Records Administration, Record Group 319, Box 19, declassification number 984082.

This is the inside of a building that was burned down by protesters at Camp Asan. Courtesy of the National Archives and Records Administration, Record Group 319, Box 19, declassification number 984082.

However, a group of young Vietnamese men, wielding sticks, stood in front of the burning barracks in order to prevent the fire trucks from entering the camp or extinguishing the fire. The security force had no choice but to react with tear gas. The protesters did not give in—instead, they continued to chant: "Return us to Vietnam." The American chief of security stepped forward. He asked everyone to put down their sticks and disperse. Still the young people did not budge, and, as they held their ground, the fire got bigger and bigger, shooting up, and painting the whole sky red.

Finally, the U.S. military police resorted to even more tear gas. Even after this, the young men reacted by throwing rocks and sticks at the police, injuring a number of them. The police shot yet more tear gas at the protesters, and the tear gas spread throughout the campground, wafting into our living quarters and causing a stampede out of the barracks. Many of the camp members had coughing fits, and tears were streaming down their faces. Women and children were crying in panic. We all congregated by the seashore, even the protesters, and the fresh air on the beach lessened the effect of the gas. Everyone could breathe more easily.

The security guards finally flooded the campground and cleared a path for the fire engines. Five minutes later, the fire was extinguished. Just outside the camp gate, the police dogs and the security personnel stood guard. They were at the ready if the protesters jumped the fence and tried to vandalize property on the outside.

After the tear gas had thinned out, the security force used loudspeakers to call upon the camp members to return to their normal routines. Most of the guards withdrew from the camp; however, a number of security personnel remained fully armed with guns and ammunition right outside the fence. Finally, the situation calmed down, and camp members returned to their rooms to sleep. The atmosphere was heavy, and it was still hard to breathe because of the tear gas.

We all felt exhausted and fed up with life. We had fled the enemy, only to have to flee again, feeling unable to go on, and now our return seemed so precarious. We didn't know what to do. Each of us was in a confused state of mind. Once again, we gathered in small groups to exchange worried words.

The representative committee, led by Hân, went to each row of houses to offer greetings and to keep up the camp members' spirits. Hân explained that some of the young men had burned down the empty houses in order to threaten the United States and scare it into finding a solution for us. He told everyone that they had nothing to be afraid of, and he urged all camp members to live calmly as before. He explained that the fire was only meant to expedite our return without causing any direct damage to the camp. We would just have to put up with smarting eyes for a little while. As for who had caused the fire, everyone knew that it was Trương Ngọc Khoa's group without even saying so.

The next day, everyone felt drained. The barracks lay in stillness, looking sad and desolate. I woke up early as usual and enjoyed my coffee and cigarettes. A few of us joined together in the mess hall, and I ran into several members of our representative committee. Hân appeared optimistic about our future. He started off by saying, "For sure, the Americans will have to react after last night's fire and disturbance. Let's wait and see."

I was much less sure. "They will advise us to wait some more," I sighed. "There is no guarantee that there will be any developments."

However, Hân was insistent. "I have done some surveying, and I learned that there is a large ship that evacuated many Vietnamese here. This ship carries the name *Việt Nam Thương Tín*—do you know it? General Herbert will meet with us very soon, and he will offer us that ship, don't you think?"

"Of course," I responded. "The *Việt Nam Thương Tín* was the biggest merchant ship in South Vietnam. It can sail long distances, and it frequently carried merchandise between the United States and the Philippines. It is the only ship like it. However, I still have my doubts about the ship solution. I don't want to make any plans until we have control over a ship."

Then, my friend Vương Long Đoàn cut in: "After yesterday's events, the United States will be frightened of us, and it will want to find a way to kick us out very quickly—you can believe me. We cannot wait for Hanoi's approval. We have to demand a ship and go back on our own, regardless of Hanoi or the United Nations."

"If we don't receive a ship soon, this endless waiting will drive me crazy," I added. "By the way, speaking of Trương Ngọc Khoa, I ask you, Đoàn, you live near Khoa, and you are also the head of the law and order committee. Can you tell us a little about Khoa and his followers?"

"Trương Ngọc Khoa lived in the same camp with me in America. At Fort Chaffee, he fought to return to Vietnam, and then in Guam, he has continued his campaign in Camp Barrigada. I have watched him in this struggle, and all the followers are just like us. Everyone just wants to return to Vietnam. There is no secret plot."

"I also heard that Hoàng Trí Mạnh was in your camp," I pushed. "Is he a VC?"

"Mạnh used to be a police sergeant in Kiên Giang. I was in touch with him many times in the camps in America and also here in Guam. He is a mature person, elderly, over fifty years of age already. He confided in me that he had supported the National Liberation Front in South Vietnam. In 1954, after the Geneva Accords, instead of following the NLF supporters who moved to the North, he remained in the South and joined the RVN police force in Kiên Giang as a secret agent. Now, he seems optimistic about our return, and he believes that as repatriates, we will be pardoned. That is what I know about him."

"But has he taken part in these protests here?" I asked.

"I saw him standing on the sidelines," Đoàn answered. "He never took part in the demonstrations."

"I heard that he is a communist mole and that he is still operating for the communists. I believe he helped stage the protests in Camp Barrigada. Is this right or wrong?"

"I know him very well," Đoàn continued. "As for rumors, people always spice up the truth to make it more interesting. In reality, there is nothing to it. I can vouch that Mạnh has never taken a direct role in the demonstrations. He lives very quietly, wakes up early in the morning to run, exercises, and then returns to his room to drink coffee and smoke cigarettes. He rarely chats with anyone, and he doesn't have any close friends."

I had pushed the matter, because I wanted to make sure the VC weren't still pulling the strings. We could not let the VC be in charge of our campaign for repatriation. Hân and my other friends all shared my point of view. We had fought against the communists for many years, and even though we wanted to return for the sake of our families, we did not want to follow the communists' lead.

Nguyen Thy Tấn asked Hân, as our chief representative, what he planned to do after the fire and the riots. Hân responded that he had been in conversation with Trương Ngọc Khoa, but he had not known that he was going to set any buildings on fire. While he didn't approve of the destruction, Hân remained committed to the ship solution.

I was still unsure whether the ship would materialize. "I don't know whether they will give us a ship or not," I explained. "Maybe they will take us to a deserted island without any inhabitants and hold us there. Those agitators Trương Ngọc Khoa and Võ Quỳnh Thiện are acting so secretly, and we don't know their true plans. If we create too much trouble here in Guam, who knows? The United States might send us to an even more isolated place."

Hân disagreed. Đoàn also believed we were closer to our return after the fire. He didn't think the U.S. government would risk allowing the protests to escalate to the next level. Our breakfast conversation had lasted until noon.

$$\sim$$

Two days later, we learned that a U.S. delegation would visit our camp. Everyone was excited about getting some fresh news. Groups gathered throughout the campground chatting with new energy. Outside the gates, several U.S. security employees were in place in case of any disturbances inside the camp.

At exactly 9 p.m., General Herbert led the delegation straight into the campground, and Hân waited at the microphone to greet them. He shook hands with General Herbert and welcomed him. General Herbert greeted us and quickly introduced Mr. Jean Sauvageot who had traveled from Washington, DC, to speak with us. Mr. Sauvageot was a thin, small man with a booming voice. He introduced himself and spoke fluent Vietnamese. Delivering a speech just like a Vietnamese orator, he said:

"My name is Sauvageot, and my Vietnamese name is Nguyễn Hữu Hai. I have a Vietnamese name, because I advised the South Vietnamese government throughout the Vietnam War. In South Vietnam, I worked in all four strategic military zones from the 17th parallel all the way down to the tip of Cà Mau. Now, I am a professor at a university in Virginia. Just a few weeks ago, I was working at the university, and I received an urgent order from Washington, summoning me to Guam to meet with you. The U.S. government gave me this mission, because I am one of the few Americans with a deep knowledge of Vietnamese psychology, sentiments, customs, and traditions. I sympathize with you, and I hope that you will sympathize with me.

"When I learned about the demonstrations here in Guam, I was not surprised. I understand that you only want to return to your wives and children. Although I am an American, my wife is Vietnamese. Her hometown is in the western part of the country, and so my second homeland is also Vietnam. My wife and I also wish to return to Vietnam someday. I want to visit my second homeland when there is peace and when there is no communism there. I also believe and wait for that future.

"The fire was one way to make your wishes known to us. However, I need to tell you that it is not a good time to return to Vietnam. The communists have taken over South Vietnam, and they are coping with many difficulties. Things are not simple. On behalf of Washington, DC, I promise you that your day of return will happen—but not yet. You want to go back in this ship, but you have to understand that we cannot act irresponsibly. Please try and understand us.

"I also want to emphasize that your demonstrations, the hunger strikes, and the fires have spoken louder than words. We have made note of all your actions. You do not need to continue the protests. Please have faith in me."

Nguyễn Hữu Hai's (Sauvageot's) declaration was persuasive. Everyone listened to it and our souls calmed down. The members of the representative committee huddled together. Then Hân responded, "I am the repatriates' representative here on Guam, and I have a few words to say. We know that our return is not simple. We have fought against the communists for years. However, no other choice is possible. If we have to wait for Hanoi's approval, then who knows when we can return? We are living here every day, every hour, thinking about our families, our wives, and our children. We cannot prolong this state of perpetual limbo. We want to make our own decisions, and the solution that we have chosen is very simple. We would like the United States to give us a ship. Then, we don't need Hanoi's approval, and we are willing to accept any consequences, including death or imprisonment. That is our choice and our unanimous opinion. That is all."

We all applauded Hân for a long time. We were one in our approval of his words.

Nguyễn Hữu Hai seemed persuaded by our resoluteness. He promised to give a full report to Washington, DC. All the American advice about waiting was no longer effective. If we remained in limbo on Guam, only negative consequences would follow for both the U.S. Army and the people in Guam.

The Americans had planned it all, and they had masterminded a plan in which they wouldn't be responsible for us anymore. They had used a few decoys like Trương Ngọc Khoa and Võ Quỳnh Thiện to demand a ship and organize our violent protests. Next, they sent this American who spoke Vietnamese, Nguyễn Hữu Hai, to visit us and measure our determination. After Hân's speech, Nguyễn Hữu Hai clearly supported our demand for a ship. It satisfied our wish, and it meant that the United States, the Guam authorities, and the UN officials would no longer be responsible for us. In the end, if the ship solution carried any risks, it would only harm us, the returnees.

Repatriates have their heads shaven in an act of protest, while banners attest to the hunger strikes at the camp. Courtesy of the National Archives and Records Administration, Record Group 319, Box 19, declassification number 984082.

From this view, one can see the organized nature of the protests and the model ship, as repatriates argue for the "ship option." Courtesy of the National Archives and Records Administration, Record Group 319, Box 19, declassification number 984082.

The following day, the hunger strikers restarted their demonstrations. The camp members painted banners with extreme slogans: "Hunger strike until death"; "We are determined to go back to Vietnam"; and "Give us a ship immediately so we can go back to Vietnam." The banners were hung across the stage and on the fences so that people passing by could see them.

The hunger strike went on for yet another day. Now, the UNHCR responded. The Swiss-Vietnamese Cảnh and a few other UNHCR employees returned to the camp. Cảnh already knew us all too well. Today was special, because he brought another UNHCR representative with him—a Mr. Smith.

"I am an American, and I have Swiss citizenship. I work for the UNHCR," began Mr. Smith. "I wanted to tell you that even though I am an American, I wanted to live and work in another country. I don't like living in America. I sympathize with you, and it is logical that you want to return to Vietnam. At the UNHCR, our responsibilities are very heavy. On the one hand, we work directly with the United States to protect you while you are waiting here in Guam.

On the other hand, we have to negotiate with Hanoi to fight for your return and safety.

"If you choose to sail back under your own power, we will not be able to guarantee your safety or protection. You will be pushing us aside even though we have done everything in our power to facilitate your return. On behalf of the UNHCR, we cannot support your 'ship solution.'

"Instead, we propose the establishment of a Vietnamese village here or in another similar place until Hanoi agrees to accept your return. You can select your own leaders and organize your own community. It will be like a separate world with organized activities just like in Vietnam, and it will only be temporary. If you agree, we will immediately start looking for an area to establish this village. We believe that this is the best solution, and we hope you will agree."

Hân stepped forward as our representative and asked whether we could have time to discuss this possibility as a group. We returned to our rooms to consider this proposal of a Vietnamese village in Guam. It was truly an innovative idea. If it could be organized by the United Nations, our community would live independently from the United States, and maybe in the future we could do meaningful work, such as establishing a company. Most of the future repatriates were enthusiastic and young, and they had many skills and occupations. With UN support and professional training, perhaps we could create a good life for ourselves. If only we could forget our past and start our lives from scratch here.

All these thoughts crossed our minds. However, it was not enough. The majority of our representatives rejected Mr. Smith's proposal. They only wanted a ship. Everyone was still motivated to return, and nothing could change our minds.

CHAPTER NINE

The Việt Nam Thương Tín

After Nguyễn Hữu Hai (Sauvageot) returned to Washington, DC, a delegation of U.S. senators and representatives came to visit our camp. The U.S. congressional members' visit was clearly momentous. We would need congressional approval for any financial support for the ship solution. For the first time, I could see that the United States was ready to make a decision.

Vũ Lê Hân began the meeting. "We regret that this visit to Guam is taking up so much of your time. As you have witnessed here in the camp, many of us are on a hunger strike. We will continue until death unless our wish to return to Vietnam can be realized. Many U.S. officials and UNHCR representatives have advised against our actions, and, to be fair, they have helped us in many ways, but, for us, we no longer have any other choice. All two thousand of us are in agreement. We have asked the United States to provide us with a ship. After receiving a ship, all the preparations and work will be our responsibility. The United States will not have to worry about us anymore. Our wish is legitimate. We would like to emphasize that we are very knowledgeable about the current situation in Vietnam. All the explanations and fears about our return don't matter to us anymore."

Trương Ngọc Khoa stood up and asked to follow Hân's speech. "We have all come to the same conclusion—we want a ship. We will continue to protest until we have a ship. We hope you will understand us and make a decision—the sooner the better."

One U.S. congressman listened and again urged us to wait calmly. Over the next few days, we were all very excited. One delegation after another came to the camp to talk with us, but there was still no concrete sign that the United States had agreed to our return. Out in the campground, the hunger strikers continued to occupy the stage. Many of them threatened to remain on strike until their death.

The threat of violence also continued. The U.S. security forces waited just outside the camp, armed with weapons and radio equipment, and they were always at the ready. Our more militant members often gathered together to display their force, and they looked aggressive. However, in fact, they did not engage in any violent actions or vandalize the camp again. They remained nonviolent in order to support the hunger strikers.

Each day developments progressed. We had banners and slogans displayed so that onlookers could see from the road. Sometimes TV and newspaper reporters came in and out, taking our pictures and conducting quick interviews with the crowds.

We painted a banner that said "Hunger strike until death" and raised it in front of the hunger strikers. Over thirty people at a time took turns sitting on the stage. No words of advice could make them change their minds. Their fighting spirit became increasingly volatile.

Finally, the U.S. officials announced a special meeting. We had already had so many meetings: Sauvageot/Nguyễn Hữu Hai, a person with oratory skills and powers of persuasion; Mr. Smith, who suggested the innovative idea of building a Vietnamese village; the congressional delegations; and now finally another meeting. It would occur in three days, and it was scheduled for 7 p.m., unlike all our other meetings.

Our militant camp members prepared to gather with new banners, a giant National Liberation Front (NLF) flag, and a huge painting of Hồ Chí Minh. The logistics committee had asked the United States for cloth, paint, brushes, and sewing machines a month earlier, but even I, a member of the representative committee, had known nothing about this plan. We wondered which of the future returnees had thought of sewing the NLF flag and painting the picture of Hồ Chí Minh. When had they decided to reveal these symbols during the special meeting?

When we saw the NLF flag and the Hồ Chí Minh portrait, most of us were astounded. We felt pain, bitterness, and humiliation, but we had to keep quiet. We did not want to ask more questions. Many of us were upset that the militant faction chose this moment to display the symbols of communist Vietnam, but we couldn't do anything. The meeting was about to take place. Our depression had reached a point of such despair that we only cared about finding a way home.

At exactly 7 p.m., the meeting began. General Herbert was there with several high-ranking men from Washington. Cảnh and Mr. Smith were there from the UNHCR, and Governor Bordallo was there representing Guam. The atmosphere appeared formal, and many faces appeared cold, reserved, and inscrutable. Our repatriate committee did not know what was going to happen. Would there be something new, or would it all just be a repetition of previous meetings?

General Herbert went straight to the point: "Camp members—I just received instructions from Washington, DC, this afternoon. We have asked you to wait calmly while we tried to find a solution. But you were still impatiently organizing protests and demanding a ship at all costs. Washington has considered your proposal, and

In this image, U.S. leaders walk toward the leadership committee of the Vietnamese repatriates. Courtesy of the National Archives and Records Administration, Record Group 319, Box 19, declassification number 984082.

A U.S. naval officer consults with the repatriate leadership. Courtesy of the National Archives and Records Administration, Record Group 319, Box 19, declassification number 984082.

the U.S. government has decided to grant your wish. It will give you the biggest South Vietnamese ship that evacuated to Guam—the *Việt Nam Thương Tín.*

"Now we want to know for sure: Do you have the same intention or not? Do you have any innovative ideas? Or do you still maintain your desire to return to Vietnam on a ship under your own power?"

The UNHCR representative cut in and reiterated the UNHCR's rejection of the ship solution. Like all the other UNHCR representatives, he sounded hurt that we could not wait any longer. He noted that the UNHCR officials had registered us on arrival and had attempted to assist in our repatriation. Once again, he urged us to wait until the diplomatic situation changed, and then the UNHCR could ensure our safe passage and reentry to Vietnam.

Governor Bordallo's words were more sympathetic. He noted his support for the UNHCR's position and Guam's ongoing hospitality. He added, "We have been trying our best to create a comfortable life for you on the island of Guam. Even though you have organized many protests and created instability on the island, we have tried to help. We can continue to protect you, and so I sincerely advise you to calmly wait on Guam."

Vũ Lê Hân stood up: "We take note of your goodwill and your help, but our position has been very clear. All of those who are waiting outside are impatiently waiting for word about their day of repatriation. We have made our choice, and nothing can change our minds."

General Herbert whispered something to the men from Washington. Then he asked the UNHCR representatives to leave, as if there had been some arrangement before the meeting. It was obvious that the Americans were in charge, and the UNHCR was only invited as a formality. Once the United States makes a decision, then the role of the UN has no value at all.

General Herbert continued: "Then the ship solution will be put into effect. Naturally, the solution will entirely be your responsibility. The United States cannot do anything if something happens to you when you return to Vietnam."

Hearing this, everyone on the representative committee applauded for a long time. The first smile blossomed on everyone's lips. The light at the end of the tunnel had appeared. The day of repatriation was near.

We were all elated. Hân announced: "We are extremely moved. We don't have any other wish. On behalf of the camp members, I can only express our sincere gratitude to you."

Then General Herbert asked for my opinion, since I would be the ship captain.

I stepped forward: "I would like to say here that I remain steadfast—I wish to go back to Vietnam. Our presence here on American soil is entirely unexpected.

We were lost and confused when we first stepped onto this island of Guam. I never thought that the communists would occupy Saigon, and all of us here left in confusion. Now, our only choice is repatriation. The simple reason is that our families, our wives and children, are still there. Now that our wish has been granted, I promise that I will fulfill my duty and captain the ship safely back to Vietnam."

General Herbert concluded the meeting after explaining the final formalities. He would call Washington immediately, and in two hours, we would meet again, and he would make the final announcement at 11 p.m.

~

Everyone was joyful and there was a thunderous round of applause. We all gathered around the yard, and the atmosphere in the camp was festive. We yelled and danced, casting aside all our sorrows. We were sure that the 11 p.m. meeting would produce results—no one doubted that. The two-hour wait only made everyone more awake and more joyful. Many people embraced each other and cried in happiness.

After two hours, everyone jammed into the open campground. We all waited in the final moments of suspense, waiting for the final decision. Suddenly there was a moment of stillness. At exactly 11 p.m., General Herbert entered the room.

General Herbert did not mince words: "I have spoken directly with Washington. At this time, I can announce that Washington has agreed to satisfy your wish. The U.S. government will give you a ship."

The sound of applause roared like firecrackers from the crowd. Outside, everyone shouted, running around the yard and announcing: "We have a ship!" Caps and hats flew into the air, and many people tore off their clothes as if crazed with happiness. We had waited so many months for this result.

General Herbert continued, "We have chosen the ship *Việt Nam Thương Tín* to transfer to you. The ship hasn't been in use since May, and, therefore, it may need some repairs. We will need some time to refit the ship. Tomorrow, I will meet with Trần Đình Trụ to discuss this ship in detail. Trụ, please gather the crew together. It will take a great deal of work to ready the ship, but there is sufficient money from Washington to do so. I will see you tomorrow."

Everyone was joyful. General Herbert smiled and shook everyone's hand. He seemed satisfied at having been able to conclude this difficult mission after so many months on Guam. He sighed with relief, and he offered me a firm and long handshake. I knew he trusted me to bring the two thousand camp members back to Vietnam.

~

A few young people climbed onto the wooden stage where the hunger strikers had sat, and they trampled on it until the stage collapsed. The young people were satisfied. Thanks to the hunger strikers, we had a day like today. We didn't need the stage anymore. This time, their destructive actions did not signal the young militants' anger and indignation, as it had earlier. Instead, it represented their joy. They were the same actions, but they carried two distinct meanings.

Men and women remained in the campground well after midnight, even after 3 a.m. No one paid attention to the passing of time. This was a sleepless night. We were looking forward to seeing our families—our wives, children, and other relations—who were still living in Vietnam. A glow of happiness covered all our faces. No words could describe this feeling. All our troubles and sorrows that had deepened over the previous few months were now replaced by a sense of joy that filled our souls.

~

The next morning, I sat down to have coffee with a few friends in my room when a U.S. Civil Affairs officer came to my barracks and asked me to meet with General Herbert. I was rather surprised that the general wanted to see me at 7 a.m., but I changed my clothes and followed him to his car.

When I reached General Herbert's office, I asked him what was so urgent. He answered that Hanoi had learned of the U.S. decision to give us a ship to return to Vietnam. The FBI had monitored its broadcast. General Herbert asked me to read the transcript of the broadcast carefully.

I read attentively. This was Hanoi's message to us and the world:

- The United States is plotting to sabotage Vietnam by sending Vietnamese who fled in April 1975 back on a ship.
- This action infringes seriously on Vietnam's sovereignty.
- All Vietnamese on Guam must terminate their intention to return by ship. Vietnam is ready to receive its compatriots, but they will have to wait until Vietnam has given its permission. They are not allowed to go back on their own.
- The Vietnamese compatriots on Guam must ensure that they don't fall into any perfidious U.S. scheme that might include an American plan to sabotage Vietnam.
- Vietnamese compatriots on Guam must take sole responsibility if they act unilaterally, without the consent of the Vietnamese government.
- The United States has to take responsibility for any act that infringes on Vietnam's sovereignty.

When I finished reading the radio transcript, I felt rather dizzy. Although I already knew that our decision to return carried serious risks, including possible death, these words of warning made me quite nervous. I was quiet for a minute, not knowing how to reply. After having composed myself, I said to General Herbert:

"General, we have known since the beginning that Hanoi has not approved of our repatriation. Still, we are determined to go back. We're also willing to pay any price, including death. For myself, I am not concerned about this message. I don't intend to change my mind. However, I will bring this message back to the representative committee, and we will share it with all camp members."

"I hope that you will read this message carefully," General Herbert urged. "I only want to help you, and I advise you to make your decision without any pressure. We will continue to negotiate with Hanoi even after we have given you the ship. Please go ahead and discuss this message with the camp members. After you have had a chance to discuss it seriously, you can give me your decision. I will meet you tomorrow."

I stood up and shook General Herbert's hand. When I returned to the camp, everyone assumed that he had called me up in order to hand over the ship.

I stepped into the room with an unexpected expression on my face. I was unable to conceal my confusion. Everybody noticed my concern, and, in turn, they all appeared worried as well. I fished Hanoi's message out of my pocket and shared it with the representative committee.

Hanoi's intelligence service was clearly paying close attention to our situation. The United States had announced its intention to give us a ship only the day before, and Hanoi immediately responded with this broadcast. Everyone listened attentively as Trần Khoa Mạc read the message aloud. After hearing the blunt words, almost everyone was in shock. We had felt so elated last night, and now Hanoi was already issuing threats. As long as we continued to live here on Guam, everyone's soul was easily affected—we were all vulnerable to a roller coaster of emotions.

Vũ Lê Hân thought for a moment and then said: "This is only a diplomatic announcement. I still believe that they will allow us back. We don't really need to worry. After General Herbert gave you this message, what did he say?"

"He said that we should look at it carefully, and, if we change our minds, please let him know. He is ready to help us. I told him I would discuss the matter carefully with the committee. This affects everyone, so we have to come to a unanimous decision."

Hân believed that we should remain firm in our position. He had no intention of changing his mind. All of us on the representative committee agreed with Hân. We were determined to go back, despite the content of the broadcast. I agreed, but I also thought that we needed to consult all the camp members, not just the leadership. If anyone wanted to change their mind, then it would be up to them. Everyone had the right to choose their own path. For me, I stood by my decision.

~

After lunch, I was finally able to lie down and rest a bit. I had been sleepless the night before, and my brain had been working continuously. I felt tired, but everyone kept stopping by my room and asking my opinion about this radio broadcast. It seemed that everyone wanted to gauge my commitment and see whether I might change my mind.

Many camp members had faith in me. It was if they had joined their fate to mine. When people get to the end of the road, they usually try to find something to cling on to, even if it's unsteady. If I went back, then everyone else would return with me. If I changed my mind, then they would follow me to the United States. Among the RVN naval officers present in Guam, many had the ability to operate the ship. However, almost everyone believed I was the only one who could navigate the ship from this island of Guam back to Vietnam. They had complete faith in me.

That evening, Hân wanted all the camp members to have a chance to hear what had been said in Hanoi's radio broadcast firsthand. He gathered the future repatriates together and asked me to speak to them. The atmosphere was so still—there was not even a whisper. Everyone focused all their attention on what I said.

Going to the microphone, I felt emotional. Even before I said a word, tears welled up in my eyes, and I choked up. I had to make an announcement that would cause everyone great concern.

I took a deep breath and began: "All of us here share one common wish, which is to return to Vietnam. We have spent a great deal of energy and fought for our day of repatriation. Today, the United States has agreed to give us a ship, so that we can go back on our own. However, as soon as the United States agreed to this plan, Hanoi broadcast its radio message. The U.S. government monitored this report, and General Herbert has shared it with me, and now I am sharing it with you. Hanoi states that the Vietnamese government forbids our unilateral return without its consent."

I then read the transcript aloud verbatim, so that everyone could hear it. I continued, "I, along with the representative committee, am still determined to return to Vietnam, whether Hanoi approves or not. We will go back and accept all the consequences. I will meet with General Herbert tomorrow, and I will ask him to move forward with the transfer of the ship. Everyone has the choice to return to Vietnam or to go to the United States. Everyone must make their own decision and determine their own fate. It's up to you. There will be no coercion. If you want to go to America, just tell the Office of Civil Affairs, and it will take care of the paperwork for you."

I also wanted to let the camp members know that we would need at least a month to prepare the ship, so everyone would have ample time to make a final decision.

After I finished, the camp members began to chant "Return! Return! Return!" and applauded my determination to go back. Almost no one planned to change their minds.

Vũ Lê Hân went up to the microphone to calm everyone down. He, too, spoke to the crowd: "The decision to return to Vietnam is ours alone. We have struggled mightily to reach the point where we are today. I think Hanoi's reaction is unsurprising. Hanoi will always oppose the United States. Hanoi sees our return as a threat to its honor, its self-image, and its sovereignty. Despite this, it is all just words. I believe if we return, for sure, Hanoi will accept us. There is nothing to be afraid of."

Rounds of applause once again reverberated across the campground. We all had a common wish. The only thing we feared was that there would be no day of repatriation.

～

Of course, after time away from the crowd, some people would be frightened into changing their minds. Since our detention, every time a disturbance broke out in the camp, a number of people had changed their minds.

This time, I felt an immense sadness throughout my soul and one sorrow followed the next. The more dejected I felt, the more I wanted to test Hanoi and its threats. I had already accepted the fact that I might die, so what else could hold me back? Every person has their own fate. Every person has their own lot. Heaven has already chosen a destiny for each person.

At this point, we still numbered approximately two thousand camp members. I was sure that a few individuals would choose to go on to the United States after hearing what Hanoi had said in its radio broadcast. It was unavoidable.

But I remained steadfast in my decision. I was unconcerned about those who had changed their minds. As long as I had a crew for the ship, I would go back.

～

The next morning, I gathered my crew together. They all eagerly waited to be assigned their duties on the ship. They were young people, and their hearts raced with hot blood. They could have decided to emigrate to the United States. All of them could have created new lives for themselves with a bright future. Instead, like me they all decided to follow their hearts. They did not want to abandon their beloved families still in Vietnam. Suffering souls all share the same state of mind, and so we easily became intimate and as close as siblings.

Only a few months earlier, my age and rank would have created an enormous social chasm between me and these young people. But today, in our new circumstances, we enjoyed total equality. They still respected and admired me as their captain. However, their respect was sincere and far more valuable than the respect I had commanded due solely to my rank and position. The men obeyed me and had faith in me. With the crew list in hand, I went straight to the point:

"Greetings. I want to speak with everyone about our roles and responsibilities in the near future. We have volunteered to sail this ship back to Vietnam, first, because of our own private desires and, second, to help everyone who shares our wish. We are no longer military men. Now, we are all on equal footing. We must treat each other as siblings. We need to collaborate and work together to navigate the ship safely to Vietnam. . . . We will work without self-interest. None of us will receive any personal benefit or payment. Like you, I volunteered for this work.

"As the captain of the *Việt Nam Thương Tín,* I do not have any formal power over you. We will work out of mutual respect. You can call me *anh* [older brother], instead of captain. When we arrive in Vietnam, we will each go our own way. But, for now, we will cherish this mission together—it is a noble and beautiful project. That is my wish."

I continued to explain how we would organize the crew for our sea voyage. I appointed Nguyễn Văn Phước as executive officer. He would be responsible for overseeing the watch shifts, and he would also supervise the repairs. Trần Cao Khải would be the engineering officer, which included the main engines, the electrical engines, the damage control system, and the anchor machine. Vương Thế Tuấn would be the navigator. He was highly skilled in electronics, and he would teach the crew how to draft navigation maps and use the radios and radar equipment on board. Hoàng Công Minh became chair of the transportation committee, and he would oversee the cables, life preservers, and life rafts. Phạm Ngọc Lộ was head of the logistics committee, which included keeping abreast of our provisions. We would need enough fresh and dried food for two thousand people to eat over twenty days. Finally, Nguyễn Văn Đàng would be our chief medical officer, in charge of health care, medications, and first aid kits, for when our passengers had headaches, diarrhea, or seasickness.

I then went on to detail the maintenance that would be required. We would need to overhaul the main engines and the generators. We also needed to create living quarters for at least two thousand people below decks. It would be tight, but there would be room for each person to have a bunk to call his or her own. We would also need an efficient galley, ready to feed all two thousand passengers every day, and a system of toilets. In short, we needed supplies and support for the daily needs of two thousand people.

The United States would provide us with all the necessary funds to repair the ship and obtain supplies for our voyage. It might cost up to a million dollars, but General Herbert had promised as much. Our demands were necessary and legitimate. After finishing the repairs, we would have to test the ship in multiday voyages and train the crew until we were confident in all the ship's machinery. That would take at least an extra week of training at sea. Finally, we would need to provision the ship with fuel, fresh water, and adequate food. It would take approximately one month to complete all these tasks. Then, we could depart.

"We have a very strong crew," I explained. "All our committee chairs were captains with long-term experience in the RVN Navy. Once we have our ship, then we can travel anywhere in the whole world."

Everyone was joyous and ebullient. No one made any further suggestions. "If no one has any new ideas, then I would like to ask you to disperse. This afternoon, I will meet with General Herbert, and our work will begin."

～

At 2 p.m. I went to General Herbert's office. He shook my hand and invited me to sit down. He poured some coffee and said: "I have been waiting for your answer. Please let me know what you have decided."

"We all discussed Hanoi's message together," I explained. "Everyone is still determined to go back home. We don't care if Hanoi approves of our actions or not. We want to return to Vietnam by ship. This morning I organized my crew and assigned tasks and responsibilities. We can get to work immediately. Please let us know when I can receive the ship."

General Herbert promised to take me to the ship the following morning at 8 a.m. We agreed that I would bring my chief mechanic and the committee chairs with me. We would begin preparing for our journey home.

CHAPTER TEN

Receiving the Ship

After meeting with General Herbert, I returned to the camp in a confused state of mind. The next day, I would have to put my shoulder to the wheel. At least with all the tasks ahead, I could temporarily forget all the thoughts that had been tormenting me over the past few months. I didn't know what would happen in the future, but for the moment I could get to work. There was plenty in front of me.

When I returned to the camp, the representative committee and camp members were waiting for me. There were even people loitering outside my bunk. Everyone observed me closely, and they seemed on edge, as if they were afraid that there might be a change. It was strange, because I was not that important, but now everyone was watching me, as though I were a VIP. At this moment, I felt as if I had become a lifeline to all the people around me. I spoke to the group: "It's done. Tomorrow I will receive the ship." Hearing that, everyone sighed with relief. The news spread quickly throughout the camp. Everyone was so elated that there was nothing left to say. I, myself, was tired and needed to lie down.

I lay alone, lost in thought, not wanting to talk to anyone. I wondered whether I would be able to see my wife and children after we returned. I wondered how the communists would treat me. It was difficult to imagine how it would all play out. The best I could do was imagine rescuing my wife and children and all of us escaping Vietnam together. Life was so complicated. Here I was in Guam, looking forward to the day of my return to Vietnam, and yet I was already planning my next escape.

I loved my homeland, my ancestral land. But now the communists controlled the country. Would they allow us to live as human beings? I had never lived with the communists. Why was everyone so afraid of them, and why did everyone leave? In 1954 nearly a million people left the North and migrated South to escape communism. They had abandoned their houses, their fields, and their gardens. They had left all their property in exchange for freedom.

But what was communism? I had fought against it for so many years but still couldn't picture how it might have changed South Vietnam. I had decided to return and face this ideology head-on. I knew I had to be ready to accept any hardships that might greet me when I set foot on Vietnamese soil. I often wondered what kind of sins I must have committed to have to suffer so. I had tried to live a moral life, but I had met with so much misfortune. My ancestors used to say, if you live morally, then you will have good things happen to you. What did this saying mean for me?

Our joy and our elation grew because the day of our return was near. We knew we would encounter unexpected hardships after our return. So many traps lay before us—how could I escape them? I had willpower, and I believed I would be able to endure any struggle. I was not afraid of hardships. I didn't mind them. I only prayed to heaven to let me return safely. I had faith in Jesus Christ in heaven, and God surely would not reject me. He would help me overcome all obstacles.

~

I was in deep thought when Nguyễn Thy Tấn came to my side without my being aware of it. He asked me to go to dinner, because it was already dark. Since arriving in the camps, I had never felt hungry. At times, I only ate one meal a day and that was sufficient. I was eating only in order to have some food in me—eating only to live. Ever since I set foot on the island of Guam, I had been living like this, living without passion.

Tấn and I ate together at a table in a corner of the room. We often confided our innermost feelings to each other. Like soul mates, we trusted each other.

I told my friend that everything was progressing smoothly. In fact, I thought that General Herbert seemed to be afraid that I might change my mind. He appeared happy when I told him that we were determined to return. After we received the ship, his mission here would end. I thought that if he had to keep working with our group, he would go crazy and have to retire to a lunatic asylum. I would receive the ship the next day, and then my work would begin. I offered to take Tấn to the ship to see for himself.

Tấn cut in: "Do you know that a number of people have changed their minds and will not be going back? After they learned about the broadcast from Hanoi, they were frightened. I went from one row of houses to another while you were meeting with the crew. How do you feel about this?"

"You and I understand each other. Even if only the two of us are left, we will still wait to return. Have you forgotten that?"

"I would go back by myself, let alone with two of us," Tấn answered.

"I never expected that a lieutenant colonel and an air force pilot like you would have such sentimental feelings. Truly you are just like me," I added. "Even if many people change their minds and go to the United States, we do not need to concern ourselves about any of them. They will not be an obstacle. The crew is determined to go along with me, and there are enough people to sail the ship back. It would only be a problem if my crew members changed their minds, and I was left alone. Then my hands would be tied. We would just look at the ship without being able to sail it."

"There's also one more piece of news I should tell you," said Tấn.

"What news? Will it have any impact on the day of our return?"

"The young people on the law and order committee received an order from someone to stay close to you and keep tabs on your every move. They are afraid that you will change your mind and will not go back. They are callow and thoughtless, and they are capable of doing something bad to you if you change your mind. Be careful and take precautions," Tấn warned.

"I have known this group for a long time," I answered. "This morning I rose early, I drank coffee by myself, and I saw a few of them loitering outside, looking at me. Then in the afternoon, when I went to the office to meet with General Herbert, someone was following me, just like a detective lying in wait for a criminal. I saw it all. These men were like cheap movie actors, and their actions were so transparent. But I don't care about them. They are like children, performing clownish acts. If I wanted to go to the United States, I would find a way, regardless of these kids. They cannot outsmart me, and I don't want to waste my energy paying attention to them. Among those of us who are returning, there are all kinds of people, good as well as bad."

Just as Tấn and I were speaking, two of the young upstarts came in. They pulled a chair up and whispered in my ear. "There are individuals who are watching you. They are afraid that you will change your plans. They have threatened to kill you if you change your mind. Have you heard about that?"

"Thank you for letting me know," I responded calmly. "I've seen that already. If you happen to be acquainted with these men, then tell them that they shouldn't threaten me. Going back is my own business. Don't disgust me, or I might change my mind. Moreover, even if I changed my mind, there would be other men here who used to be ship captains. They are not as experienced as I am, but they still have the ability to sail this ship back. Besides, the United States has planned everything. Everything is ready for our return."

When I went back to my room, Vũ Lê Hân, Vương Long Đoàn, and a few members of the representative committee were there, waiting to hear more details about my meeting with General Herbert. Hân said, "We came to see you, because General Herbert will only speak directly with you. He doesn't have to work with our committee anymore. Please let us know what we need to do to prepare the ship."

"Of course, I will let you know any developments. You still represent our camp. My only responsibility is to sail the ship. We will have to spend some time training the crew, repairing the ship, and supplying it with fuel, food, fresh water, etc. Plus, we need to fix the machinery and make the ship livable for two thousand people. It will take at least a month. Tell everyone that this waiting period will not be like the months of limbo we have recently endured. We will leave when the ship is ready. There's no need for any more impatience."

Then Hân asked me, "Do you have any ideas about why Hanoi doesn't want us to return?"

"I don't think anything about it. Even if it means death, I will still go back. You already know my intentions."

Đoàn chimed in, "But once we are in Saigon, Hanoi wouldn't dare to sink our ship. The whole world knows about this. Our safety is all but assured."

"I also think so," I agreed. "If they shoot us to death, then we will have to accept it. We are all RVN officers, but I will be responsible for the most serious crime, because I dared to take you back. So if they decide to kill us, they will shoot me first. Next will be Hân, who worked at the presidential palace and who is the leader of the repatriates. Then it will be Đoàn, who also worked at the presidential palace, and then Tấn, who was an enemy pilot, etc. I am condemning you on behalf of the VC, so that when we return, we won't be shocked."

At exactly 8 a.m., General Herbert picked me up as promised. When we reached the docks, we saw the *Việt Nam Thương Tín* anchored in the distance. This was the first time that I had seen the ship with my own eyes. In Vietnam, I had heard about this ship, but I had never had the opportunity to board the biggest merchant marine ship in Vietnam. It had carried merchandise overseas, usually between the United States and the Philippines, and it had only occasionally docked in Vietnam. It weighed 12,000 tons and was 140 meters long with six holds for merchandise. It had been built in Italy and sold to South Vietnam a few years earlier. It was still new and in good condition.

No flag was flying from the great ship's mast. This ship no longer represented a sovereign nation. Only a few months earlier, the yellow flag with three red stripes flew from its mast. Now, that flag had been lowered, because that country was no more. The ship had taken evacuees from Saigon and brought them here, and the men, women, and children who had been on board had now scattered to the four corners of the earth.

The ship was empty. Except for the *Việt Nam Thương Tín,* all the other warships and merchant ships that evacuated Vietnam on April 30 now belonged to

The *Việt Nam Thương Tín*. Courtesy of the National Archives and Records Administration, Record Group 319, Box 19, declassification number 984082.

the United States. In contrast, the *Việt Nam Thương Tín's* destiny was still tied to Vietnam. I thought to myself that a ship also has its own fate. For the crew, a ship was the same as their house or their family. Each sailor had two lives: one on land, where he lived in a house with his wife and children, and one at sea. The ship was a second home, where members of the crew lived closely like siblings, especially when they had to wrestle with the waves and the wind and the open seas. There was always a great feeling of camaraderie at sea.

The motored raft carried us out, and we climbed onto the abandoned ship. The atmosphere was still, with no one wanting to say a word. I thought about my lot. General Herbert led us on an inspection tour into every area of the ship from the engine room to the pilot's bridge. I had the impression that he had been here many times in order to be familiar with every space on the ship.

Finally, I spoke: "I see that the ship needs a lot of repairs. General, can you tell me the estimated budget for the repair work?"

The *Việt Nam Thương Tín*. Courtesy of the National Archives and Records Administration, Record Group 319, Box 19, declassification number 984082.

He responded quickly, "Don't worry. We have allocated approximately a million dollars for this ship. A plan is ready, and today, I officially hand the ship over to you. Starting next Monday, we will meet every day to proceed with the overhaul. I will prioritize the repairs and the provisions, and you can bring the crew on board."

"General, I was here in Guam three years ago for an overhaul and then a second time to receive a U.S. ship for the Vietnamese Navy. This work will be similar. I am ready."

General Herbert explained that he would be an intermediary and assist me with the shipyard authorities. He would be present at all the meetings and ensure that we received the assistance we needed. This sounded perfect to me. I had already mapped out our plan to repair and ready the ship. I would sketch out each day's tasks, and I would be responsible for keeping track of all the repairs. If there were any obstacles, then I would go to General Herbert.

A few years earlier, I had commanded a ship that stopped in Guam for repairs. At that time, I still had everything. I had felt great pride in my responsibilities as a captain in the RVN naval uniform. Now, my days were filled with similar tasks, but I was a different person. I was lost. I had nothing left, and only a vacant sadness occupied my soul. Looking up at the sky, I could only see black clouds covering the whole sky.

Usually, I would strive for impressive achievements and aim to build a bright future. But this time, it was the opposite. I was working, but my intuition told me that the future would be dark.

~

The vehicle entered the camp gate and stopped in front of the row of houses where I lived. I again saw familiar faces, and they were waiting for me to give them fresh news. I was quiet. I didn't want to say anything to anyone. I saw Vũ Lê Hân, and I uttered just two words, "Already done."

Then, I pulled him into my room, so I could speak to him alone. I told Hân that I had received the ship and requested an overhaul. After the repairs were completed, we could leave Guam and return to Vietnam. Hân replied positively to the news and told me that everyone would be very grateful for all my work. Now I had something to say. "I don't know whether they will be grateful or if they will blame me for their future problems. However, I will always do my best, because I want to return more than anyone."

Then I explained the process. We would have weekly meetings, and General Herbert would help us at each step. I would need all of our committee chairs at each meeting, and they would be updated on the preparations and the state of the ship. My job was to focus on the technical side and make sure all the machinery was running properly. We also had to make the ship habitable for two thousand people at sea. We would have to be meticulous.

Hân reassured me that I could focus on the ship. He would collaborate with the representative committee and take care of the camp members. We would work closely together throughout the weeks ahead.

Then, I started to think through all that had to be done. The voyage would last at least ten days. The crew would sail day and night, and so they could not do anything else. We would have to be well organized. The fate of two thousand people lay in our hands. We would have to live up to our sense of duty. If something untoward happened on board the ship, especially to a woman, then we would all lose our honor.

I told Hân we had to focus on discipline. With such a large number of people on board, it would be difficult to keep track of everyone's actions. Thus, discipline and organization were essential. We had to organize down to the minutest detail.

~

On Monday morning, the bus arrived and everyone was ready. We drove to the meeting, and General Herbert himself was there. He shook my hand as I stepped out of the bus. He was always so thoughtful.

I decided I needed to ask General Herbert a difficult question: "General, could I ask you a question? Hanoi has forbidden us to go back. In your opinion, what do you think will happen when we return? Will I be safe?"

He replied graciously, "Given what I know, you can go back. However, once you are in Vietnam, it will be hard to escape the troubles there. To be honest, I cannot picture the VC officials' reactions when they see your ship entering Vietnamese territorial waters. I sympathize with your decision, and at the very least, the whole world knows your story. Hanoi must recognize international opinion. They wouldn't dare harm you. I think that you can return in safety."

I was not so optimistic, but I had prepared myself. I answered that I was ready to accept the worst, no matter what.

Again, General Herbert respected my feelings. He added, "I understand you. However, there is one thing I would like to say privately. Please, whenever you need my help, I am always ready. Don't hesitate to speak to me about anything."

His words carried a lot of weight. In my experience, Americans were very willing to help other people, and they usually tried to assist in a way that supported others in making their own decisions. The Americans never imposed their viewpoints on me. The way I understood it, if I changed my mind, General Herbert would still help me.

"Thank you, General. You have helped me a lot already. Today we are here, and it is a major achievement. I don't need anything else."

Next, we all gathered in the meeting room. Inside, U.S. naval officers sat on one side of the conference table. The other side was left vacant for us. I was moved because this meeting room was familiar to me. I had sat here on my previous trips to Guam, but at that time, I had walked into the meeting room in a captain's uniform. This time, I wore only a pair of jeans and a short-sleeved shirt. My informal dress reflected my own sense of dejection and demoralization.

We sat down. There was a name card at my place titled "Captain." Yes, I was a captain out of necessity. Opposite me was the director of the naval shipyard on Guam. Next to him was the U.S. commander of the naval force on Guam. General Herbert presided at the head of the table. In this very formal atmosphere, it was clear that the United States had prepared for our return. There were so many high-ranking officers involved. Looking over at our side, we looked less impressive. We had also been high-ranking officers, but now we were just remnants of a defeated military force. We were all wrecked ciphers. Still, we were able to show some pride. Here we were sitting at a meeting on an equal footing with high-ranking officers from the U.S. Navy.

The director of the shipyard stood up and shook my hand. He announced, "On behalf of the United States, I am responsible for the repairs of your ship. I promise that I will complete this work as quickly as possible, so you can return to Vietnam. I ask you to have faith in me. Our primary mission is to maintain the Seventh Fleet; however, today I received a special decree to prioritize the *Việt Nam Thương Tín* for you." He went on to outline the many tasks that had to be completed before our departure. In addition, one officer would take charge of logistics, and a doctor and nurse would supply the ship with medical supplies. We had a lot to accomplish in a short time.

After the workers completed the repairs, they would conduct a test run to ensure all the machinery was ready for long-distance travel. We would also have time to train our crew, so we would have confidence in operating the ship on our own. Only then would the Americans officially transfer the ship over to me.

I stood up to respond to the officers. "These plans are more than adequate. I sincerely thank you all for having helped us to fulfill our dream."

The meeting adjourned, I left the room with a lingering pride. At least, I could still see the high-ranking American officers' respect for my current position, even if it was only an empty title.

The next day, we began to work for real. At 8 a.m., we boarded the ship. All the machinery was disassembled, cleaned, and tested for accuracy. Broken parts were replaced. The painters set up scaffolding around the ship in order to paint the hull. Other workers erected the living quarters, the kitchens, and the restrooms. Everyone worked enthusiastically, and it proceeded smoothly. Time simply flew by. At 4 p.m., we returned to the camp by bus.

Three weeks passed by swiftly. In no time at all, the repairs were well under way, and the living quarters and kitchens were completed. The captain's room was equipped with a new bed, a new mattress, and many conveniences. Of course, the captain always had separate quarters to sleep and eat, but this time, I didn't feel any excitement over this special treatment. I observed the custom only for the sake of appearances. I did not move into my own room on the ship but, instead, preferred to remain in the camp with my friends. During this time of loneliness and loss, the thought of my captain's quarters only made me feel more bereft than before. Therefore I waited until the very last day to pack my things and move into this room.

When I had free time, Nguyễn Thy Tấn and I would exchange confidences. We truly sympathized with each other and shared the same thoughts. Although we only met in the camp, because of our circumstances, we had become very close.

On Sundays, we would go to church together. I was a Catholic, and Tấn was a Buddhist. However, I believed that Christ and Buddha were both supreme beings, and it was valuable for religious people to worship and pray together. I went to his Buddhist temple, and he went to church with me. At this moment of despair, we could turn to Christ or the Buddha and ask for their blessings. I usually prayed silently during quiet moments by myself, but Tấn would go to the middle of the yard every day and turn his face to the sky. He would mumble prayers without paying any attention to those around him. He had this all-powerful faith. When he prayed, he only saw the Buddha in front of him. We prayed to both Jesus Christ and the Buddha, and if both of them could bless us, then it would be all the better. Certainly, our prayers had reached the ears of Jesus Christ and the Buddha. That was why we were about to enjoy the day of our return.

At the camp, the Americans cared for our spiritual needs as well as our physical well-being. Father Tiến, a priest, celebrated Mass every day, and he, too, had decided to return to Vietnam. Catholics believe that Jesus Christ is present everywhere, and the future returnees included a lot of Catholics. Therefore, it seemed as if Jesus Christ had arranged for Father Tiến to return with us and be at our side to conduct Mass every day and remind us to always worship Jesus Christ and to pray.

On this Sunday morning after church, we paid Father Tiến a visit. We chatted for the whole morning, and he asked us when we could begin our journey.

I answered politely, "Dear Father, we should be able to leave in about one more month. Father, wherever there is Christ, you can be happy. Since Christ is everywhere, and your followers are nearby, you already have everything."

"I know that you and the other men miss your wives and children," Father Tiến added, "but I abandoned my church. I abandoned my parish, and my parish members are like my children. Therefore, I miss them like you miss your wives and your children. My mission is to be a priest. Just like you, I have a responsibility. When I abandoned my parish, all of my followers were left behind. I don't know whether there is another priest who can stand in my place to say Mass for them."

Father Tiến was sixty years old, and throughout his life, he preached to faithful Catholics. He taught his congregation how to worship Christ and live an ethical life, an honest life, and a straight life, as Christ had taught his disciples. He had decided to leave, because he didn't think he could live with the communists.

I asked Father Tiến, "Do you have any news of Vietnam? How have the Catholics been treated since the communists have taken over the South?"

Father Tiến answered, "I am just like you. It's difficult to imagine how the communists are treating the Catholics. I only know one thing for certain: communism always opposes Catholicism. The communists advocate atheism, and they are fearful of religious people and their faith. But apart from their faith, Catholics serve society like anybody else. In the communist world, there are still people who follow Catholicism. It is not like ancient Rome when Jesus Christ suffered and died. But the communists are cunning. They make sure that the Catholics don't have enough time to go to church, and they oppress their spirits indirectly. They make people struggle to address their daily needs and obtain food and clothing, and therefore they have little time for Christ or religion. In general, Catholics find the communist world stifling."

"In my opinion, Father," I answered, "if we return and are thrown into jail by the communists, then you still have Christ by your side. But Father, you are getting old and if you are sent to prison, will you have enough strength to tolerate it?"

"Deep in my heart, I want to return," Father Tiến replied. "I have a few nieces and nephews in America who have written to me to change my mind. They want me to go to America. I'm so undecided. Did you know that the number of repatriates changing their minds is increasing every day? At least a hundred of them have started the process to go on to America."

"Father, I know that. Going back is my own decision. Those who choose to return or stay have no influence over me. I am determined to go back."

The next Monday, I went back to work, and General Herbert and I conducted an inspection of the ship. General Herbert was satisfied with the progress of the repairs. Walking side by side, we chatted in a friendly manner. I decided to ask him another question that had been on my mind.

"General, there are a number of people who have given up. They are no longer going back to Vietnam. Are you aware of that?"

"Of course, I am, because whenever someone changes his or her mind, I am the one who expedites the process. What about you? Are there any changes?"

Of course, if I changed my mind, it would cause trouble for him.

"I have thought a lot about making this decision. The majority of those who have changed their minds have done so because they are afraid of the communists. They no longer dare to go back. As for those of us who are determined to return, we are willing to risk our lives. We no longer care. I'm one of those people, General, you can rest assured."

General Herbert continued with his warmth and generosity. He expressed how much he respected me and that he would always be willing to help me. I appreciated his friendship and trust.

Next, General Herbert surprised me. He continued, "When you go back, I have a special gift for you."

"Thank you, General. Being able to go back to Vietnam is the most precious gift already. I no longer need anything else."

He insisted, "I will have a uniform made for you. You will be dressed properly as the captain when the ship leaves the harbor."

I was stunned by this offer. "What for, General? I will just wear these clothes until the day I go back. Military uniforms no longer have any symbolic meaning for me. I threw away my military uniform the moment I stepped onto Guam. All of our status and position has been washed away. 'Captain' is just a hollow title now. I'm no different from anyone else."

"I have always admired and respected you," General Herbert continued. "I would just like to offer you a token of that admiration with the uniform. You have given up everything in order to search for the truth in your life. This decision speaks to the power of your conscience. However, I wonder whether, when your goal is achieved, it will live up to your expectations. I truly want to help you, but given your decision, I don't know what else I can do except support you in your journey."

"General, you have sympathized with my situation. That makes me happy already. I have the feeling that we are indeed soul mates. We understand each other."

General Herbert's regular presence on the ship made the workers quite productive. All the tasks were finished in good time.

One day, the U.S. officer in charge announced that the repairs of the *Việt Nam Thương Tín* were complete. The ship was ready for its test run, a twenty-four-hour journey around Guam. He added that we were particularly fortunate with our maintenance crew. Two of our crew members had been the *Việt Nam Thương Tín*'s original mechanical and hydrodynamic workers. They had left Vietnam on the *Việt Nam Thương Tín,* and now they would return on this same ship. Both of these men were familiar with the operation of the main engine and the electrical generators.

Next, the logistics officer explained how they would supply the ship. They would fill the freezers with fresh and dried food. As for fresh water, there wasn't enough time to fix the water spigots. They had rusted over from a long period of disuse, and the repairs would be complicated and take many weeks. Instead, we would use large plastic containers for fresh water, and they would be stored in designated areas. It would be necessary to ration water while at sea, but we already knew this well. The U.S. officer suggested that we designate one person to be in charge of dispensing fresh water each day for personal use. If we each conserved it, it would be more than adequate.

As for lodgings, there were sufficient pillows and blankets and space for each person to rest. Regarding medical needs, there would be medications supplied and sick beds in the nurse's cabin. There were also individual life preservers and rafts, and they had all been tested in case of an emergency.

Then the officer asked me how long I thought it would take to travel from Guam to Vietnam. They needed to know the estimated number of days to properly supply the ship. I explained that the journey was about two thousand nautical miles at a speed of ten miles per hour. If we were able to maintain this speed, the trip would take ten days and nights. However, in order to prepare for storms or any trouble with the machinery, it would be best to be provisioned for at least an additional ten days. General Herbert advised that we stock the ship with enough provisions for thirty days. If we changed our minds after we reached Vietnam's territorial waters, he wanted to make sure we could return to Guam.

I thought to myself, obviously, this gentleman has a lot of interesting ideas. His thoughts and plans go beyond my understanding. Now that I was on the point of returning to Vietnam, he was prepared for the possibility that I might bring the ship back to Guam!

I decided to respond. "Thank you, General, for thinking for us. I hadn't thought about the extra provisions, and, to be honest, I don't wish for such a situation to occur. I believe that the officer in charge of logistics has made adequate provisions."

General Herbert concluded by thanking everyone and adjourning our meeting. Everything was almost ready.

I went back to the camp and wrote down all the tasks I needed to complete the following week. The day of our return was imminent. There was no longer anything to worry about, at least for the time being. The beginning is always the hardest. We had surmounted so many obstacles, and I was sure that we would have many more difficulties in Vietnam. But that was for later. We could only plan one step at a time.

Back in my room, lying down to rest and glancing to the side, I saw Tấn lying with one arm across his forehead, as if he were lost in thought. I asked him to let me know what he was thinking: "Friend, what is so special about today that you are in such deep thought?"

"Of course, there are many things to tell you, but seeing that you are just back from the meeting and you seemed so tired, I thought you should just rest. Tonight when we eat, I will look for a quiet place, and then I will tell you many things. You have been so busy with the ship that you haven't been paying any attention to activities inside the camp."

"What is there to pay attention to? Now that our day of return is fast approaching, we should set aside everything else and focus on the ship," I replied. "The repairs have progressed nicely, and next week, there will be a test run. Then everything will be ready."

That night, after we were done with our meal, Tấn pulled me out to the deserted shore. He wanted to talk in private. We usually had to be on the alert whenever we talked with each other, because among the repatriates there were both "true" and "false" friends. We didn't trust everyone, and therefore, we had to be extremely cautious in both words and gestures. How could we fathom people's hearts? And how could we know who among us might be VC spies watching our every move? I was the captain, and this position would draw most of their attention. They might write up a report and give it to the VC authorities. Even though we had no plots, no plans, no politics, we were cautious about what we said aloud.

We sat down on a stone bench, looking at the sky and the sea. The firmament was clear, with only a few white clouds, and the sea winds were blowing strong. It was a poetic scene, but it did not match our inner feelings.

I wanted to know what was on Tấn's mind. "So, you took me out here to lull my soul into a dreamy world?"

"What kind of dream?" Tấn answered. "A part of our hearts has already died, even though you and I have truly romantic souls. But now is not the time. I brought you out here because I have several things I want to tell you."

"Just go ahead and tell me."

"Do you know how many people have left?"

I answered sharply: "Of course not. I don't concern myself with who has stayed and who has gone."

"Well, the number has grown to more than two hundred people. This might continue until the day the ship sets sail for Vietnam."

"We can just ignore them. It has nothing to do with us. The ship is ready, and we are still going back, right? We are returning in order to solve our problems, don't you agree?"

"Of course," Tấn replied, but he chose his words carefully. "Of course, I am like you. But this news has created turmoil at the camp. We won't know until the day of our return how many people will go back to Vietnam with us."

"Well, even if a thousand people choose to go to the United States, we will still have a thousand people who want to return to Vietnam."

Then Tấn got to his real question. "I just wanted to let you know. As for me, it is not important, but there is a question that is being raised—usually, when a ship goes to sea, it flies a flag on its mast. What flag will fly on our ship?"

"I hadn't thought of that—but you are right. The ship sails under a flag, and when it is at sea, the ship is considered under the sovereignty of that nation. But our country has fallen to the communists. Our ship is no different from a ghost ship. It doesn't represent anyone or any place, and therefore, we don't need a flag. When a ship travels in international waters, it doesn't need to fly a flag at all times. It needs to fly a flag only when it enters a specific country's territorial waters. Our ship is a special one; therefore, it can go without that symbol. I don't need to pay attention to it."

Tấn had more to say. "The representative committee hasn't told you anything, then?"

"I have told them that I will be in charge of operating the ship. I let them take care of all the activities at the camp. What have they prepared?"

"This is a painful issue, but I need to let you know. They have sewed together the National Liberation Front flag, and they plan to unfurl it when the ship leaves the harbor. They have also made banners and drawn a large picture of Hồ Chí Minh to display on the ship. In this way, they plan to curry favor with the VCs."

"If that is so, then it's truly sad, but what can we do now? Perhaps, we can talk to the leaders of this group, but if they are just opportunists, then we cannot do anything about that. They will not listen to us. We have decided to return because of our wives and children, and we're willing to accept any consequences that may happen to us. This is the first consequence that we have to accept. Truly, we have lost everything. Our nation no longer exists. We have been humiliated. We can no longer do anything. Our country is lost, our families are dispersed, and we ourselves have been broken. The best thing is to forget about ourselves. I have chosen to be blind, deaf, and mute. It is the best thing to do for the time being. The more we think about it, the more painful it will be. We are already so wounded. And once we have returned, we will have to meet with even more shame. Yet that is the road we have chosen."

Tấn had more to say. "I know, but I wish we were only common soldiers with just superficial knowledge. Then there would be nothing to talk about. Even though our positions don't exist anymore, we were high-ranking officers. Our ideals and our honor have been trampled. How can we avoid feeling outraged?"

"I agree, but what can we do now?"

"Of course, there's nothing we can do. I just feel overwhelmed and angry, and I needed to confide in you."

"We should just forget it. I have told you that these malcontents at the camp are only acting a part. Each human being has a true face and a mask. Only when something critical happens will we see their true faces. They are trying to play games with the communists, but they will end up gaining nothing. You can see their opportunism everywhere. They deserve our contempt."

"Yesterday, after I went to the Buddhist shrine to pray," Tấn went on, "I stopped by to visit Father Tiến. He left for America this morning. He sent you his regards and his good-bye. He thought you were too busy, so he didn't try to say goodbye. Also, he left silently. He didn't want anyone to know. He had received so many letters from his nieces and nephews in America, and they kept urging him to go to them. Eventually, he gave in."

"I myself advised him to go to America. It is a good thing that he changed his mind. He doesn't have any family in Vietnam, except for his parishioners. But wherever he goes, he will have his followers. Christ is everywhere."

CHAPTER ELEVEN

Leaving Guam

On Monday morning, the two hundred-person crew prepared for the long-distance test run at sea. We boarded the ship, and everyone knew his place. As the captain, I gave the order to start the main engine, and within five minutes everyone was ready. I stepped into the control tower with General Herbert.

The atmosphere was quite formal, just as it had been when I was a real captain, but today, I was just a reluctant captain. As for the tasks at hand, we were still experts. We had been sailors in the RVN Navy only five months earlier. I could see that after we put our shoulders to the wheel, everyone became more alert and enthusiastic.

I gave the order to weigh anchor. The ship gradually sailed away from the wharf, leaving the U.S. officers and the dock behind. I waved good-bye to everyone and maneuvered the ship out to sea. Sailing away from Guam, I sketched out our itinerary on a chart. The test run was twenty-four hours, during which we would circumnavigate Guam twice. With our plan documented, I went down to the dining room and drank a cup of coffee with General Herbert and a few other high-ranking U.S. officers in charge of the repairs.

As I drank my coffee, smoked my cigarette, and spoke with the officers, it appeared as if I was my former self again, a captain. But in reality, I was deep in thought and sorrow, and my mind was elsewhere. In this state, I worked like a machine. In fact, I thought we all resembled corpses without souls.

Then General Herbert spoke, bringing me back to reality. He remarked, "I knew you were experienced, but I didn't really believe you had enough expertise to control a ship as large as this one. Now that I can observe how you maneuver and navigate the ship, I can see your skill. You order the crew in such a calm manner. I can tell you are an expert captain of the highest caliber."

"General, you are praising me too much," I responded, even though I was proud of his acknowledgment. "As a matter of fact, I have had more than ten years commanding warships. Even though the *Thương Tín* is bigger than most warships, in principle and practice, they are all alike."

Then the director in charge of repairs reported that the engine, radar, communication equipment, pumping system, and anchor were all in good working order. However, the ship would have to sail at a high velocity continuously for twenty-four hours. Only then would we know for sure whether the ship was seaworthy.

Next, General Herbert and I decided to tour the ship and watch the crew in action. We observed the men in the engine hold, the radar post, and the cockpit. In each location, the sailors worked diligently and conscientiously. The ship was in the correct position, and the crew followed the itinerary exactly as I had drawn it up. I felt reassured. General Herbert noted the crew's skill and trustworthiness, and we agreed that they were ready. They had worked hard, because they, too, wanted to return to Vietnam.

After sailing for twenty-four hours, the ship returned to the harbor. Everything had gone smoothly and without a single glitch. Even though I had worked without sleep, I felt fine. Hope began to flow within me, as I realized the date of our return was fast approaching.

After the test run was complete, the U.S. officer in charge announced that his duty was done, and the ship was ready. General Herbert had a grim expression, with only a half smile on his lips. Still, he shook my hand in praise. He continued: "Tomorrow, you and the crew can move on board the ship and prepare for your departure."

I felt so grateful. "General Herbert," I answered, "yes, we are ready. Thank you for your trust and faith in our mission. I feel you are always at my side."

~

Enjoying a deep sleep for a few hours, I woke up feeling refreshed. Then glancing over at the bed next to mine, I saw Tấn with his arm across his forehead, looking as if he were deep in thought, and his face reflecting his sorrow. I called his name, and he shot up as if he had been awakened from a dream. "You can smile now, Tấn," I said. "The ship is ready—we will leave in just a few days."

Tấn was in shock, not knowing whether it was good news or bad news. Of course, he had been looking forward to this day, yet he was fixated on all the misfortunes that might occur on his return. He was sad and pessimistic, and he knew there would be many hardships in Vietnam, but he still felt compelled to return. He wasn't carefree as other people were. He only nodded without answering me. His emotions were all tangled up. He was glad to hear of our imminent return, but his joy was mixed with thousands of worries weighing on his mind.

I tried to calm him down. "Tấn, do not worry so much. At least, you are returning as only one man among many. You are not the captain, and so you will have far less trouble than me. I will be a target for the communists, and I am sure I will bear the brunt of their anger. Certainly, the VC will be suspicious of me, and they will interrogate me. But even so, I don't pay any attention to those thoughts. I will deal with it when it comes. Right now, this is the worst. It is impossible for things to get any worse. Please smile, even if our smiles carry tears, at least they can lighten our sorrows."

Alert and refreshed, I went to meet the representative committee. I told everyone about the successful test run. The crew had worked well as a team, and we were ready to sail. It was time for the camp members to pack their bags and prepare themselves for the journey.

Hân expressed his joy and pleasure in our accomplishments. However, I wanted to make sure everyone was aware of the risks. I continued, "I'm not sure whether I have done a good thing or a bad thing, so don't thank me too soon. After we reach Vietnam, we will know whether we should be happy or sad. Everyone should prepare themselves and be ready to accept the consequences. I have to board the ship and make arrangements for our supplies. Whoever wants to go with me can come."

All in the camp were joyous. Everyone packed their belongings quickly and prepared to leave. After so many months in the camp, we had collected a great deal of stuff. Every day, camp members stood in line to receive all kinds of provisions. They wanted to bring everything onto the ship, and they didn't know what to keep and what to throw away.

Of all the preparations, organizing and storing fresh water was the most difficult. Drinking water had to be pumped into twenty-liter containers. Each person would receive one container per day, but that added up to sixty thousand containers to be used by two thousand people in thirty days. We would also need to have extra water in case of emergencies and for everyday cooking purposes. We would also have to tell people to conserve water. It was to be used sparingly for drinking, washing, and brushing their teeth. We were providing more than enough per person, but people would not be able to take full baths every day.

On board the ship, the pace of activities was very hectic. Cranes lifted cargo from vehicles onto the deck of the ship and then down to the storage units. The crew placed food in the hold in separate compartments for dried food, vegetables, and fruit. Everyone worked enthusiastically. Each man was proud of his assigned duties, contributing to the common task. Our work ethic was great because each person was doing the work he wished. No one was looking for any special privileges.

I gave the representative committee a tour of the ship. Everything was neat and tidy. I showed them the sleeping areas for the passengers, the kitchens, and the restrooms. I wanted the committee to explain the ship's layout to the camp members so they would be prepared and know how to behave in an orderly manner. Even though they had come to Guam by ship, we needed to remind them how to act and behave on board.

We also needed to consider the two hundred passengers on board who were women, children, and the elderly. Safety and order would be very important during the voyage, and we had to pay particular attention to it, especially because there were women on the ship. I wanted to make sure the women had private berths. Hân agreed to work with the camp leadership to maintain order on all fronts.

Before we could embark, the ship needed to have a final, independent international inspection to comply with maritime law. The next day, a delegation led by a Dutch officer boarded the ship to inspect it one final time to ensure its seaworthiness. After reviewing each crew member and the machinery, the delegation pronounced itself satisfied.

The atmosphere at the camp was festive, and many of the repatriates had radiant expressions, innocently thinking about reuniting with their families and homeland. However, there were also gloomy, worried faces among us. Should they go home or not? This was the moment of decision.

On October 15, 1975, almost six months after we had arrived in Guam, we were preparing to return to Vietnam. We had left Saigon in April 1975, in a panic, in confusion, and in despair. These six months of waiting had seemed like six centuries, but time had kept moving forward, and the earth kept spinning. For six months, I had waited in sorrow. I couldn't imagine that we would finally be able to board the ship and go home.

The next day, I would leave Guam, this lonely small island in the middle of the Pacific Ocean, so distant from every continent. In some ways, Guam's isolation reminded me of my own separation from my loved ones. For these six months, I had lived like a parasite, day in and day out, stretching out my hand to receive food like a beggar. My life had had no meaning whatsoever. Tens of thousands of people had left Saigon in April 1975, and now thousands of people were going back. Those who had left and those who were returning all had the same sorrows, losing our country and losing our families. We were all lost and isolated.

Those who went to the United States would, of course, meet with many hardships at first, but at least they could make their own decisions regarding their future. They would have the opportunity to advance in a free land. But among those of us who were returning, no one knew what our struggles would be like.

We would leave Guam without any regrets. We wanted to return. But our worries remained with us, too. We did not know what the future would bring.

Before boarding the ship, each of us would have to go through one final procedure. At first, it appeared similar to the process of going through customs and baggage inspection before going abroad. However, in reality, the United States created a final procedure in which everyone would have to make a final decision: to return to Vietnam or to go to the United States.

I had to go through this same formality like everyone else, no more and no less. At last, it was my turn to enter the room and meet with a U.S. staff member who sat at his desk with a list of returnees. The American asked me for my full name and date of birth. I answered, and he checked my name. Then he asked, "Do you want to say anything before boarding the ship? If you change your mind and do not want to go back to Vietnam anymore, then let me know. Now is the moment for you to decide."

I simply said: "Of course, I want to go back."

The U.S. Civil Affairs officer was also brief: "In that case, please go through the door on my right."

I silently went through that door. On the other side, a bus was waiting to bring the repatriates to the gangplank of the ship.

Each office had one entrance and two exits, whoever went back to Vietnam would go out through the door on the right. Anyone who changed his or her mind and decided to travel to the United States at the last minute would go through the door on the left. Buses were waiting outside both doors: one led to America and the other back to Vietnam. The Americans had given us one last opportunity to decide whether to go on or to go back. It was entirely up to us. Even though it appeared to be a simple formality, it was our final moment to decide our fate. We had a choice. Since we met with the U.S. officer alone, we didn't know who among us chose to go to America at this final juncture.

Tấn pulled me aside at dinner. He told me, "I see that you are always busy preparing the ship, but I had time to observe and look into what the troublemakers are up to. There have been strange things happening on the ship. Are you aware of them, Trụ?"

"I have been working so hard, and I try to ignore those young men. You can tell me now."

"Just climb up to the deck behind the command post and see for yourself. They have tied a huge picture of Hồ Chí Minh onto the railing, and the National

Liberation Front flag has been raised on the ship's flagpole. Now you are the captain of a VC ship, and you don't even know it."

I chose my words carefully. "Knowing nothing would cause us less pain. We are going back and giving ourselves up to the VC. We were defeated long ago. What could we do? The representative committee perhaps is aware of their actions, but they didn't dare to ask our opinion about this matter. I understand their psychology. They want to curry favor with the VC. However, we don't serve that flag. Our goal is to go back to our wives and children—that's it. We are not responsible for their actions or their shamelessness. You and I are entirely free of responsibility. We understand ourselves even if no one else understands us. Am I correct?"

Tấn was quiet and added: "Of course, but I feel so ashamed."

"What can we do? I would prefer the flagpole to remain empty. That would represent the true meaning of our ship. As for the portrait of Hồ Chí Minh, we can ignore it. If they worship Hồ Chí Minh, then that's their business. It has nothing to do with us. Those opportunists can be found anywhere, anytime."

The gangplank was still bustling with activity, and the repatriates were boarding the ship with all their belongings that they could carry. That evening, two buses carrying people from Fort Chaffee, Arkansas, a refugee camp in the United States, arrived. Some of these men and women had been sponsored by Americans to start a new life, but then they had given in to depression and decided to return to Vietnam, too. They arrived just in time for the ship's journey.

The morning after the ship was loaded and everyone had boarded, General Herbert arrived. He informed us that, instead of the more than 2,000 people we had anticipated, the number of those actually on board was 1,652. Over the past few weeks, at least 500 people had changed their minds.

Now, it was time to check the weather report. The meteorologists spotted two storms concentrated over the ocean. One was three hundred nautical miles west of Guam, and the other was five hundred nautical miles northeast of Guam. Both of them were moving northwest at a speed of ten nautical miles per hour. This meant that if we set out on our voyage that day, one storm would chase us from behind and the other one would be in front of us. If the ship could maintain speed, then it could avoid both storms. It would be my decision when to start the voyage.

General Herbert handed me a number of documents, including the radio frequencies of the weather stations in the region as well as that of the Seventh Fleet in case of emergency. I appreciated this assistance, but I told him, "I hope I won't have to call on the Seventh Fleet for help. I don't plan to contact them unless the engine breaks down, and the ship cannot sail. However, I don't believe that will happen. Our test run was sound, and we have made careful preparations for the

Young repatriate men board the *Việt Nam Thương Tín* with their belongings. In these images, one can see the youth of the average repatriate. Courtesy of the National Archives and Records Administration, Record Group 319, Box 19, declassification number 984082.

voyage. Everything has been favorable. General, thank you one last time, and can we soon start the journey?"

"My mission can be considered accomplished," he replied. "However, I still am responsible for your ship until it has entered the territorial waters of Vietnam. That's why I've asked the U.S. Navy to keep an eye on it throughout the voyage. But, yes, you can leave this afternoon."

As we were talking, someone announced that a number of reporters with cameras had come to the wharf to meet with me, including representatives from the U.S. press, the Voice of America, the BBC, and Australia. I greeted them at the gangplank. The questions started at once, and I did my best to answer them.

"Please tell us about your thoughts before returning to Vietnam."

"I feel happy because this has been my dream."

"Why are you returning?"

"I'm going back because of my family, my wife, and my children."

Young repatriate men on board the *Việt Nam Thương Tín,* waiting to disembark from Guam and return to Vietnam. Courtesy of the National Archives and Records Administration Record Group 319, Box 19, declassification number 984082.

"We have heard that Vietnam has not permitted your return. Why are you still going back?"

"We know that, but we still want to go back. I'm ready to accept all the negative consequences that may happen to us."

"Do you think that the communists will sink your ship if you try to enter the territorial waters of Vietnam without their permission?"

"I don't think they will dare do that. You are here interviewing me, and so the whole world will learn of our story. The VC must be wary of the pressure of public opinion from around the world. Furthermore, we all are determined. Even if they sink our ship, we don't have another choice. We are Vietnamese, and our families still live in Vietnam. As for the communists, how they want to treat us is up to them. We don't need to know, and there is nothing for us to be afraid of. Next question."

"I have often interviewed people who have escaped from communism in order to find refuge in a free land, but this is the first time I am interviewing someone who is going back to a communist country. Please tell us your thoughts on this matter."

"Just like everyone on this ship, I am not abandoning freedom in order to return to communism. I would like to emphasize that we are returning to our families, our wives, and children."

"What makes you think the communists will allow you to reunite with your wives and children?"

"I cannot envision this, but I still must return. Even if they imprison me, one day I will meet my wife and children. If I continue to live here, then I will never see them again. Vietnam was divided into two countries, one free and one communist, since 1954. I migrated from the North to the South in 1954, and for more than twenty years, I was not able to meet any of my relatives who were trapped in the North."

"Are you returning voluntarily or under coercion?"

"I'm returning voluntarily, and it's been entirely my decision without any pressure whatsoever. If right now, I changed my mind and decided to go to America, I still have that right."

"I see that there's a communist flag and a picture of Hồ Chí Minh on the ship—what does this mean?"

"Your question makes me nervous, and I'm not quite sure how to answer. Please understand, I only saw this picture last night, because a friend pointed it out to me. I was shocked when I saw it. Even though I am the captain, I don't control everyone on board and no one asked my permission to fly that flag. I only know that we have united in our struggle and our desire to return to Vietnam. We have been living together in the camp for nearly six months, and I know one thing with certainty—there are no communist infiltrators among us. Instead, you need to realize that we have a few opportunists within our group, and they are using the flag and the picture of Hồ Chí Minh to serve their own purpose and self-interest. We are about to return to a communist-controlled country, and so no one wants to stand up against these symbols. That's why everyone has remained silent. However, deep in our hearts, many of us are ashamed and deeply mortified, but we cannot do anything about it. In fact, we have suffered a great defeat. Next question."

"What role is the UNHCR or the UN playing in your return?"

"The UN doesn't have any role at all. In fact, the UNHCR has done its best to help us. It tried to act as a liaison between the United States and Hanoi, but it was a fiasco. Even with the UNHCR support, Hanoi refused to accept us back. If we wait for Hanoi's permission, we might have to wait ten or twenty years, and we cannot afford to wait that long. We had to fight in order to have this ship. The UNHCR is not involved."

"What is the opinion of the UN and the United States regarding your return?"

"You can ask them directly, but the U.S. government and the UN have always encouraged us to wait until Hanoi has given us their permission. They have tried to prevent us from going back, but they have failed."

"We thank you, Captain, for this interview. We wish you a safe trip."

"Thank you all."

After the reporters left, I turned to meet with Tấn, who had been waiting to talk with me. I spoke first: "Now we are ready to leave at 1 p.m. sharp with 1,652 people. By the way, have you seen Trương Ngọc Khoa and Võ Quỳnh Thiện on board the ship?"

This was why Tấn had wanted to speak with me. He said, "They stayed behind and went on to America already."

"I was suspicious of these two men from the beginning," I sighed. "Do you see how sharp I am? I just observed their actions closely. They were obviously working for the CIA. They could do things so easily. Not only did they decide to go to America, but I'm sure they earned U.S. dollars while they were here."

Tấn was more surprised. He told me, "For me, it was so unexpected. They had led the protests for our return, yet in the end, they changed their minds."

"It's easy to understand," I countered. "The Americans didn't want us to wait here in Guam indefinitely. If it kept dragging out after they had fed us and taken care of us, it would have caused trouble for them. Of course, they had to find a way to get rid of us as soon as they could."

Tấn was still confused. "Yes—they are getting rid of us, but it is also our own desire to go back to Vietnam."

"Exactly," I sighed. "Khoa and Thiện worked for America, and, in the end, it turned out to be good for us. They didn't do us any harm, and if they hadn't fought so hard, then maybe right now, we wouldn't have a ship to go back with."

I kept on thinking aloud. "We leave tomorrow at exactly 1 p.m. My work is almost done. The captain's greatest responsibilities are in the preparations before the voyage. Most of the work at sea will be done by the crew, and I will be free much of each day. You can come up to my cabin, and we can exchange confidences throughout this long voyage. You are the only person here I really trust. On reaching Vietnam, I don't know whether we will we have the opportunity to sit and confide in each other. We will have to put on an act when we step into the communist world. Whenever we talk with each other, and a third person appears, we will be forced to be on our guard. We will no longer have the freedom to talk."

Reporters interview the repatriate leadership before they depart on the *Việt Nam Thương Tín*. Courtesy of the National Archives and Records Administration, Record Group 319, Box 19, declassification number 984082.

"I can only trust you, too," Tấn agreed. "It's so funny, whenever we are talking, there are always a few people loitering nearby, eavesdropping on our conversation."

Tấn was always deep in thought, and his sorrow was reflected on his face. He missed his wife and children so much that I had never seen him smile. Throughout our months on Guam, he often told me that we were going back because of our love for our wives and children, but we didn't know whether we would be of any help to our families or if we would cause them more hardship.

CHAPTER TWELVE

The Return Voyage

At noon, I gathered the crew together and reminded each of them of their duties. We would maintain a speed of ten knots an hour throughout the trip, and I estimated we would arrive in Saigon within nine to ten days. We would be able to sail even more quickly if we had favorable weather conditions and all our machinery worked properly.

On the wharf, an officer was ready to untie the ship from the dock, and a number of reporters gathered to take pictures of the scene. General Herbert walked up the gangplank to meet with me. He shook my hand. He had come to say good-bye for the last time. Accompanying him was an even more senior U.S. official, Mr. Keely.

Mr. Keely spoke to me, "We have spent a lot of time working for this day. General Herbert accepted this mission on my behalf, and he has completed it. I came to represent the United States and to wish you a safe trip."

At this point, Mr. Keely handed me a Samsonite suitcase and continued, "This is a special gift we would like to present you with before you start the journey. Please open it. It represents our admiration for you as a captain."

I accepted the gift and opened it. Inside the suitcase was a dark blue captain's uniform with embroidery on the cuffs and golden stripes. "I sincerely thank you and General Herbert for this touching honor. However, I must decline this thoughtful present. Even though I value your gift, it may cause problems for me in Vietnam. Perhaps you understand."

"But it is only a suit, and I don't think you will run into any trouble when you go back," Mr. Keely replied.

However, I had to refuse. "Again, I thank you and ask you to take it back." I returned the Samsonite to the officer. Finally, Mr. Keely seemed to understand and accepted the suitcase. I said my last good-byes to General Herbert, and they both exited the ship.

I raised my hand to wave good-bye to everyone on the wharf. Within fifteen minutes, the ship had sailed out of the harbor. We left Guam and set course to sail directly westward.

~

An immense sadness flooded my soul with all the memories of misery, longing, and waiting we had experienced in the Guam refugee camp. Farewell to the island. Farewell to all the friends and family who had evacuated with me on April 29. I had left with many of my wife's relatives: my mother-in-law, my wife's older sister, and my wife's younger siblings. I had lived closely with her family for many years and had established loving relations with all. I was leaving everyone to return to Vietnam by myself. They, in turn, would have to struggle with a new life in America. They would face a language barrier, a new climate, and new customs and traditions. We each had our own sorrow.

Why did it have to be like this? I felt pain throughout my body. Tears welled up in my eyes, and my mind was in turmoil. I didn't know what I was doing anymore. I was still sitting in a captain's chair, commanding a large ship with the fate of more than 1,500 people in my hands. Together with them, I was returning to my wife, my children, and my homeland. However, I didn't know whether I was returning to my family or stepping into the world of the dead. When I looked behind me, I could see Guam disappear below the horizon. It was only three hours since we had left, but already I was surrounded by only the sky and the sea. The ocean was immense, the sky was blue with white clouds, and the Pacific Ocean was as calm as its name implied.

Human beings are so minuscule compared to heaven and earth. We are not even as big as a grain of salt in the ocean or a grain of sand in the desert. But then, human beings continue to have conflicts and struggle with life. The Creator enabled humans to be superior to all other animals because of our brains. But, given our intelligence, why couldn't we live in peace and harmony? Instead, we have devoured one another and become savages. Take Vietnam. It is a relatively small country with approximately four thousand years of civilization, yet we have known so many years of war: some wars caused by foreigners and others caused by internal animosity. The Vietnamese people have been trampled upon from one generation to the next, all because of the petty ambitions of their leaders. These men should have prioritized the welfare of the people and the nation.

Every time a man has stood up to declare he's fighting for a "just cause," it has caused our country pain. Words such as "for the nation and the people" are just a façade, and these slogans hide personal ambitions and cunning. As for our present situation, the communists proclaimed that they were fighting the Americans to save our country and liberate the people. However, after they chased the Americans out of Vietnam, countless Vietnamese fled to escape this new regime.

More than 1,600 other people and I were returning to be with our families. In many ways, my life had lost all meaning, and so I didn't care how brutal or cruel the communists turned out to be. As human beings, we all have to die—we cannot escape that. Even if I have to die upon my return, why should I be afraid?

At 8 p.m., I saw that the ship was still not being affected by the storms. We were in a calm sea with a gentle breeze, and it was quite favorable weather for a ship voyaging across the ocean.

At 5 a.m. the following day, the pilot and I went to the bridge, measured the altitude of three specific stars, and pinpointed the position of the ship. It was following the route that I had originally drawn on the map. We were in the middle of the ocean, and all land masses were outside the radar's range. I toured the ship and saw that the crew members were performing well. The passengers were sleeping in their berths, and those who were not accustomed to the sea were exhausted by seasickness. I reminded the nurses to look after each passenger and to hand out medication for motion sickness to those who needed it. The people who were well enough walked back and forth on the deck, looking up at the sky and down at the sea, as if they were tourists.

Several days later, we could see the Philippine mountain ranges on the horizon and the San Bernardino Strait in front of us. The sun was slowly disappearing behind a mountain range ahead of us. Before entering the territorial waters of Vietnam, we had to cross this strait. It would take a full day and night to thread our way through the Philippine Islands and reach its western shores. I had to stay awake and work twenty-four hours straight, because we had to navigate this winding route with mountainous islands on both sides. Near the shore, we could see the twinkling lights of Filipino fishing boats. This image made me think about the fishing boats in Vietnam that I had often seen at sea.

When the ship entered San Bernardino Bay, I saw a ship from the Seventh Fleet follow us. I understood that this ship had been ordered to be at the ready as my ship crossed the strait. By the time we reached the strait, I was exhausted, and navigation was difficult. Most ships had permission from the Philippine government to cross through its territory, but for my ship, no rules applied. According to international law, my ship was violating the Philippines' sovereign waters. However, our case was exceptional, and the United States had already contacted the Philippine authorities so they knew about our voyage.

Next, I received the latest weather report about a storm in our vicinity. It was nearby; however, we were still not in its path. The storm had caused severe damage to some areas of the Philippines and continued to move in a northwesterly direction. When we were about ten nautical miles from the shore, the sea became violent, and there were Category 5 winds, which are hurricane-force. Waves splashed up on the bridge. The passengers and a few crew members became frightened.

Everyone waited for my response. The waves alternated in washing over the ship, and water flooded the deck. I knew that the storm was not endangering the ship. It was moving northwesterly, away from the hurricane. It had enough power to last for only one more day. A ship like the *Việt Nam Thương Tín* was built to stand up to hurricane-force waves. I had faced waves like these before, and I knew there was no danger. I continued in the same direction and reminded the disaster committee to make sure all the watertight doors were locked, so that the seawater wouldn't flood the rooms below deck. I also reminded the deputy captain to calm the passengers, and tell them that if they got seasick, they should just lie down and rest. The waves would let up the next day, and everyone would be well again.

In fact, almost everyone got seasick. The passengers lay down in their rooms, unable to eat anything at all. The deputy captain handed out motion sickness pills and made pails available for them to vomit in. For those who were really strong, their sickness would subside when the waves calmed down, and they wouldn't need any medication at all.

Then, the nurse who was in charge of the health committee ran up to the bridge to let me know that one person had died. Who was it? I needed to know immediately.

"An old woman who has been sick for the past few days," the nurse answered. "She hadn't eaten anything. I gave her an injection and took care of her for the past few days. I thought that she only had a cold and that she was seasick like everyone else. I never thought she could go this quickly."

I had to be practical. I told him that a body bag was stored at the nurse's station. The nurses needed to wrap up the old woman and then bury her at sea. According to maritime law, a person who dies on a ship must be buried at sea within twenty-four hours, so that the body doesn't infect anyone else on the ship. I observed the burial rites from my command post. The woman was Nguyễn Thị Nại. We had a minute of silence to remember her, and I quietly prayed to God that her soul would soon find its way to heaven.

Mrs. Nại had been a traditional Vietnamese mother, down-to-earth, and honest. Her son had been an officer in the RVN Army, and he had reached the rank of major. However, he had married a city girl who didn't like village life. During the evacuation, the whole family—the son, his wife and children, and his mother, Mrs. Nại—had left together. Events had come to a head in Guam, the daughter-in-law had mistreated Mrs. Nại to such a degree that she decided to go back to Vietnam, believing that in this way she could protect her son's happiness. She was sad because she loved her son very much, and she was humiliated from being so mistreated by her daughter-in-law. However, on board the ship, she had refused to eat, and a few days later she had become so feeble that she could not tolerate the waves. In the end, she died. It was such a painful story, full of selfish people without a strong moral foundation. Her corpse was lowered into the vast sea. We didn't know where her soul would drift to.

The ship had a truly bizarre fate. When it had originally left Saigon in April 1975, carrying evacuees, it reached Nhà Bè before heading out to sea. The VC shelled it from the shore near Vũng Tàu and damaged the hull. In the melee, the VC killed the well-known author Chu Tử. Now that the ship was returning to Vietnam, another person had died. Perhaps Hà Bá, King of the Water, was demanding a sacrifice in order for the ship to reach the shore.

Farther out at sea, the waters calmed down. The sky was clear, and the ship no longer pitched and rolled. The storm had moved away. The passengers had recovered, and no one was still seasick. I let everyone know that we would reach the coast of Vietnam in just one more day. They were jubilant. Many of them climbed up on deck to look for the shore, even though land was still beyond their range of vision. In all four directions, they could only see the flat horizon.

I was lying down and resting in my room when I heard a knock on the door. Hoàng Trí Mạnh asked to meet with me. Here I need to remind the reader that Hoàng Trí Mạnh was a VC, and his identity had been uncovered by a number of camp members. He had gone on to America with the refugees, but now, like us, he was returning. Throughout his time in the camps, Mạnh had lived quietly, and he had not taken part in the repatriate protests or spread any communist propaganda.

Mạnh wanted to speak with me: "Perhaps you are surprised to see me, because you don't know me, but I know you well, and I respect you. Now that the ship is about to reach Vietnam, I wanted to confide in you."

"I already know about you," I replied. "I have heard many people talk about you. Is there anything else you want to tell me about yourself? Truly, about the real you?"

Mạnh understood what I was referring to. "To be frank with you," he replied, "you have heard that I am a VC, is that right? That is true. Until April 30, I was still working for the National Liberation Front. I was a mole for more than twenty years. As a young man, I joined the Kiên Giang police force. At first, I was just a plain police officer, but I was soon promoted to corporal. I kept tabs on the local police and relayed relevant information to the Front."

"Then why did you evacuate Saigon on April 30?" I asked. I was curious why a VC would leave at the moment of victory.

"On April 28 I unexpectedly received an order from my higher-ups to leave with the evacuees. There were no details, just the order. I was told: Just go to America, and someone will contact you later with an assignment. I didn't have time to tell my wife and children, and I just packed my bags and left with the evacuees. I went all by myself to Guam and then Fort Chaffee, Arkansas. I waited quietly for several months at Fort Chaffee, but no one ever contacted me. When the repatriates began protesting at Fort Chaffee, I decided to sign up to return. At that time, I was still able to keep my identity and politics secret. No one knew my background. I didn't join the protests, and instead I stood on the sidelines."

I was curious. "When you were in Guam, you witnessed the repatriates' protests. You have worked for the communists for many years. Did you see communist party members instigating the protests?"

"I don't think anyone shared my mission. The protests, the demand to be returned, repatriation—those were entirely your wishes alone."

"What do you think will happen to us when we reach Vietnam? Do you know?" I asked.

"I worked for the NLF and against the Americans to save our country. Even though you collaborated with the enemy, we are still all Vietnamese. Now that the Front has won, I believe that there will be reconciliation between our two sides. Since I left with you, I don't know what the current situation is like, but I believe we will return to safety. Frankly speaking, I admire you. You are a sensitive person, full of sincerity, and you have sacrificed everything for the love of your wife and children. I promise that I will be a witness and attest to your character with the new government. You chose to return to Vietnam because of your personal sentiments, not because you are plotting to sabotage the new government. When we arrive in Vietnam, I promise that I will help you if circumstances allow."

"This is quite unexpected—the first communist that I have ever met turns out to be a person on my ship. What will you do when we reach Vietnam?"

"I will explain to the new government why I returned. The NLF ordered me to follow the evacuees and to wait for an order in America. However, I never received any instructions and decided to return. I will also have to report on the events that led to our return. I believe the authorities will understand you and will grant you mercy. I hope that you will have to spend just a short time being investigated, and then all of you will be able to be reunited with your families."

"If only you were the person who could decide. Then I would feel reassured. It is my wish to be reunited with my family and to start my life afresh. But I don't know what will happen. I have resigned myself to my fate."

"You shouldn't be pessimistic," Mạnh replied. "Life is still long, and no one can deny your sincerity. I wanted to speak with you and calm you down. Even though you remained quiet in the camp, you couldn't hide your worries. You are such a pensive man. I admire you a great deal. Please, for the moment, believe in me."

"Thank you. At least you have helped me with a few ideas about what may happen during the first few days back in Vietnam."

I shook his hand and saw him to the door.

CHAPTER THIRTEEN

Arrival at Vũng Tàu

After nine days at sea, the ship had traveled two thousand nautical miles without encountering any obstacles, save for the one day of strong waves and winds off the coast of the Philippines. We were only one hundred miles from Vietnam, but neither our eyes nor our radar could detect the coast.

Suddenly, an airplane appeared in the sky and circled our ship many times. I looked up. Because of my time working with the Americans during the Vietnam War, I could recognize it as a P2V reconnaissance airplane. I realized it was from the Seventh Fleet, checking to see if I needed any help. General Herbert had told me that he would be responsible for us until the ship safely entered the territorial waters of Vietnam. However, there was no need for me to contact the Americans. The P2V circled a few more times without seeing any reaction from me, so it turned eastward and disappeared into the sky.

On October 24, the first mountains of Vietnam appeared on the western horizon. The ship was just over thirty miles from the coast. I announced that we were entering the territorial waters of Vietnam. Everyone rushed up to the deck to admire the view of our homeland. Many people were worried about what would happen next. The mountains became bigger and bigger, and the radar told us that we were only twenty miles from the shore, and then fifteen, and then twelve. Now we were in Vietnam's territorial waters. Our ship entered Vietnam's waters, but we were the only ship at sea. I did not see even one other ship in the area, not even a fishing boat.

I was taken aback, because our ship, a foreign ship, had entered the territorial waters of Vietnam, and the VC were not there to stop us. There was no obvious response, and the radar picked up only a few small boats near the shore. The ship slowly sailed along the coast of Vietnam, passing Phan Rang, Phan Rí, Phan Thiết, Bình Tuy, and then Vũng Tàu. I saw only a few fishing boats. It was deserted—so unlike the past, when I patrolled this coastal area, and twinkling lights from the fishing boats covered the whole area. Today the weather was auspicious, but the fishing boats were all gone, and the sea was deserted. I wondered about the VC's ability to control the coastline. In my head, I started planning how to escape Vietnam by boat with my family after I arrived at home. I would find a way to get my wife and children onto a boat, and if this was all the security along the coast, we could easily escape Vietnam.

At 6 a.m. the next day, a flashing beam from Vũng Tàu appeared in front of us. I was sitting in the captain's chair, when suddenly Vương Long Đoàn, the head of the law and order committee, approached me and reported that someone had requested that I turn around and not enter the harbor at Vũng Tàu. I was surprised and asked why.

Đoàn answered, "I don't know why, but suddenly this man panicked and yelled out loud in the hold. He asked to meet with you and request that you turn around. We prevented him from coming up here, and we have tied him up and posted a guard. I'm here to tell you so that you know what's going on."

"Well, he could have an intuition that something bad is about to happen. What kind of person is he? Do you know?"

"He is still very young, all by himself, without friends or relations. He is kind of aloof, and he has kept to himself. No one knows anything about his background."

I was not unsympathetic, but we were going to move forward. "Perhaps he is scared thinking about the VC. We should stay calm and get ready to give ourselves up. He has his own reason for being frightened, but now that we are here, we no longer have any choices, save to keep calm. You need to explain this to him, so that he will understand the situation and avoid causing a commotion on the ship."

My ship had entered the harbor of Vũng Tàu, and we still didn't see any VC ships. It was bizarre. Could a big ship such as the *Việt Nam Thương Tín* enter from a foreign country, and the VC were not aware of it?

After we dropped anchor, it took us half an hour before we could establish contact with the Vũng Tàu control tower. I radioed to say, "We are the Vietnamese returning from Guam. Please tell us what we have to do."

The response from the other end was: "Where is the island of Guam? I don't understand what you are saying."

I tried again. "The island of Guam is about two thousand miles east of Vietnam. It is under the control of the United States. We evacuated on April 30, but now we have returned on the *Việt Nam Thương Tín*. We are anchored off Front Beach. Look at the naval map of Vũng Tàu, and you will see the position of the ship. If you don't understand, you can report it to your superiors. Your superiors may know more about our ship."

"Stay where you are and wait for our orders. And keep the radio on," the voice on the Vũng Tàu tower answered.

This contact person sounded like a jungle man. I found it difficult to talk with him on the radio—he spoke with a heavy, Northern accent, and I could barely understand him.

It had only been a few months since the North's victory, but Vũng Tàu had been completely transformed. It looked decrepit and run-down. It was South Vietnam's central harbor, and during our time it had been overflowing with ships. I remembered that there was rarely space for foreign ships that wished to enter Saigon Harbor. Now, it was empty! A dead harbor! We were the only ship in sight.

I picked up the binoculars and looked out onto the streets of Vũng Tàu. Again, the empty and abandoned scene sent chills down my spine. It was 9 a.m., but the streets were still. Here and there, you could see a few people traveling on bicycles, but no swimmers were on the beach. The kiosks were still standing, but they were all closed. The communists seemed to have established total control. There was no tourism, which meant that the population either didn't have the money or wasn't allowed the freedom to travel and vacation as before.

Viewing Vũng Tàu's desolation, I imagined life in Saigon. It had to be similarly quiet. Everything had changed so much. In the past, I had taken my ships on many missions far away from Saigon, and every time, after the mission was completed, I had sailed through Vũng Tàu. In those days, when I saw flashing lights from the Vũng Tàu lighthouse, my soul would stir with longing for reunion with my family. And now, it was the same lighthouse, the same space, but it was a different time, and my soul no longer was aglow with happiness. Now it was steeped in worries. I was only about one hundred kilometers from my wife and children, but I wondered whether I would be reunited with them in the next few days. Would the communists leave me alone and let me live with my wife and children? It was so difficult to predict.

Just after 10 a.m., three small military ships, formerly belonging to the RVN Navy's coastal patrol, sailed toward the *Việt Nam Thương Tín*. These ships were familiar to me but not the men. The crew members were VC sailors from the North, and the ships flew the flag with a yellow star on a red background. Finally, the small boat flashed its lights at us.

"Tell us the name of your ship, and where it came from."

"It is the *Việt Nam Thương Tín*, coming back from Guam," I flashed with the light signals.

"How many people are on the ship?"

"1,652 people."

"How many Americans are on the ship?"

"No Americans."

"How many foreigners?"

"We are all Vietnamese."

"Name of the captain."

"Trần Đình Trụ."

"Who gave you permission to come here?"

"It is our wish to come back."

"What type of people are these 1,652, and why are they on the ship?"

"We are the people who evacuated from Saigon on April 30, and now we would like to return to Vietnam. Most of us are former military personnel from Saigon, and we are together with a small number of civilians."

"Are there women and children?"

"About two hundred elders, women, and children."

"What weapons do you have on the ship?"

"There are no weapons at all."

"Tell everyone to go down into the hold and stay there. No one is allowed on deck. Then lower the gangplank. We will board your ship and search it."

"We are ready."

So the three military ships slowly approached us. One sailed to my right, one sailed to my left, and one came up alongside the *Việt Nam Thương Tín*. All the sailors pointed their guns at us, ready to fire. Five men climbed aboard. The captain was in the lead, a revolver on his hip, and the other four carried AK-47s. I remained on the bridge. The captain and the two guards carrying AK-47s came forward, and the other two stood on either side of the stairs.

This was the first time I had met a VC naval officer from the North. Here was an officer from the communist Navy. He was wearing a yellow uniform, and it was wrinkled. He wore a pith helmet and a worn-out pair of black shoes. It had been six months since they overran the South, and now they controlled our ships. Probably, our RVN naval personnel who had been left behind trained them to operate these ships.

After I introduced myself, the VC captain took out a pen and paper to take some notes and, in a heavy Northern accent, began a preliminary interview. He had not been in the South very long. Another interrogation began with the same questions as before. Then the VC asked whether he could search the ship.

I had a crew member escort them as they conducted their search. The captain, together with one of the guards, remained at the command post, still deep in thought. He asked me a few more questions, this time asking me about my former job and my family circumstances.

"Your voyage has been very long. Are you tired?"

"I'm fine. I don't feel tired."

"Where's your family?"

"In Saigon."

"Who are they?"

"My wife and our three small children."

"The country has been unified. Peace has been restored. One day you will be reunited with your wife and children."

On hearing his words, I felt reassured; however, I remained quiet, and spoke only in response to a direct question. I didn't ask any questions out of curiosity. This officer's duty was just to meet with me and escort my ship. Maybe he didn't know anything else beyond that, or perhaps he knew but didn't dare to say too much about it.

After the VC had finished their search, they returned to the command post and their captain. They had found nothing. The captain continued:

"Now please get ready to weigh anchor and follow me."

"Please let me have the itinerary, so I can prepare the trip on our charts."

"Just get ready to sail northward."

I had the crew prepare the ship to sail northward without knowing whether he meant North Vietnam or elsewhere. I had enough naval maps in order to go anywhere. Next he commanded: "Weigh anchor and start sailing. You will sail in front, and my ships will follow. My sailors and guards will remain on your ship, and we will be in touch via radio."

The VC captain gave his orders, and from that moment, the captain and his two guards were always at my side. It was obvious that I was under arrest.

The Vũng Tàu lighthouse faded slowly and sank below the horizon. The sea that day had strong waves. It was the season when the northeast monsoon winds began to blow on the Eastern Sea. These conditions did not affect a ship as large as the *Việt Nam Thương Tín,* but the small VC patrol boats pitched and rolled as if they were losing control. They began to drift away from the ship, and the VC captain kept asking me to decrease our speed, from ten knots per hour to eight and then six. It was ironic that the three VC ships couldn't even keep up with the ship they were supposed to monitor. That was the skill level of the VC Navy! Yet despite their weakness, we were the vanquished. Suddenly, I was gripped with sadness, thinking of how many years the RVN military had trained and prepared us. However powerful we were, the VC had destroyed us in an instant. We had run away from an army that had only mediocre abilities and poor technological means.

The VC captain was having difficulty with his ship because of the poor weather, and one ship had a broken engine. He requested that I pull his ship along, slowing our ship down. I ordered my men to shoot a nylon line over to the VC ship with the broken engine. Then we began to tow it. These actions gave me pause. I had returned to the enemy because of my wife and children, and now I was helping the enemy escort me to an undisclosed location. After we arrived, who knew what would happen? However, I believed in maritime law. An emergency rescue at sea is always a noble act, and the captain is always responsible for any accident that may happen at sea. I could not let them struggle with the sea, not even my enemy. Thinking this way, I was willing to help them and pull their ship to safety. The VC captain thanked me in admiration. In fact, from the first moment, he had been polite and respectful, and he had never insulted me.

The sea and winds were powerful, and I was pulling another ship, so our speed decreased a great deal. I had charted a course far from shore in order to avoid the reefs near Bình Tuy. It was nighttime, and we could not see the coastline or the mountains. The VC captain saw that we were far from the shore, so he asked me where we were. I pointed it out on the naval map and told him the location, the direction, and the current speed. He looked at the charts but didn't seem to understand. He grew suspicious and requested that I navigate the ship closer to the shore. Maybe he thought I was going back to Guam and bringing his ships with me. However, it was foolhardy to change direction at this point. I was taken aback and explained, "I've charted the shortest, most direct route. What is wrong?"

The captain kept questioning me, "Are you sure of your position? Are we in the correct position?"

"If you don't believe that I am on the right route, would you like to determine the position? Please look at the radar screen. You can also test it with the depth finder."

I showed him the points on the radar screen and the sonar equipment. We were in the position I had pinned on the chart. I also pointed out to him the direction on the compass and the map. Everything was transparent. If he was a naval officer, he should recognize our position right away. He was supposed to be a captain, but he seemed to understand nothing and doubt my explanations. I didn't know what else to say to him. He just looked at the sea in the dark and guessed that I was sailing in the wrong direction. He insisted that we change course.

"Change to a northerly direction for me," he demanded.

"Why?" I asked.

"Just do as I say."

I was annoyed with his stupidity. He was the captain of a warship, but he knew nothing. Perhaps he thought a ship was like a fishing boat, and he could sail wherever there was a body of water without knowing his position. I didn't care. Really I didn't want to know how the VC trained its Navy, but this man's lack of knowledge and skill amazed me. I pulled him over to the naval map and used a ruler to plot our current position. Then I showed him what would happen if we shifted to the north.

"If we move to a northerly position, we will sail right into this reef," I tried to explain. "The reef is not even one meter below the surface of the water. If I change our direction as you wish, then one thousand people will be buried at sea, do you understand? I already told you we are on the right path. Don't doubt it."

He felt confused and ashamed, and he didn't know what else to say. He was still suspicious of my intentions, but he had no alternative but to let me decide.

The weather remained stormy, and so even though we were traveling only two hundred knots, it took us two full days. On October 28, I finally dropped anchor at Cầu Đá Harbor near Nha Trang. With my binoculars, I looked around the harbor. I didn't see any other ships or boats, save for one small ship with the same red flag with a yellow star on it. Looking down from the gangplank, I saw rows of houses on the mountainside with closed doors and not a soul around. The atmosphere was so chilly that it was hard to understand. No cars or bicycles were on the roads, and the town looked abandoned. Nha Trang, the city of white sands, like Vũng Tàu, used to have a lot of tourists coming and going. The mountains were still there, and the sea kept its deep blue color, but it was a dead city. Not even one swimmer was playing in the waves. Instead, a caravan of Soviet trucks was on the road, flanked by police wearing pith helmets. This was our reception.

After we dropped anchor, the VC captain asked me to prepare the charts so that I could prove we had sailed from Guam back to Vietnam. Hoàng Trí Mạnh, the VC who had been a mole in South Vietnam, asked the VC if he could come with me. Deep in his heart, I think he wanted to testify to my good character and intentions. The captain agreed to let him go with us. We boarded a raft that took us to another ship. Once aboard, I realized that the men there wanted to take me to a room where I would be by myself. They stopped Mạnh at the bottom of the stairs, and he was not allowed to meet the VC officials with me as he had wished. I was alone.

~

In the room below were approximately ten people with serious expressions, waiting for me around a long table. An empty seat was saved for me. All the men around the table were high-ranking security officers from Hanoi who had just come to the South. It seemed like a trial—and the men were ready to indict me. As it turned out, they had decided on my sentence even before we left Vũng Tàu. They were going to judge me first, and then I was certain that all who had come back would also be tried.

One of the officers invited me to sit down in the empty seat. Waiting for me was a cup of hot tea and a pack of Thăng Long cigarettes, made in Hanoi. He offered me the tea and the cigarettes as he introduced himself.

"We are from Hanoi," he began what was sure to be a long speech. "I would like to emphasize the fact that Vietnam is completely independent. The country has been reunified, and from now on it will be one country from north to south. The Vietnamese have defeated the United States and chased the Americans out of Vietnam forever. There will never be another American in Vietnam. Those of you from the South Vietnamese Army—it is clear you were only puppet soldiers. And you returned from America without our permission, infringing on the sovereign rights of Vietnam. We do not have to accept you back. However, we will offer you clemency and welcome all of you."

Then he continued, "Perhaps you heard that the communists would take revenge on you, and there would be a bloodbath when we took over the South. Because of these rumors, many panicked and fled the country. In reality, you have been fed poisonous, American imperialist lies. We sympathize with you, and we will show you that those were only rumors, twisted propaganda. In fact, all the puppet soldiers and officials who stayed in Vietnam have been treated humanely—we haven't killed anyone. Everyone still lives a normal life, and they will become honest citizens. Sooner or later, you, too, will become honest citizens. Perhaps you still remember the Vietnamese proverb 'We go back to bathe in our own pond, because whether murky or clear, our pond is still the best.' In any case, there is nothing for you to be afraid of."

I sat and listened, observing every single face, as I smoked my cigarette and sipped my tea. I heard the VC's words, but I did not know what actions would follow. And yet, at first, I actually felt reassured, and, in any case, I had prepared myself for all possible consequences. Most importantly, I remained tranquil in front of these grim faces. The men were mostly between the ages of forty and fifty, and they were all high-ranking VC officers. Looking closely, I recognized a rather familiar face, wearing a VC naval uniform. He was about fifty years old. He stared back at me, acknowledging the familiarity and the fact that I could not place him. He explained: "Perhaps you don't know me, but I have known you ever since you were a cadet at the naval academy in Nha Trang. I worked for the RVN naval academy for many years. It's such a coincidence that we meet again here. When you were a captain, I heard about your reputation. Today, I'm still working at the academy, but with new responsibilities; otherwise nothing has changed."

I realized that he had been a VC mole working at the South Vietnamese naval academy for many years. We had never suspected him, and he had even been an RVN enlisted officer working in the Office of Internal Affairs and the Naval

Training Center at Nha Trang. I hadn't known him personally, but I had seen his face many times. Every time my ship was on a mission and we stopped in Nha Trang, I made a point of visiting the academy. He was usually in the office, and that is why I recognized him. Now, the tables had turned, and he was in a position of power over me, conducting the questioning and the investigation.

"How was your voyage? Was it exhausting? How many days did it take to sail from Guam?"

"The voyage lasted ten days, but I'm used to it, so it was not tiring at all."

I answered him, while handing over the naval charts that accounted for our itinerary. I had drawn our route on the map and tracked the ship's position on a daily basis. It was just a formality, because in reality, he had never worked on a ship at sea. He didn't understand the naval map at all; however, he pretended to be knowledgeable and continued asking me questions about the logbook. Then another officer began interrogating me.

"Please tell us the reason you came back."

I repeated what I had already said several times. "I came back because my wife and my children live in Saigon. My family is totally dependent on me, and they cannot survive without me. Even though I had the opportunity to go to America, I couldn't abandon my family and live by myself in a foreign land. I returned because of my conscience and my responsibilities. I didn't have any other choice."

"You have been fighting against the fatherland and our people for more than a decade. Weren't you afraid we'd seek revenge if you came back?"

"I'm not afraid. I'm willing to accept any consequence that may happen to me."

"When we conquered the South, all the puppet soldiers and officials had to report to the revolutionary government. Did you know that?"

"I have heard about it, but I don't have much information."

"You should know our policy is to punish those who run away, not those who return. Do you believe that you will receive clemency from the revolutionary government? Can you tell us your intentions on returning to Vietnam?"

"I think that I will report to the new government just like all those who remained behind."

"You seem sincere; however, since you have come back from America, we will have to investigate you carefully. Perhaps you understand that this is not a simple issue. We only hope that you will answer all our questions without hesitation. You no longer have anything to hide. You will be reunited with your family after you have answered all our questions. The essential thing is that you be sincere, because if you conceal anything, we will know. You commanded this ship, so more than anyone else, you must know about everyone who has returned with you. So, first of all, we want to know the kinds of people on the ship and the purpose of their return."

"They are all like me. We were all evacuated to Guam. There was a UNHCR office that allowed those of us who wanted to return to Vietnam to sign up. I think that all the other repatriates shared my wish, which is to return to their mother-land and their families."

The VC pushed on. "How can you be certain that they all share your aspira-tions? What about those who are still single?"

"We lived together in the refugee camp for over six months. Everyone knew almost everything about everyone else. You can ask each person, but I believe we all came back for our families."

"It is a big ship, so there had to be meticulous preparations. We want to know how and why the Americans organized your voyage. We also want to know what the Americans are plotting."

The VC was obviously not convinced by the truth. I tried to explain our situ-ation on Guam, and that we, and not the Americans, insisted on our return. "We had to protest in order to get this ship. It was not organized by the Americans. It was all organized by us, the Vietnamese."

"You don't seem to understand my question. Your return was well organized, and so the Americans must have had a larger plan. The Americans chose you to be the ship's captain. When the Americans transferred the ship to you, what secret mission did they give you?" He continued with a more threatening tone. "We must add that the revolution confers clemency on all, but only if you are sin-cere in all your declarations—especially you. We know that you committed crimes against the fatherland and the people, so this is your chance to do something to pay for your crimes. We hope that you will think carefully and be sincere with us."

This coercive interrogation began to make me feel uncomfortable. They were beginning to launch into specific accusations. However, I was able to recover my composure. I knew when I had entered this room that I wouldn't have a defense lawyer.

I replied, "I don't understand your implication that I accepted a mission from the Americans. I can be honest and say that I came back entirely voluntarily. My decision had nothing to do with the Americans, and they never gave me a secret mission."

"Before you left, did you know that Hanoi broadcast a message stating that you were not permitted to return? We learned that the Americans were plotting to sab-otage Vietnam even after they had been defeated and withdrawn from Vietnam."

"Yes, I heard the message. We all knew about it. But I still decided to come back, because we thought that we were Vietnamese, and so we could always go back to Vietnam. We knew we would have to report to the government like those who had stayed behind. We never had any intention of committing any type of sabotage, and so we were not afraid of coming back."

"So, you knew that you were not permitted to come back, and you still returned. That means there must be a plot. Even if it's not your plot, there is an American plot somewhere. This is the main point that we want to know about. Unfortunately, I see that you haven't told us everything yet—you haven't been sincere. We want you to have time to think, and you can answer more questions later. In any case, you're still in a confused state of mind. Really, we understand, we just need the answers. Please stay calm, consider our questions carefully, and report back when you're ready to be sincere."

I quickly realized there would be a lot of trouble for me. They had forced me to accept responsibility for crimes I hadn't committed. I knew there were many ways to torture and coerce a captured person into acknowledging their "crimes." The VC were so paranoid and suspicious. The Americans had withdrawn from Vietnam because of their own strategic self-interest. The U.S. military was the strongest in the world, and it had surely had the ability to defeat the VC. The Seventh Fleet alone could have leveled Vietnam. The Americans had pulled out of Vietnam for their own reasons.

Vietnam was such a small and mediocre country compared with the rest of the world. Why would the Americans continue to plot against the VC? And if they were going to disrupt the new government, they would never do something as conspicuous as sending a ship of suspected men back to Vietnam for that purpose. It made no sense. These VC were still so terrified of the Americans. That's why they were still suspicious.

I sat still and took out another a cigarette while waiting for more questions. I knew there were no plots, and the truth was always the truth, regardless of the VC's allegations. After the bird has been put into a cage or the fish has been put into a tank, there is nothing left to do but stay calm. The questions now came at me faster than before.

"When you left Guam, how many Americans were there on the ship?"

"There were no Americans on the ship."

"If there were no Americans, how could you steer the ship by yourselves?"

Again, it was a silly question, but I still answered clearly and explained, "All of my crew members were RVN naval personnel with substantial experience at sea. There were plenty of skilled men who wanted to return."

"On what day did you leave Vietnam?"

"I left Saigon on April 29."

"That was almost six months ago. Where have you been since then? What have you been doing? What has your contact been with the Americans?"

"I left Saigon and joined the ships of evacuees, arrived in Guam, and stayed in a refugee camp there. I didn't do anything, and I didn't contact any Americans. Every day I stood in line waiting to receive my food and waiting for the day I could come back."

"How can we believe this?"

"All of us who came back stayed in the camp like me—your investigation will tell you that much."

"Tell us how you felt when you arrived in Vietnamese waters. What is your wish now?"

"I feel content. My only purpose is to be reunited with my wife and children."

"Of course, you will see them, but only after we are done with you. Just remain calm, think, and feel assured. Now you can return to the *Việt Nam Thương Tín* and wait for our orders."

I left the room. Outside, two guards were waiting to take me back to my ship. Hoàng Trí Mạnh appeared pensive and as though he had something he wanted to say, but could not. As for me, I felt as if I had been under house arrest ever since we dropped anchor at Vũng Tàu. The VC captain was always by my side, as if to watch and isolate me, so that I wouldn't be able to talk with anyone else.

When the raft pulled alongside the ship, I saw a whole slew of VC police, all wearing yellow uniforms, crowding the deck. While I was being interrogated, the VC had boarded the ship and gotten hold of the list of all the returnees. They began to classify us, and they called our names out one by one and divided us into small groups. Then they took us ashore and pushed us into the covered vehicles that had been waiting for us.

When the VC called each name aloud, the person would step forward with their luggage and wait for their turn to leave the ship. After about half an hour, my name was called. I calmly stepped onto the stairs like everybody else, carrying only a small suitcase with a few personal possessions. Stepping onto the raft, I didn't want to turn around and look at the ship, where I had spent all my energies ensuring our safe return to Vietnam.

At this moment, I felt no emotion—none. In the past when I had left a ship, I had always had a feeling of nostalgia. For a sailor, a ship is like a second home, and I never wanted to say good-bye to it.

This time, I was the captain of the *Việt Nam Thương Tín* for only ten days. My duty had ended. I had fulfilled my own wish and the wishes of the people who, like me, had wanted to return to Vietnam. Even though the time had been brief, we had struggled together and journeyed back together. We had so many shared memories.

Now, as we disembarked, no one said a word. No one said good-bye to anyone else. One by one our names were called, and armed men escorted us off the ship.

Our memories remained locked in our own minds.

From that moment on, I no longer spoke with anyone from the ship.

CHAPTER FOURTEEN

Reeducation Camps

The VC transported us to the Stone Pier in Nha Trang. When we reached the wharf, not a soul was in sight. The covered security trucks were the only vehicles on the road. The emptiness sent chills down my spine. The police were carrying weapons. No one spoke to anyone else. We became prisoners the moment that we climbed into the vehicles.

We drove for about fifteen minutes to a prison in Nha Trang. A police officer called out our names again. My name was called at the same time as those of two other men. The VC divided us into groups of three to five people. My group consisted of Đỗ Kiến Từ, Văn Đình Hoạt, and me. Từ and Hoạt had both been majors and helicopter pilots. In silence, we were taken to a small cell, just two meters wide and four meters long with four straw mats spread out in each corner. There was barely enough room for four people to lie down. One straw mat was still vacant, set aside for a fourth person who would join us later. We stepped into the cell, and then we each sat on our straw mat and looked at one another without knowing what to say. The VC locked the door, but we had a small window, so natural light could still shine into the room.

Occasionally, we heard the sound of a truck pulling inside the yard, and the vehicles kept coming and transferring the ship's passengers to this jail. Certainly, there were other prison camps as well, because this camp had room for only a few hundred people. Two VC stood guard, one young and one old. The young one carried an AK-47, and the older one had a bag hanging from his shoulder.

The older guard spoke first, "You will be staying here while you complete your paperwork. Whenever you leave this room, we will be your guides. Every day you will be able to go outside and wash your face and brush your teeth. In the evening, you can take a bath in the corner of the yard. When you need to urinate or defecate, just knock, and ask a cadre to open the door for you."

The first evening, the VC took us out one by one to search our bodies and our luggage. Each of us had to take off all our clothing, including our underwear. We had to bend down and show them our buttocks, and they would shine a light into our anus to see if there was anything hidden in there. We had to open our mouths wide for them, and they looked into our mouths as if we were being examined by a dentist. Our personal belongings were searched thoroughly as well. They even dissected our cigarettes, tearing up the wrappers and pouring the tobacco into a nylon bag. They kept all our belongings and handed us two sets of camouflage shirts and pants. In fact, these were RVN marine uniforms the VC had confiscated after April 30. Now, they were giving them back to us as prisoner uniforms.

The first night of my life in prison, I was allowed to lie down on a straw mat on the cement floor. Feeling exhausted, I closed my eyes and soon fell asleep. I only remember that I slept very well. There was nothing for me to think about. I just had to resign my fate to my Maker. I didn't know whether I would ever be able to see my wife and my children. Nevertheless, I still believed that, as long as I stayed alive, then our reunion would happen one day.

At 7 a.m., the guards opened the doors. All of us gathered around the well to wash our faces and brush our teeth. We had to wait our turn to pull up a bucket of water and then divide it among ourselves, filling up our tin cups. Whatever we did, we were escorted and watched over by the guards.

I was waiting for my turn to draw water when Hoàng Trí Mạnh came near and whispered to me: "Everything went wrong. It's a disaster. I never suspected that they would have this about-face. They don't even believe me—a person who worked for the Revolution for years. I wanted to support you and be a character witness, but they doubt me, too. They interrogated me last night for a long time, and I had to fight with them because they made so many nonsensical accusations. These men are all from Hanoi, and I'm from the South. I don't see anyone from the NLF here, and so I can't explain anything to them. To tell the truth, I don't understand what's going on myself. Please stay calm. I am sorry I cannot do anything to help you. I don't even know what will happen to me. I only hope that you will sympathize with me."

I accepted Mạnh's kindness and tried to reassure him that I had resigned myself to my fate. Even though he had only said a few words, Mạnh kept looking around as if he were afraid of being spied upon. He quickly said good-bye and went to another part of the yard. After the time for brushing our teeth and washing our faces was over, the VC locked us back up in our cells. We lay down and waited the whole morning until mealtime. Ironically enough, our first meal was so welcome, hot rice with braised fish and cabbage soup. It was an authentic Vietnamese meal. Even though it was simple, I thought it was delicious after six months of eating only American food.

That evening, a cadre wearing a pith helmet opened the door and spoke to us in a very quiet voice. He spoke with a Northern accent and went from room to room as if trying to gauge our reactions: "Now that you are back in Vietnam, you can stay calm. Study a few lessons, and after that you will return to your family. You have to study just three basic lessons. Perhaps you have heard rumors about revenge, about a bloodbath, and so on and so forth, but you can see that we will treat you kindly. Vietnam is reunified, the American enemy is no longer here, and we are all Vietnamese. There is the folk verse, 'Like squash and melons loving each other, people in the same country should love each other even more.' We will rebuild our homeland and make it wealthier and stronger."

He used a lot of euphemisms in order to calm us down. He mentioned the absorption of these three lessons without telling us what the lessons were and how long we would have to study. He seemed to be purposefully vague.

I decided to make conversation. "Did you just come here from the North?" I asked.

"That's right. This is my first trip South. My job is to work with you returnees. After it's done, I'll be going back to Hanoi. You also speak with a Northern accent. Where is your hometown?"

"I left the North in 1954, and I lived in Saigon for a long, long time, so I no longer have a hometown. Have there been many changes?"

"Of course. There is electricity in the countryside, and there are houses with tiled roofs. There are no longer thatched huts as back in 1954. Perhaps one day you will be able to go back to your hometown. Then you will know." He pulled out a pack of Thủ Đô cigarettes, which were made in Hanoi, and he offered me a smoke.

I held the cigarette and smoked greedily, inhaling deeply each time for the smoke to seep into my heart and my lungs. I hadn't had a cigarette since last night, and the VC had confiscated the cartons of Pall Malls I had brought with me from Guam.

Then, the Northern cadre announced that everyone would study in the auditorium the next day. It would be our first lesson in the reeducation program. He left the room, and the guard locked the door behind him.

In the morning, I missed my coffee and cigarettes. My hand felt empty without a cigarette, and I was craving one just like an addict, with a dry mouth and listless limbs. I began to understand what it meant to exist without material pleasures. I understood the value of all the things that I had taken for granted.

My mind was still hazy when the guard opened the door and told us to gather in the auditorium. Before us was a flag with a yellow star set against a red background, a portrait of Hồ Chí Minh, and VC slogans strung up around the auditorium: "There is nothing more precious than independence and freedom," "Hồ

Chí Minh the Great," and "Independence, Freedom, Happiness." I remembered these slogans from when I was little and the Việt Minh first organized.

Then a middle-aged man took the lectern: "I am the education cadre with responsibility for working with you this morning. First, the reeducation program is for all of you—you were all puppet soldiers and puppet government officials in Saigon. Now, we have a revolutionary regime, so everything is brand-new. Our country is entirely different from before, and, therefore, your reeducation is essential. Our purpose is to help you become honest citizens who can contribute to the rebuilding of the fatherland. All of you will have to undergo this period of reeducation. Only after you have learned the ways and policies of the Revolution will you be able to assimilate into the life of the people. I want to emphasize one point. You must be confident and embrace the Revolution. This will improve your studies and help you progress. Then you will be allowed to be reunited with your family. The other puppet soldiers have already begun their reeducation program, and most of them have already returned to their families and their normal lives. Today I want to introduce the camp regulations. Our country has many laws, and there are also many laws in the camp. You must understand the rules, and you have to obey them."

One by one, he explained the camp rules and regulations. In total, there were thirty-six rules, with twenty additional rules regarding the new life and culture of revolutionary Vietnam. Everything was regulated, from how we had to address the cadres to how we had to behave while working. And we had to accept and embrace all the policies of the Revolution. All revolutionary rules were unquestionably correct. The revolutionary government could do no wrong. The essential thing was to have complete faith in the new government.

Later in the afternoon, a VC officer called me into a small interrogation room. This was a high-ranking cadre, well past middle age. He invited me to sit down in the chair opposite him and offered me a cigarette. He spoke with a Hanoi accent, very polite and soft-spoken. Then he pulled out a file with an envelope in it. He handed it to me, "Please open it. Is that a picture of your wife and children?" I accepted the letter and photos of my wife and children. My heart was overflowing with emotion. I was unable to speak. The letter contained only a few lines from my wife, "You are back. The kids and I are very happy. Please feel assured. At home, the children and I are all healthy, our lives are normal, and there is nothing for you to worry about." There was a picture of my whole family, sitting on a swing inside our yard. Tears welled up in my eyes. It was obvious that my wife was told what to write. Unlike letters that people normally write, this letter did not contain the truth. My wife and children looked the same, but their expressions were joyless.

"Yes, that is my wife's handwriting," I said. "And this is a picture of my wife and children."

"Did you know that your wife and children tried to commit suicide? If the Revolution hadn't come to their rescue in time, they would all have been dead."

"I didn't know anything about that," I replied.

"When you left your family, they returned to the house. They didn't know where you were, where you went, or how to get in touch with you. In a state of despair and fear, they took medications to try to commit suicide. Of course, all these negative rumors about the Revolution were just propaganda and twisted truths. Fortunately, the Revolution came to the rescue and saved their lives. Now, your wife and children believe in the Revolution. We took this picture two days ago."

"The Revolution has liberated our people and chased away the American invader. Life has returned to normal," the cadre continued. "As for you and the repatriates, even though you have been led astray, when you have shown remorse and repentance, we will accept you as well. Everyone has to go through reeducation in order to become honest citizens. As for you, we have studied your background. I have your file in front of me—it details what you have done, your military positions, and your family background. We already know it thoroughly."

He was not done yet. He kept speaking to me in the same tone. "We will ask you to write about yourself, and we hope to see your sincere deposition. I hope that you will sincerely report everything that you have done and will do, so that we know how to help you. You are the person who navigated the ship and brought more than a thousand people back to Vietnam. We have to pay attention to you first. That's the reason we met with your family and gave you their letter and pictures. But you don't have to worry about your family. We will take care of them. In return, the Revolution hopes for your sincerity. I need to elaborate on this point. The American enemy lost the war, but they still haven't given up. They are still plotting and scheming to sabotage Vietnam. Your return is one of their plots. We know you must have returned with a special mission. We want to know their plan, so you can help the Revolution. Please stay calm, and think carefully while you study. Tomorrow, I will go back to Hanoi. Do you have anything to tell me now?"

"Thank you for the letter and the picture of my family," I replied. I had nothing else to add.

~

This was my first meeting with a high-ranking VC cadre. He was polite and civil with bright features, and soft-spoken in order to convince his listeners. And I did feel somewhat reassured, because at least I had seen recent pictures of my family. His words seemed to be encouraging, not threatening.

They wanted to know whether I had accepted a covert mission from America. Of course, this was absurd. I had never received a mission from anyone. So far in our group, I was the only person who had received any news about his family. I felt lucky. However, the VC did this because they hoped to exploit my feelings and use the letter from my wife as bait, a gift, to extract information from me. Of all the repatriates, I was the one of whom they were most suspicious.

I had been in my cell for only five minutes when another guard returned most of my personal belongings to me. They had confiscated my personal documents, my identification card, my officer's card, my driver's license, my Vietnamese money, my watch, and my pen. As for my Pall Malls, they had taken the wrappers off each cigarette. Instead of a box of cigarettes, I had a bag of tobacco. I had to find some rolling paper for the tobacco before I could enjoy smoking again.

In the morning, the VC called us into the auditorium again. The second lesson was about the heroic Vietnamese people, who had defeated all the invaders, from the Chinese enemy to the French enemy to the American enemy.

In the evening, I was called to go and give my deposition again. This time, I met with two young cadres. One spoke with a Northern accent and one with a Southern accent. This was the first Southern accent I had heard since returning to Vietnam. Both of them wore civilian clothes, but they were clearly high-ranking, well-educated security officers. They sat at two separate tables approximately a meter apart. I sat down in a chair right in the middle, facing the two tables. They took turns questioning me, and they wrote down all my responses. It was entirely different from the polite older man who had questioned me the day before. These two men took turns attacking me. They wanted me to admit that I had received an assignment from the CIA.

"First of all, the revolutionary government's policy is one of leniency," the first cadre began. "There is no retaliation, so you can rest assured. You have started to learn the rules and regulations. The first rule is that you must always be honest with us. You must confess to all your crimes. We have your file here on the table. We know about you already, and so you cannot hide anything. Please tell us your highest rank, your positions, and your final unit."

I answered their questions. "During the last few years, I was a commander, and in 1975, I was the deputy commander of the Fifth Coastal Zone posted out at Năm Căn, Cà Mau."

"When did you leave Saigon? And by what means?"

"I left Saigon on April 29 on a naval ship."

"You ran away taking state property. This is a crime. Do you realize that?"

"At that point, I was no longer the captain. I was only a passenger on that ship."

"Where did you go to from Saigon? And what did you do during your time away?"

"I left Saigon, and the ship sailed to Subic Bay in the Philippines. After that, everyone was transferred to an American ship, which sailed straight to the island of Guam."

"What island is that? And where is it?"

"Guam is an island in the Pacific Ocean, about two thousand nautical miles east of Vietnam. It is under the control of the United States. I stayed on Guam until we were allowed to return. I didn't do anything there at all."

"On what day did you leave Guam?"

"October 16."

"Did you stop anywhere? And, if so, for what purpose?"

"We didn't make any stops. I sailed straight to Vũng Tàu."

"How many people were there on the ship? And what kind of people were they?"

"There were 1,652 people. The majority of them were military personnel. I already reported all this information the first day I spoke with your officers."

"We know, but we want you to report it many times, so that we can check it against your first report. When you were in Guam, which Americans did you work with? And what relationships did you have with them?"

"I wasn't in touch with anyone from America."

"You said you didn't work with any Americans, but then how do you explain the ship? Where did you get it, and why did you get it? How could you get it without any support or contact with Americans?"

"I was only in contact with the person in charge of transferring the ship. Our contact was entirely professional, focusing on the repairs and the supplies needed to go back to Vietnam."

"Apart from the Americans in charge of the ship, were there any other Americans you met with in Guam?"

"No."

"When you left Guam, the Americans gave you a small suitcase. Who was that American? And where is that suitcase now?"

I sighed. "Perhaps one of the other repatriates has told you this. As a matter of fact, the American who was in charge of all the returnees presented me with a captain's uniform before we set sail. It was a blue suit with embroidered yellow stripes on the cuffs, and he wanted me to dress like a captain during the voyage. He presented me with the suitcase, and when I opened it, I saw the uniform. However, I declined the gift and gave it back to him. Everyone on the bridge witnessed this exchange. You can ask any member of the crew, and they will tell you the truth."

"Tentatively, we believe you, but, of course, we still have to speak with many more people. We need to learn the true nature of the Americans' plans for your mission."

"There was no American mission. The Americans were just trying to satisfy our desire to return to Vietnam. I just happened to be the person with the most naval experience and the ability to steer the ship."

"Who assigned you to be the captain?"

"Nobody assigned me. The camp members knew my background, and they voted for me to be the captain. I accepted this responsibility because it was my wish to return to Vietnam as well. I didn't care about the position of 'captain.'"

The cadres seemed stumped. "Your answers are so simple, but it doesn't make any sense. Why would the Americans give you such a large ship without an ulterior motive? Truly, we cannot understand this."

"I have explained that this ship was only the means to an end. We all wanted to return, and the ship had no value for the Americans."

"You are not being honest on this point. If the CIA has given you an assignment and threatened to harm you if you disclose it to us, please remember, they cannot touch you here. You have returned to the Revolution. Also remember that you entered Vietnam without the Revolution's permission, and that is a crime in and of itself against the Revolution. You used to hold a gun and fight against the Revolution. Now that you are here, I would suggest that you consider how you might contribute to the Revolution and atone for your crimes. Only then can we protect you and your family. As for the CIA, they are back in America. They cannot do anything in Vietnam anymore. So think carefully and tell us everything. Hiding things will only put you at a disadvantage."

"I have already answered your questions truthfully. I don't work for the CIA, and I don't have anything to hide from you."

"Then why did you come back?"

"Because my wife and children were still in Vietnam."

"If your family hadn't stayed behind, would you have returned?"

"I can truthfully tell you that if my family had evacuated with me, I would not have returned out of my fear of you."

The cadres were frustrated, and they became more manipulative. "We cannot figure you out. Perhaps, you hope that one day the Americans will return to Vietnam, but that will never happen. You puppet soldiers followed the Americans. You fought against your fatherland, you fought against your people, and you betrayed your nation. Do you know that you committed a crime?"

"I lived in the South and joined the military in order to defend the fatherland. I believe that if you had lived in the South, you would be just like us. You would have been forced to join the RVN military, but that doesn't mean we were fighting against the fatherland. We love Vietnam, too, and, unlike what you think, we didn't love America."

"Obviously you don't recognize your crime. And you still don't realize that the Revolution was just. After the reeducation process, you will understand. Since you have studied the first lesson about the rules and regulations, you should remember that among the thirty-six items that you have to memorize, there is one that says you must report all your crimes and all the crimes committed by other people that you know. So, please tell us, when you were in Guam, which Vietnamese repatriates interacted the most with the Americans?"

"I never paid attention to other people's business. When I was in the refugee camp, I kept apart from most people. I was so depressed. And I never saw any Americans in the camp until we prepared the ship. Then there was some interaction with the Americans, and, as the captain, I probably interacted with the Americans the most."

"You keep saying that you know nothing, but, given your position, it doesn't make sense. Please try putting yourself in our position. Would you believe us? We want to emphasize one thing. The revolutionary government is smart, and it has a clemency policy for puppet soldiers, but clemency only comes to those who are sincere. The revolutionary government has liberated the people and defeated the American enemy. We want to know about the American plan to sabotage us, so we can defend the fatherland, which would include defending you at this point. Once you understand, you will collaborate with us and help us destroy the enemy plot. And when you help us, it means that you will help your country, yourself, and your family. Please consider this carefully, and report on everything you know about the American plot. That is our only request. This is your best opportunity to redeem yourself. If you don't redeem yourself, then how can your crimes be erased? For those who have committed crimes, we ourselves don't have the right to sit in judgment, but the people will judge you. You should remember that. We are only acting on behalf of the people."

The two of them took turns attacking me. It was like they were machines. I listened to them and only heard words like "revolution" and "the people." The communists usually used euphemisms to lead you astray. They never used the word "communism." Instead, they said "revolution," a word that always sounded more positive. A "revolution" means renovations; all revolutions brought new promise for the people, erasing injustices and oppression. Hearing the term "revolution," the listener was more easily persuaded, and the VC chose each word carefully in order to influence us and sway us to their side. However, I knew every time they said "revolution" and "the people," in reality they meant communism. The VC spoke of judgment by the people and a people's court, but, in reality, the people were not involved, just the VC and the communist government.

～

I responded to their attacks again: "I have answered all your questions truthfully. I abandoned a life in America, full of great prospects for myself, in order to come back here and accept any punishment, so that my conscience wouldn't be tortured. As soon as the first men began to question me in Vũng Tàu, I could picture my trial. I will accept any trials or judgments, but please don't try to coerce me into saying things that aren't true. I have nothing to conceal from you. Time will give you the answer."

"Your ship carried the NLF flag with a picture of Chairman Hồ and slogans about the spirit of the Vietnamese people. Tell us, who among you organized these things? Who painted the picture?"

"I steered the ship, but I did not make all the decisions. A committee of representatives organized all the internal camp activities. Vũ Lê Hân was the head of the committee, and the artist was Bình. I did not know about the flag and the painting until I boarded the ship for the final time."

"What kind of person is Hân?"

"I only met him when we were waiting in the camp together. He expressed the same wish to return to his family that I did. Other than that, I knew nothing about him."

"What kind of person is Bình?"

"I don't know much about him either. I didn't speak with him during my time on Guam. I only knew that his wife and children were stuck in Vietnam, and he wanted to return just like me."

"Let me tell you that all those paintings and slogans, as well as the NLF flag, were just a veneer to cover up your evil plots. Your activities cannot deceive the Revolution."

"You can think whatever you want. After the investigation, you will see more clearly." I remained steadfast.

"We have been working with you for several hours, but we don't have the answers we need. I hope you will continue to think about our conversation. You will meet with us again."

～

I returned to my cell exhausted and depressed because of the coercive interview. It all seemed so silly. I had never thought about the things that they wanted to know, so what kind of argument could I make against them? My only choice was to stay calm and to accept what would come next. It was as simple as that.

On the third day, we learned the next lesson. This lesson was about labor. Every communist was proud of the term "labor." The Labor Party of Vietnam; labor is glory; labor produces wealth; labor enriches the fatherland, and so on. The chief cadre stepped up to the platform to lecture us, boasting that he came from the working class, and his family had been the poorest farmers for three generations. Now, he was an officer in the People's Police. I cannot understand this sort of pride. Then, he said that we had never known the meaning of labor. I cannot understand how he could look at us and say such a thing. Maybe the VC were just parrots. The Communist Party had molded these people, so they did whatever they were told to do.

In the evening, I was led to yet another interrogation. This time, I was brought into another sparsely furnished room with only a wooden table and chairs and a pile of folders in front of a VC. I sat in a chair opposite him. He fished for a pack of North Vietnamese cigarettes and invited me to have one: "So you learned the third lesson today? There are three basic lessons in the Revolution's reeducation program. I hope you will make progress quickly, and soon you will be an honest person, integrating yourself into the new life and the new culture."

He used a lot of terms that sounded strange to me. I didn't understand what he wanted to say. What did an "honest person" mean? And what was this "new life and new culture"? He kept speaking:

"Tell me your impressions after a few days of reeducation."

"I listened attentively like everyone. Of course, under this new regime, there will be new things, but I will get used to them without any difficulty."

"After your first two sessions, I am told you still haven't told us the truth. We will let you have more time to think. I will leave paper and pen here with you, and you will sit by yourself, think carefully, and write your own confession. I hope that you will be sincere and give us the precise information about your activities and your background. In addition, you must write about those who came back here with you, the activities they were engaged in, and whether they were involved in any plots. Try to remember all the details and write about each person—the more information, the better. Start writing, and when you are done, I will come back to get your deposition. I will leave a pack of cigarettes here for you to smoke. If you need anything else, you can tell the cadre to come get me."

When he was done, he left the room, leaving me by myself with a sheaf of paper. Sitting by myself, I felt relieved because at least I didn't have to respond to their questions. I started writing about events I no longer wanted to remember, but it was much better than having to answer their silly questions.

My deposition was quite long. I went all the way back to 1945 and wrote about my life until the present. I wrote about attending elementary school as a child and when I joined the military. I wrote down the names of my military units and commanders and noted my tasks, my ranks, and my positions in the Navy. I also wrote about my family, including my wife, my children, my relatives, and even my parents and grandparents. I tried to recall everything, and it was easy for me, because I remembered everything. As for reporting on other people's crimes, in my opinion, no one had committed any crimes, and that was the truth. I wrote slowly, and it took me two hours to finish. While I wrote, I smoked one VC cigarette after another. Even though the VC cigarettes didn't taste or smell good, it was still relaxing to smoke.

~

In my cell, everyone asked me about my interrogations. They wanted to know what the VC had asked me, because they knew they would be next. Từ and Hoạt told me they needed to learn from my experiences.

"It's nothing," I explained. "They asked me about my family background and my activities, and they told me to report on other people, but I had nothing to tell them. The thing is, they think I work for the CIA and am on a mission to sabotage Vietnam. Can you believe that? It's so ridiculous. I just have to stay calm. I don't know what will happen next."

"How did they carry out the investigation?" asked Từ.

"They sat me down and questioned me, and then they told me to write a deposition. The VC were sort of soft-spoken and occasionally even seemed polite. They haven't been rude or arrogant yet. The men who questioned me were officers from Hanoi. They seem to have been carefully trained, and they were relatively respectful and didn't insult me. The problem was that they wanted me to say specific things, and they wanted me to be truthful, but even when I was honest, they didn't believe me. Their main goal is to find out if any of us have been working for the CIA, but in my opinion, this is foolish, because none of us work for the CIA at this point. Everyone is going crazy because of their families, but they don't realize this."

Then Từ asked me if I had seen any signs that they might release us or let us see our families.

It was hard to tell, I explained. They didn't give me any signs one way or the other. I thought that Từ and Hoạt would be able to blend into the crowd better than I could, so I told them they should have better luck than I had. Since we had dropped anchor in Vietnam, the VC had kept their eye on me, and I knew I was on trial. I still didn't know how long they would hold me, and I guessed it would be at least five years until they released me.

Từ continued to press for more information. "You were born and raised in the North, and so you have some experience with communism. Since I'm from the South, I don't even know what communism is."

"No. I'm just like you. In 1954, I fled the North, and even though I was in the South Vietnamese military, I never faced the communists directly. I don't have any experience with communism either. I never really paid attention or tried to understand communism. It's true—I never thought I'd have to confront the communists like this."

The fourth day came, and then the fifth, and one by one people were called and interrogated by the VC. As for me, I was questioned twice a day, once in the morning and once in the afternoon, and cadres took turns questioning me. All of them made me write my deposition again and again. I wrote it many times for many different people. They wanted to see whether my testimony from one day would resemble the one on the next day, and they were looking for any inconsistencies. The communists were suspicious by nature, and they didn't even trust one another, which is one of the reasons they had so many people question me. However, all my depositions were the same. I wrote it so many times that I knew it by heart.

Weeks went by, and then a month, and we still lay in our cells. Each morning, we went to the well to brush our teeth and wash our faces, each day we ate our meals, and each night security guards locked us back into our cells. During this time, the VC used the rice and other food we had stored on the ship for our two meals a day. There was more than enough food from the ship, and so the VC hadn't even spent a *đồng* to feed us yet.

The investigations dragged on, and the VC called on each person to make his deposition many times. For them, nothing was urgent. They kept interrogating me twice a day for more than a month, and they did not stop asking me about my supposed work for the CIA. However, they never beat me, and, instead, they used sweet words to try to persuade me to change my answers.

After the first week, the VC moved seven or eight people to another location, rumored to be Chí Hòa. The men might have included Hoàng Trí Mạnh and Vũ Lê Hân, but I didn't pay close attention. We guessed about the transfer, because during our mealtimes everyone noticed that these men were no longer there. In reality, no one knew where they had taken them or what they had done to them.

A month and then two months went by, and I was still called upon to write my deposition each day with a new cadre. In time, every cadre in the camp knew me. They all asked the same questions and lectured me about the Revolution, about defeating the American enemy, and so on. I had the impression that I was listening to a cassette tape over and over again. It was so boring, and they all sounded like parrots. Each one of them boasted about the mythical victory, about the people's heroes, about the great Hồ Chí Minh, and about how there is nothing more precious than independence and freedom. They called the French "former colonialists," the Americans the "new colonialists," and the Russians and the Chinese "our brethren." They repeated the old proverb "If you open your lips, your teeth will get cold" to justify our need to defend our new so-called comrades. That was all they knew. As for members of the South Vietnamese Army, they called us minions and mercenaries. They didn't seem to realize that they were the minions of the Russian and Chinese imperialists. Right now, they depended on the Russians and Chinese more than we had ever depended on the Americans.

After about three months of interrogations, more than a hundred cadres had questioned me, but, in the end, all my depositions were the same without variation. They hadn't been able to find anything new or questionable in all my testimony. In the end, a very high-ranking cadre invited me into his room and offered me some tea, saying:

"I just arrived here from Hanoi two days ago. I have been assigned to meet with you face to face," he began. "First of all, I would like to let you know about your family. Your wife and children are doing fine—the Revolution takes care of them, so you don't have to worry at all. Please be patient and collaborate with us for just a little while more. It's been three months, but I hope you can sympathize with us and understand why we are keeping you here. We want to have a firm grasp on all the facts about the American plot to sabotage Vietnam. However, I am very sorry that you and the other passengers have not yet been sincere or told us about the American plot. I have read all of your depositions. You have been sincere in many things. Our files on your family background and your activities match your own testimony, and so we can see that you have shown us your goodwill in telling the truth in these areas. However, you are still trying to conceal your American assignment from us. We have known about your assignment the entire time you have been here, but I want you to think for yourself and to share it with us voluntarily. We have waited for you for nearly three months, and we are disappointed in your responses. Hanoi sent me here in order to help you testify one more time. Perhaps you are still concealing information because you don't trust the Revolution. I want to tell you sincerely that the Revolution always has clemency for those who admit their wrongs. The Revolution never retaliates. Just think it through. If the Revolution were after revenge, then we would have already shot all of you. It is the people who want revenge. The people have condemned you, and so we must protect you and help you absorb the ways of the Revolution. The Revolution has gathered all of you together with the single purpose of protecting you."

I thought to myself that this is the voice of a Janus-faced person. They arrest and imprison us and then say it is for our own protection. It was truly silly. The

VC spoke out of both sides of their mouths and believed whatever they said would be right. The French have a saying, "La raison du plus fort est toujours la meilleure" or "Might makes right." We hadn't committed any crimes, but they forced us to admit them. We didn't collaborate with the Americans, and they kept saying that we did. So, it was best to just let them say whatever they wanted. There was nothing to argue about and nothing to worry about either.

The VC cadre continued, "I want to help you. We understand that if you had an assignment from the Americans, they must have threatened you to keep it secret; however, please trust us. There are no longer any Americans in Vietnam. If the Americans learn that you have revealed their secret, we will protect you. They cannot do anything to you, I guarantee it. This is the time to tell us the truth. This is your opportunity. We have been waiting for your answers for three months already, and you still talk in circles. I promise that if you make a sincere deposition, it will just be between you and me, and no third party will learn about it. Please be brave enough to tell me everything. What do you think?"

Using all his tricks, he tried to coax me to write a new confession. By this point, I was quite familiar with this kind of mediocre coercion. Inside, I was laughing, but I showed nothing. I told him: "I have been called up here every day for you to investigate me. I still have only one answer for you: I returned because of my wife and children. I cannot answer differently as you wish, because I have already answered sincerely. I have told you the truth, but you are still suspicious and think that I work for the CIA. I recognize that you are a high-ranking officer, and, therefore, I would like to venture an observation—you have specialized in the field of security and intelligence, and so perhaps you know about the American CIA. I don't. I only know that the CIA stands for the Central Intelligence Agency of the United States, I don't know anything else. If you really think that I work for the CIA, then you have a very low opinion of the American intelligence agency. Do you really think they would use a person who was so obvious that you could guess it immediately? I know that the CIA has had an oversized hand in international relations. However, the CIA is not so mediocre and second-rate that it would try to use the returnees for espionage, particularly not someone so obvious as the captain. Think about my observation. Consider whether or not I am correct. In my opinion, it's obvious that the repatriates came back entirely because of their families. We left in a panic on April 30 and lost our families. Now we have come back to them. It's that simple."

Perhaps he realized that my idea sounded logical. He decided to stop questioning me and took me back to my cell.

The next day began in a somewhat unusual fashion. It had been morning for a while, and everyone realized that our cells hadn't been opened for our daily washing and breakfast. We started to wonder why and ventured guesses—maybe today we would be released and could return to our families. Then around 9 a.m., our cell doors were opened, and we received an order to gather together in the auditorium. Everyone waited anxiously. Everyone had been questioned multiple times; however, none of us had been beaten or tortured. It had been exactly three months, and no one had received any news from their families, except for me.

The camp supervisor was wearing simple civilian clothes and spoke with a Central Vietnamese accent. He addressed our group: "It's been three months since you've been here, and we are very happy that we have succeeded somewhat in conveying the meaning of the Revolution to you. Most of you have studied attentively and proved that you have made some progress. We applaud this spirit in you. It means that our mission has been accomplished on behalf of the party and the state. Today, I would like to add that you must have complete faith in the Revolution. We are done with the political training period, but you should recognize that the more people learn, the more they realize how little they know. Uncle Hồ said that we have to learn forever. Learning is like an immense ocean; how can human beings learn it all? The next component of your learning program is labor. All of you will be taken to a new location so you can learn the value of work. Labor and reeducation are the responsibility of each citizen. Before you go back to live with your families, you must participate in manual labor. With the Revolution, every citizen has to work, and we cadres have to labor, and so you also have to labor. We all have to labor. Then, and only then, can the country gain material wealth. Labor is glory. Labor produces wealth and enriches the fatherland. You must learn this by heart. Until now, you have only known how to hold a gun, and you don't understand what labor is—but you will learn. You will learn to become honest citizens and integrate yourselves into the Revolution, the fatherland, and your families. That is our aspiration. It is the aspiration of the Revolution, the aspiration of your family, and your own aspiration. We will be transporting you outside the city to work. Please understand our reasoning and don't think incorrectly about it. It will have a bad influence on your learning. You will go to a new camp, where there is a lot of land and adequate living and working conditions. It will be a good environment for you to learn to labor. Before you go, I wish you all good health and peace of mind. Go back to your rooms and pack your personal belongings."

Everyone was shocked. We thought after the interrogations, we would be released. Now we learned that we would be taken to a new location to labor, not knowing where and what form of work it would be. I began to worry about this camp supervisor's words. He was circumspect and spoke like a person who has been duped and deceived. He told us to labor well and to study well, but what did "well" mean to him? I had been honest throughout the last three months, but they didn't recognize the truth. Now I would have to labor "well," whatever that meant. Deep in my mind, I had accepted that I would be imprisoned for at least five years, and it seemed that this would be the case. So I was composed and only waited to see what would happen next.

At least, the interrogation period was over. I didn't think that they would force me to write the repetitive depositions any more. I seemed to have passed the first stage. Even though the road was long, if I kept walking on it, I would reach the end. One day, I would meet my wife and family again. That was my final purpose. Being in a hurry wouldn't solve anything. I had to accept my fate.

I packed my bag. It was just the same suitcase I had been carrying with me since April 30. I had a mosquito net, a blanket, and two camouflage outfits. It was not much, but I did not need very much.

The cell door opened. The cadre called out each name, and a VC carrying a gun escorted us to the trucks. A convoy of covered trucks was waiting for us outside the gates of the camp. We were hauled onto the vehicles like a pile of goods, each truck carrying about thirty people, and everyone sitting squeezed against one another. They also handcuffed us together. It was the first time we looked just like prisoners. In my heart, I felt depressed, but to remain brave, I stayed focused on my family. With my wife and children as my focus, I was filled with extraordinary willpower.

CHAPTER FIFTEEN

Moving from Camp to Camp

We were now no different from blindfolded prisoners who are led away to their fates. We could still see one another's faces, but we could no longer observe anything outside the trucks. Armed police were in every truck, and we were jammed together. A bucket was in the back of the truck for us to urinate in, and we would pass it around to whoever needed it. We were shackled together, so when one person urinated, the person with whom he shared handcuffs would also have to stand up and witness his bodily functions.

Most people had nodded off. The truck bounced as it traveled along the bumpy road. Sometimes when the truck veered hard, the urine spilled out of the bucket and onto the floor of the truck. We started to smell the stench of life under communism. The air was stifling.

The convoy kept moving until late afternoon. When it stopped, the VC took off our handcuffs. They ordered us to step out of the truck. The VC guards stood alongside the road, carrying AK-47s, looking serious, their eyes filled with murderous intent.

We were in a mountainous, forested area. Before transferring us into this camp, the communist cadre introduced it by saying: "Here is the school, the reeducation labor school for you."

It was so ironic that it was almost funny. It was a prison camp, but they called it a school. Going to prison was called going to school. Perhaps only the communists knew how to manipulate this very special kind of wordplay. When the VC first occupied the South, they had talked about school, not prison camps, therefore after the surrender the naïve people in the South didn't realize that they were being sent to prison. Now, we were in the Xuân Phước reeducation camp, or concentration camp, in Tuy Hòa Province. During the war, it had been a secret VC base. The camp was isolated from the local population, which was several kilometers away. It was only us and the security personnel guarding the prison. This camp was new, or, to be more precise, it was not finished yet, and so the roofs and walls were made of leaves, the bunks had makeshift doors without any locks. A barbed wire fence surrounded the camp, as did four guard towers, one in each corner.

We were newcomers. We didn't know what would happen next. They didn't have to lock the cells or build strong doors, because the VC knew that none of us had any intention of escaping.

We were herded into the makeshift huts. Bamboo beds lined both sides of the room, with room for thirty people in each row. Each person was provided with a straw mat to sleep on, lined up one next to another. At the head of the beds were bamboo shelves for personal belongings. We strung up mosquito nets along the barbed wire that hung from one end of the room to the other. The bamboo creaked and rocked, so when one person turned even slightly, everyone was affected, but none of us complained.

We were all alike. Everything was the same. The communists called it a new cultural lifestyle. It was essential for us to forget everything in order to cope with reality. Human beings have to adjust in order to survive. Nothing would make me afraid or worried again.

The next morning, the cadre in charge of the camp lectured us about the re-education program. He didn't mention how long we would be there; instead, it was just like what had transpired at the prison camp in Nha Trang. Each camp had exactly three lessons. The key difference was that here we were required to engage in labor, called reeducation labor. He declared, "We have a responsibility to educate you in the reeducation program. Today we will begin with the regulations. Today's lesson has thirty-six regulations and twenty decrees about your new cultural lifestyle. If you learn well and labor well, you will soon be reunited with your families. It is that simple. I will also emphasize that you must have total faith in the Revolution. Together, we will fulfill the duties assigned to us by the Party. Our camp is organized into three areas, Sections A, B, and C. All the people here are the same people who came back on the *Việt Nam Thương Tín*."

I realized that when we arrived in Nha Trang, we had been dispersed to many different camps to be investigated. Now, we were all concentrated in this Xuân Phước camp. Section A was for those of us who had been officers, intelligence agents, or police officers. Section B consisted of petty officers belonging to all the branches of the military. Section C was for enlisted men. Each section was divided into labor teams of thirty to forty people.

The chief cadre continued talking along the same lines as the Nha Trang cadres: labor is glory; labor produces material wealth; labor enriches society; and so on.

Everything in this camp was ordered in steely discipline, including the way we ate, the way we talked, the way we addressed the cadres, and the way we labored. When we addressed the communists, we had to say, "Dear Cadre." We had a weekly schedule: Every day we woke up, we brushed our teeth and washed our faces, we exercised, we had breakfast, and we gathered to go out and work. At noon we came back for lunch and afterward continued to labor. In the evening we went back for dinner, and then we gathered in our rooms for self-criticism until late into the night. On Sundays, we could rest.

Each team selected a team leader, and the VC called this "self-government," even as the VC cadres stood behind us and observed all our activities. During self-criticism, the VC usually hid behind the door in order to eavesdrop and hear what we said. In addition, they usually selected a few members from each team to spy on us and report any activity that could "harm" the camp or went against the Revolution. Within a short time, they were able to control the camp, our thoughts, and our actions. Nothing escaped their eyes. We all began to distrust one another. No one dared to live truthfully anymore. We all began to live a lie. Some people worked to avoid all trouble, while others hoped that if they played the game, the communists would grant them clemency and allow them to return to their families. Others worked the system in order to enjoy extra perks and privileges.

In other words, each person put on a mask. No one could understand anyone else. The communists succeeded in what they called reeducation. The first step was to transform an authentic person into a false person. This happened quite quickly.

As the saying goes, "Hold your breath while crossing the river." We tried to adapt to the "new cultural lifestyle," but it was a farce. Yet, regardless of the difficulties and hardships, human beings could overcome anything through willpower.

Our living quarters were dirty beyond imagination. The food was of exceptionally poor quality. In the morning, they served us one sweet potato; at noon, they served us two sweet potatoes or a few ears of corn or cassava; and the evening meal was the same. Obviously, prisoners did not need meat, fish, and vegetables. We experienced hunger and hardship, but every day, we still had to carry a hoe out to the field to toil. "Labor is glory; labor is to produce material wealth." We had work quotas, and the security personnel carried guns. We all worked hard in the fields. There was no other way. The VC not only transformed us into false people, but they transformed us into beasts.

Truly, if a farmer took his water buffalo out to plow each day, and he saw that the water buffalo was tired, the farmer would let it rest. After the water buffalo was done plowing, the farmer would feed the animal, even if only grass. The water buffalo needs to eat enough to have the energy to continue plowing in the coming days. In the camp, we were no different from a herd of water buffalos. Each day we had to go into the fields just like beasts of burden. The only difference was that we were fed just enough to stay alive, but we never had a full meal. Over time, all the nutrients in our bodies were depleted. With only sweet potatoes and cassava to eat, no one had the energy to think about anything other than a bite of food. We had all been tamed. No one still had the ability to protest.

After our labor, we could only throw ourselves onto our stinking sleeping mats. The stench had become so familiar. We no longer even had enough energy to converse with one another. Talking would require calories.

Life continued like this for three months. Every day in the camp was like every other day. They had investigated us and forced us to work, but they still didn't have any evidence that any of us were working for the CIA.

Then, six months into our captivity, the VC began to let us write letters to our families. Each month, we were allowed to write one letter, and the VC opened and read our letters before sending them. We had to report that we were fine, that we were healthy, and that we were being reeducated. We were not allowed to tell the truth about the reality of our life. Instead, if we wanted to be sure that our letters reached our families, we had to praise the Revolution. We all wrote about how the camp provided us with plenty of food, cool and clean living quarters, healthy fun and entertainment, and so on. We wrote to our families just so that they knew we were still alive, and we hoped that this provided our families with some strength for enduring the situation.

Next, the VC began to let our families send supplies. Perhaps the communists realized that we no longer had the energy to toil in the fields. They permitted our families to send us three kilos of extra food every three months, so that we would have enough energy to produce "material wealth" for the camp. Sadly, very few of our wives could even support themselves, so how could they think of sending us supplies? As a result, only a few of us received token packages. We saw the packages as symbols, gifts wrapped up with love and devotion. However, our wives and children were not permitted to visit us. Our families' human rights had been taken away. We had no more freedom. The year went by, and we adapted to this type of extreme hardship. The communists always told us to study and work hard in order to be reunited with our families, but there was no sign of any reunions.

Many people still believed and did their best, hoping that they would soon be allowed to go home. But then, no news came, and we saw no sign that they would release us. Reeducation meant that we remained at the camp indefinitely, without knowing how long we would be there. Every day we cleared forests, and the land was gradually transformed into vast fields of sweet potatoes and cassava. We planted sweet potatoes and cassava to feed ourselves, and the communist state never had to pay a single *đồng*. We even produced a surplus that supported and fed the cadres and the security personnel. But even if the crops were abundant, we still couldn't satisfy our hunger because the VC still rationed our food.

Along with performing agricultural labor, we also were organized into construction teams: floor builders, carpenters, bricklayers, and so on. The men who made the floors had to go into the forest and cut down trees, the brick team built kilns to produce bricks, the carpenters built doors, and the construction team built camps. All of us had recently been warriors, from commanding officers to enlisted soldiers. During the war, we had been armed to fight the VC, now we held hoes and knives under the barrels of the VC security personnel.

We had built the camp ourselves and produced our own food. The longer we stayed, the more secure the prisons became, complete with sturdy-looking houses and brick walls. Anyone who had any intention of escaping from the camp would find it very hard indeed.

～

We remained at the camp for eighteen months, and no one had been released including those who had held the rank of private second class. One morning, as usual, we stood in line for breakfast. The mess hall had a bamboo roof covering a large piece of land, with planks set up as tables. Looking toward the camp gate, I saw a convoy of about ten covered trucks. No one knew why they were there.

After breakfast, we each grabbed our bag and slung it over our shoulders, as we did every day. We had sewn the bags ourselves, using pieces of old fabric, each fashioning our own style. In the bag, we kept a washcloth, a bar of soap, and a pair of briefs, so that we could go to the stream to bathe before returning to the camp. We were not that different from a gang of beggars in a kung-fu novel by Kim Dung (Louis Cha).

Unlike in our normal routine, on this day a security guard read off a list of names of those who would be transferred to a new camp, and my name was among them. Of the 120 people whose names were read, most were majors, lieutenant colonels, captains, colonels, and those who had belonged to the intelligence agencies and special police. We stood in line to board the trucks. The men who remained continued as they normally did and went out to the fields.

Again, the VC shackled us together, and we climbed into the trucks. The convoy departed, and nobody knew where it would be going. At noon, it stopped at the foot of a mountain for us to get out. They allowed each of us to eat a loaf of bread and use the toilet. Then we reboarded, and the convoy hit the road again. At night, it stopped at a prison camp in Đà Nẵng. We ate and rested there overnight, and early the next morning, we continued our journey. We were not told where we were going. We only knew to obey the order, climb onto the truck, and climb down, all while our hands were still cuffed together. Then the convoy drove over the Hiền Lương Bridge, which spanned the Bến Hải River and the 17th parallel dividing North from South Vietnam.

Finally, the trucks stopped. The VC leader told us to get out of the trucks and gather at the side of the road: "This land belongs to the socialist North. You will rest here, and after that, you will continue your journey. You have to go North, because the Party is concerned about you. You have committed crimes against the people, and we are afraid that the people will take revenge on you. Before releasing you, the Party also has to educate the people, so that their hatred for you will dissipate. There will be better and more favorable conditions for you to learn in the North. You need to understand this in order to be reeducated."

Truly, I didn't understand this line of reasoning or their false language. They called imprisoning us "protecting" us. We had been in only two camps, and at each one, we had heard the same rationales. These security guards had all been produced from the same mold. Yet in the final analysis, however paradoxical the situation was, we couldn't respond. If the VC called a right foot a left foot, we would still have to accept it. The nonsensical could become sensible; the unbelievable could become the truth.

When we were done eating, we returned to the trucks and the journey. This time we were no longer handcuffed, because we were in the North. The VC lifted the canvas that covered the truck, and this improved the stifling atmosphere considerably. We could admire the scenery outside and see the desolate scenes along both sides of the road. Along the mountainside, we saw rows of sweet potato and cassava fields, but we didn't detect any houses or streets. We saw almost no passersby and no traffic. The Northern people had been trained to be informers whenever they spotted a stranger in their neighborhood. The VC were no longer afraid of our trying to slip away. North of the 17th parallel, we would not be able to escape the communist web.

We were transported to a camp in the Tân Kỳ District of Nghệ An Province, the birthplace of Hồ Chí Minh, the founder of Vietnamese communism. The camp lay deep in a jungle valley about thirty kilometers from the Laotian border, and it was surrounded by high mountains. What protection!

We were taken into the camp. After passing through the opened gates, we reached a dilapidated row of houses. The walls were covered with moss, and inside were two rows of bunk beds made out of wooden planks. At the far end was a small room for the latrine. The VC squeezed all 120 of us into this room. It was crowded, with only a few dim lightbulbs and an overpowering stench. They provided each of us with a straw mat, but we had much less space than in the last camp. Here the mats overlapped, so each man no longer even had a sleeping mat to himself. At the Xuân Phước camp in Tuy Hòa, we had believed that we were in a reeducation camp, but at this camp in Nghệ Tĩnh, it was clear we were in a prison camp. The VC still used the word "reeducation" and prison interchangeably, but this was essentially a prison. The term "reeducation" was only aimed at deceiving people who were too naïve to understand the manipulation of the VC. The word "revolution" was used instead of the word "communism," "reeducation" was used instead of imprisonment, and forced labor was called "glorious labor." The communists used all kinds of euphemisms in order to sound gentler and more generous. We got used to the VC's words, but in the end, we understood their true meaning.

Our trials were only just beginning. Again, the communists gathered us all together in a group and promised that if we studied hard and made progress, we would be released. But they never defined "progress," which meant that there would never be any progress.

Sometimes, the VC released a few people, in order to create trust and encourage some prisoners to feel hope. Most of the men the communists released had relatives who worked for the Revolution.

The communist parrots took turns lecturing us. Just as at the Xuân Phước camp, we learned the camp regulations on the first day, followed by lessons about history, and then, lessons about studying and manual labor. In other words, our daily lives followed a prisoner's regimen. Each day there was forced labor, and our three meals consisted of sweet potatoes in the morning, sweet potatoes at noon, and sweet potatoes in the evening, with only cassava or the hard corn usually fed to cattle for variation. Even the sweet potatoes were rationed out in small amounts, and we never had more than two hundred grams per meal. After a while, we were physically weakened to the point that the surplus fat on our bodies had been completely depleted. We were allowed to eat only enough to survive, except for the days of Tết, when the VC granted us some rice with a few pieces of braised meat and a small bowl of vegetable soup. As for clothing, each year the communists provided us with one outfit made with rough fabric from the North. If you wore this uniform out to the field for a few days, it would soon be tattered because of so much manual labor. Our only relief was that the VC allowed us to wash in the stream.

Our life dragged on from one month to the next, from one year to another. Time kept flowing, but our lives didn't change. Each month we were allowed to write one letter home, and every three months, our relatives were allowed to visit us and bring some supplies. But most of our families were so poor that they couldn't send us any additional food. How could they, when they themselves were hungry?

The population was starving. When we went without rice and had only corn and sweet potatoes, the VC explained that this type of hardship could be found everywhere. They blamed it all on the American enemy and the war that had destroyed the country. They said that Northerners had suffered hardships that were similar, if not worse. The VC told us that during the war each grain of rice was broken into four equal parts: one part to support the army fighting for the fatherland, one part for the liberation forces in the South, one part for the people in the North, and one part for our fraternal countries, Laos and Cambodia. This is why we didn't have any rice. In general, this was the way the VC explained things to us.

After more than two years of imprisonment and this starvation diet, we became thoroughly exhausted and emaciated. Still, every day we had to carry our hoes into the fields to perform hard labor. In the winter, it was even more brutal, and when it rained, we had only a simple piece of nylon fabric to cover our shoulders. At night, the fabric became our blanket, covering us up and providing us with some warmth. Regardless of the weather, we were never allowed to rest.

Starving people was a powerful strategy. We thought only about food. We had no energy to think about anything else, let alone protesting. Some people lost their sense of morality and informed on other camp members in order to survive. Their willpower to resist was gradually extinguished. In fact, the communists exploited this as a kind of weapon, not just against us prisoners but also against their own population.

After having lived for thirty years under the communists, Northerners had to put up with hardships and food rations no matter how hard they worked. There was never any surplus. Even the guards were not very different from us. For example, when we had two sweet potatoes for a meal, they could have five to seven potatoes. They had more food than we did, but they still only had sweet potatoes. They also didn't have any meat on a regular basis, only approximately a kilo per month for their whole family. Other than the ruling elite, the population was victimized by the regime.

The communists had molded the military and the security personnel into powerful tools, and these soldiers only knew how to obey decrees from on high. With their short-sighted, narrow-minded thinking, they could consider only the Party, and they had no knowledge of the outside world. They couldn't differentiate between the good and the bad or between right and wrong. They only knew how to have complete faith in the Party. The Party was absolute in everything. After we had spent so many months with these security guards, I came to the realization that they deserved to be pitied more than hated. Their work was also a kind of imprisonment. The only difference was that they could carry guns and go back and forth between the inside and outside of the camp—that's all. Their families were also desperately poor, and they had to sweat for their food.

Some days we traveled quite a distance from the camp. We had to cut the elephant grass at the edge of the jungle or cut the bamboo up in the mountains. We went through the nearby villages, and we could see the people's desolation.

I recalled spending my childhood in this same Northern countryside. Over forty years later, things seemed to have gotten worse. I could imagine how the wealth in the South would be lost, and the people in the South would become like the people in the North. The Northerners couldn't see the dangers, because communism had been instilled in them from such a young age. They had never witnessed or experienced anything other than what the communists had said. The communist cadres usually said that the American imperialists had taken our people back to the Stone Age. But what about them? Why couldn't they see that it was communism that had taken the people back to the Stone Age? The longer we were "reeducated" in the camps, the more we could see the communists' exploitation and treachery. They might have cursed American imperialism, but what they were doing was far worse.

CHAPTER SIXTEEN

Winds of Political Change

At the beginning of 1979, communist China attacked Vietnam. All the reeducation camps close to the Chinese border were moved down to the southern part of North Vietnam. Most of the prisoners in these camps were RVN officers who had worked directly for the Saigon regime. These camps had been managed by the communist army. Now, the military handed the reeducation internees over to the police, because the army had to fight against China in the North and the soldiers of Pol Pot in Cambodia. Therefore, a large number of the prison camps in Lào Cai, Yên Bái, and Hoàng Liên Sơn were relocated and combined with the camp where I was staying.

It had been several years since I had returned to Vietnam, and I finally had the opportunity to speak with my fellow warriors who had been trapped in Vietnam. Through everyday conversations with them, I understood communism more clearly. These friends of mine had witnessed every event since the first day the communists took over the South. They had been deceived by the communists. The communists had told them that in order to receive clemency, they needed to identify themselves. After they had reported to the communists, the VC had encouraged them to pay a sum of money to go and study and promised them that they would be reunited with their families in a few days. Instead, the communists had taken them to the Chinese border, where they had been imprisoned until now.

I had begun to realize that the communists had spared us the death penalty but had instead imposed on us the penalty of living. The communists didn't allow us to die easily. As in many Northern camps, the prisoners in this camp suffered from starvation. While performing labor in the jungle, they would eat wild fruit wherever they saw it, but when they returned to the camp, they fell severely ill, and, in the absence of any medical treatment, they would die. There were days when dozens of people died at the same time. If they had died right after the communist victory, at least they would have died quickly and easily. All of us understood the policy of concentration and reeducation; it was reeducation until we died. We had no hope that one day they would release us. We could only believe in fate, in a miracle, that would allow us to return. Without the war with China, one by one we would have been transferred to the border camps just like the other high-ranking RVN officers. They wouldn't let anyone stay in the same camp for long, and they constantly moved us from one prison to the next.

Prisoners who still had a nation had hope. They would enjoy the standards for prisoners of war according to the Geneva Accords, and, at the end of the war, an exchange of prisoners of war would take place. We were entirely different: we were stateless and thus had no hope at all. The only road to take was to resign ourselves to fate. We maintained our faith in heaven, in the Supreme Being, but often when we turned to heaven, we received no reply.

Time passed, one year after another, and we became accustomed to life in the camp. We lived in a strange world, like insects, like birds, like wild animals. We lived without being allowed to distinguish between right and wrong. Our clothes were mere tatters patched up, and we toiled in the cold under the barrel of AK-47s. Even when I was in a deep sleep, I had nightmares. Horrendous dreams. When I woke, I was drenched with sweat. But when I was wide awake and opened my eyes, I looked straight at my current life and saw the spectacle around me. It was even more horrendous than my nightmares. It was the pure truth. I looked at the dirty mosquito nets, strung up one after another, and I smelled the stench that we had to take in year after year. It had become so familiar that it didn't register anymore. An oil lamp cast its weak light at the end of the room, and I could see those people who had been powerful in their own region, now lying in rows, sleeping deeply after days of forced labor. We were all living in a bizarre world, surreal, unlike anywhere else on this planet.

I usually thought that human beings, with all their willpower, could overcome anything. I was not afraid to face reality, but I was like everyone else. We had been able to adjust to this macabre life. Occasionally, I had the time to think about my wife and children, and I felt a pain in my heart. My wife and children had committed no crime, but now they also had a hard life in this communist world. How could my wife and children find the will to withstand all the suffering? I did not want them to know hunger. I only wanted them to know peace and calmly wait for me. I prayed to the Supreme Being. I asked Jesus Christ to put my wife's burden on my shoulders. Even though my shoulders were small, I still had enough strength to carry more. On the days that I was mistreated physically, I felt as if my prayers had been answered. I worked harder without feeling tired, and occasionally I would feel content.

Yes, it was just like that. I had never known manual labor before, but now each day, I carried water buckets on my shoulders for the vegetables. I had to walk down a hill to a pond and then climb back up to the gardens to water the vegetables.

I did it hundreds of times a day. Only with my faith in the Supreme Being could I overcome these hardships. I saw this miracle clearly. With my faith, I believed that humans could not harm me. The communists could not harm me. Only the Supreme Being could do that to me. But how could the Supreme Being harm people? The Supreme Being only challenged me. Jesus Christ saved the hardships for me, so that I could overcome them. If the battle is hard, then the victory will be glorious.

While I was in the camp, I made friends with many people who had been my superiors in South Vietnam and who had more experience living in the communist prisons. These people usually sat down and analyzed current events. The communists could not survive, and in the end, only the truth could exist forever. They believed that we should wait calmly, what had to happen would happen. I was also fortunate enough to meet a priest, Father Lan. This man lived very tranquilly, and imprisonment meant nothing to him. Wherever there were Christian disciples, there he would be. He was a young priest full of forgiveness and compassion, and he never showed fear, even when he witnessed barbarous acts in the camp. He regularly stayed by my side and explained the trials that Jesus Christ had prepared for human beings. Father Lan strengthened my faith and helped me spiritually. Whenever he received supplies from home, he shared his food and cigarettes with those of us who were too poor and received no supplies. His generosity made me admire him.

I witnessed six Tết in prison. The Vietnamese New Year was an occasion for the security guards to take a break. I had the impression that these sacred days were held solely for the security personnel who ran the camp; they were no longer for us. Nevertheless, we could relax and avoid a few days of forced labor during the New Year holiday. It gave us time to store up our strength as much as we could. During the days of Tết, we were permitted to eat rice, rice cakes, some braised meat, and candy. Well, it was not exactly candy, and it could even be said that it was the dirtiest candy in the world, but when I ate it, I had the impression that I had never eaten any candy this sweet in my whole life.

One day followed the next, and the months and the years went by. There was still no sign, no news to indicate that we would be released. Every year during communist celebrations, the VC released a few people, but those who were released all had special relationships with high-ranking communists. Sometimes we received bits of news from the BBC and Voice of America that our relatives secretly smuggled into the camp. There was news about the United States, the United Nations, and groups fighting for human rights. These snippets were passed from one man to another and often changed in the telling. We felt hopeful when we listened, but whether all these rumors would prove true was another thing.

Everything was beyond our control. Sometimes three or four of us would sit down, drink some hot tea, smoke, and discuss the news to pass the time and alleviate our depression and despair. Those were the days when some of us received letters from home, often containing something nutritious for our health and our souls. That was all that we could hope for. After our manual labor, exhaustion would overcome us, and we would fling ourselves into a deep sleep, and no one had the strength or the alertness to think anymore.

Whenever a prisoner's relative visited the camp, the cadre would call out that prisoner's name and then that person could stay behind and not work that day. That was our only wish. Every morning, everyone anxiously waited for any names to be called. We looked forward to getting any extra food to boost our health, a break from our labor, and the opportunity to hear news about our family and current events.

Finally, one morning my name was called. I was elated. By this point I had been in prison, separated from my wife and family, for over six years. Many of my fellow prisoners had had visits from their relatives, but this would be my first time. Throughout my journey, my goal had always been focused on seeing my wife and children again. My wish had been granted.

When I saw my wife and my children, they were still in fairly good health and that made me happy, but there had been some decline. There was a long table, at which I sat opposite my wife. A security guard was present as well, and his job was to spy on our conversation. We sat looking at each other more than we talked, only understanding each other through our eyes, through our awkward smiles. Tears streamed down our faces, and our hearts tightened. I asked, "How are you and our children?"

My wife replied, "We are fine. How are you?"

I responded with a question, "How is life going?"

"Very tough," my wife answered, beginning to reveal more information. "Large meals alternate with tiny meals. Some of our furniture was taken the day you left, and I have been selling the rest gradually in order to buy food. The children are still going to school. Are you fine?"

"Of course, I'm weaker, but we have become accustomed to our current life. Please rest assured that you don't have to worry about me. The most important thing is to stay calm. You should try to take care of yourself and the children. I will be back someday. Then we will make plans. Just as rivers have bends, people have their ups and downs. Please, don't worry and don't be sad. I am used to hardship. I know hunger, and I can stand it, but I don't want to see you and our children go hungry. Visiting me this once is enough. I know it is in a remote place, and you have very little money. I don't want to see you and our children suffer anymore because of me. Since sending me extra food means that the children will have less, please don't worry about sending me extra supplies. Just take care of yourself and the family."

I was able to make only some casual conversation, and then visiting hours were over, and I had to return to the camp. It was such a hardship for our wives and children to come and visit us. We were able to meet each other for just an hour, and our conversation was controlled. We couldn't say what we wanted to say.

Back in the camp, I carried two bags of supplies that my wife had given me. My heart was heavy. Even though it was good for me, I knew that it meant less food for my wife and children. It was so painful. Loathing flooded over me. Without the communists, my life would never have come to this. Before, my life had been peaceful and filled with happiness. I had enjoyed a roomy house and a beautiful wife and well-behaved children. Everything had been turned upside down. I no longer had the ability to do anything useful for my family, and, worse yet, I made my wife and children suffer more, because they had to save some of their meager food to share with me.

I wish I had not returned. By now, I would have established a new career in America and had the ability to send money home to help my wife and children. The communists had begun to allow relatives living overseas, including America, to send money and supplies back to their families in Vietnam. By the time I learned about this, it was already too late. When I made up my mind to return, I had never expected that such a thing could happen. I had drawn on my earlier experience from 1954. Between 1954 and 1975, families in North Vietnam and families in South Vietnam had no contact. Yet this history did not repeat itself a second time. That is fate. How can humans escape their fate?

At the beginning of 1981, we moved to a new camp in the South. The trucks took us to a train station in Nghệ Tĩnh. Our train had many cars, and it carried thousands of prisoners from many camps, including Nam Hà Camp, Camp Number 6 in Nghệ Tĩnh, and Camp Number 3 in Tân Kỳ, where I had been held. This unusual camp transfer was unexpected. No one knew the reason. We only knew that we were moving to a camp in the South, and this made everyone happy. Normally, the communists took us far away from our families, the farther the better for them. This time, they were doing the opposite, but they must have had a reason.

A rumor circulated that after they moved us to the South, they would release us in waves. We had a long discussion, and we analyzed the issue. I had endured the blackest days of my life. There had to be a day when it would all go away. Life had to change someday. It would make no sense for it to be like this forever.

When the train arrived in Quy Nhơn, the cars split. A few cars went southward to camps Z30C and Z30D, and the other cars went up to a higher plateau and Camp Gia Trung. I was taken to Camp Gia Trung. This camp was built on a hillside, and it looked decent and clean. The houses had tiled roofs, and we could see that the camp was bigger and more beautiful than the residential houses in the region. Six years earlier, reeducation prisoners had built their own prison, which imprisoned them inside. Even though Camp Gia Trung was located in the South, all the guards, soldiers, and officers were from the North.

It was a notorious camp run by evil security personnel, trained in the North, whose hearts were filled with hatred. The security guards just wanted to beat up any prisoner they saw. One slip-up from us, and they would beat us up. They would even beat us for standing in lines that were not straight enough. One prisoner was looking up at the sky by a fence, and a cadre saw him and thought he was planning on contacting former RVN officers, even though the fence was right next to his barracks. The cadre fished out his key ring and beat him with it, causing gashes and bleeding from his head. This man was taken aback, not understanding why he was being assaulted. He just hugged his bleeding head, returned to his room, and asked us to help him bandage up the gashes. The communists beat us in order to terrorize us and to teach us the meaning of fear.

The communists also made use of the common civilian prisoners, whom they trained to rule over the political prisoners. These civilian prisoners had also been RVN soldiers, but they were imprisoned because of ordinary crimes, such as burglaries, robberies, and homicides. These men mercilessly beat up the political prisoners who had formerly been their superior officers. They became the VC cadres' minions, and all for some little personal perks: they could enjoy big meals, they could walk freely inside the camp, and they didn't have to hold a hoe. Also, whenever our families brought us extra provisions, our packages were searched by these petty collaborators. They paid close attention to all the delicious and precious food items we received, and they would get "donations" from us, which they then offered to the VC guards. The cadres always talked about revolutionary ethics, but they committed robberies without ever dirtying their hands. In order to survive and be left alone, we had to give in to them and hand over the valuable food we received from our families.

Terrorizing us, beating us up, coercing us—these were the sharp weapons the prison guards used to maintain iron discipline in the camp. No one dared to do anything except follow the rules. The atmosphere was suffocating. We couldn't make a move without their observing it. Their spy network spread over the whole camp.

We could be very feeble or very sick, but as long as we could still eat and talk, we had to carry our hoes out to the fields to perform labor. No one dared to report an illness, because if you were sick, you had to meet with the security personnel and answer their questions, and this could make you sicker. Asking to take a day off was not a simple matter at all.

~

Terrorizing us, trampling upon us, and starving us—none of this caused us to feel discouraged. We had been RVN soldiers, and we could put up with all kinds of hardships and risks. We had enough courage to overcome everything. We still believed in a brighter tomorrow. These dark days could not go on forever. We kept ourselves informed of international events and were able to see that communism would collapse sooner or later. On that day, we would be released.

During this time, our relatives were able to visit us and bring provisions more frequently. They also brought more optimistic news with them. They acquired information from the BBC and the VOA as well as from our relatives living abroad. We learned that America had been negotiating for our release. The international association for the protection of human rights was also fighting on behalf of political prisoners, not only in Vietnam but elsewhere in the world. The day of our release couldn't be far away. It would definitely happen. I was even more reassured when I learned that my family had been receiving supplies from our relatives in America and Australia. I no longer feared that my wife and our children would starve.

It became easier to breathe in the camp. We had found our faith, and although we had to labor and couldn't show our opposition, we were happier. Most of us had been receiving supplies from family members, and then these individuals would share with those who went without. Starvation no longer ran rampant. We prisoners even shared exotic foods and foreign cigarettes with the security guards. They had learned to appreciate these tidbits, and so they became closer to the prisoners and terrorized us less. Their initial hatred began to decrease, and in time, they became partially aware of their responsibilities toward us and recognized the nonsense of all the tasks that they were carrying out.

We were also able to receive news from the outside world. When our relatives visited us, we found out about fresh developments. Positive news buoyed us, but sad news about our families came frequently as well. The most painful thing in the life of a reeducation prisoner was that we knew the communists trampled on the dignity of our relatives. These communist cadres had tried to infiltrate each reeducation prisoner's family in order to find a way to destroy it. They succeeded in breaking up many marriages, because many of the prisoners' wives could not think clearly enough and fell into their traps. This phenomenon was like a catastrophic hurricane sweeping away the foundation of every family.

Vietnamese women had lost everything by this point. When their husbands went to the reeducation camps, they had to take care of the small children all by themselves. With their property going up in smoke, they alone had to do their own job and their husband's job under the blackest circumstances. They had to deal with treacherous communist cadres who spied on them night and day in order to sabotage their families. Most of the women proved to be courageous and defended their families even in the face of sacrifice. However, sometimes, they lacked willpower. Because of women's weaker nature, they could be gullible and not have enough strength to deal with reality. They lost hope that their husbands would be released one day.

〜

Our relatives increasingly brought more optimistic news with them. We learned that General John W. Vessey Jr. (ret.), President Ronald Reagan's special envoy, frequently went to Hanoi to negotiate with the government about the remaining American soldiers missing in action (MIAs). At the same time, he advocated for the release of all RVN political prisoners. This was accurate news. We were full of faith. Sooner or later, international pressure would force the communists to release all political prisoners.

The world situation had also shifted. The Soviet Union had shown signs of changing. The Vietnamese communists were no longer pawns controlled by the Soviet Union to further their global ambitions. Moreover, Red China had become an enemy of the Vietnamese communists. They were no longer two brotherly nations.

After over forty years, the Vietnamese communists had taken the country back to the Stone Age. While they claimed that they had made the country richer and more beautiful, in reality, they had done the opposite. The country fell deeper and deeper into poverty and misery. Wherever the communists went, they only caused destruction. There were no new buildings or construction. The people in the countryside still had to carry a hoe on their shoulders and walk with a plow behind a water buffalo. City dwellers lived in darkness. The majority of them were jobless, and even if they had a job, they could still afford only two meals a day.

Life lacked conveniences from running water to lightbulbs. The entire country was plunged into grinding poverty, and the communist government didn't have a plan to improve people's lives.

Social order was turned upside down. The country had more prisons than schools. Only the People's Army and the People's Security Personnel were powerful. They could put down any protest and maintain the privileges enjoyed by the Communist Party members. The communists had instituted one-party rule, and they monopolized patriotism. Law meant the law of the strong. The more ignorant the people were and the poorer they were, the easier it was for the communists to rule over them. Young people had no future. College graduates who didn't come from Communist Party members' families found it hard to find a place in society.

People all over the country wanted to abandon their homeland and escape to anywhere around the world where they could find freedom, employment, and a peaceful life free of hunger. From the South to the North, everywhere people were organizing to cross the border to escape communism. It seemed understandable for Southerners to flee, but after decades under communist rule, even Northerners began to understand the true face of communism, and they also began to flee the country. The Vietnamese people carried a profound love for their homeland, but in this era, they fled as never before in their history.

On Sunday, we usually had the day off. We would gather together, share our extra food, such as Chinese sausage, dried shrimp, cabbage, and instant noodles, and enjoy a meal among friends. It was frugal, but it seemed more precious than all the luxurious meals we had ever tasted before. The atmosphere in the camp was more open, and so camp members had more opportunities to exchange their innermost thoughts with one another and discuss current events over tea and cigarettes.

One Sunday, we were just chatting together when a cadre came in and announced that we had to get ready to be transferred to a new camp. This was the fifth time in my prison life that I would be transferred. For some men, it was their tenth time. We had become accustomed to it; life in any prison camp was pretty much the same. We learned that we would be transferred to Camp Hàm Tân, a camp in the South very close to Saigon. We were elated. All of us would be closer to our families, and it would be more convenient for our relatives to visit us and bring food every month.

The convoy of covered trucks appeared on the camp grounds. All of us were ready. We looked no different from a gang of beggars. The longer we stayed in prison, the more patched-up our bags became. We climbed onto the trucks in pairs, sharing handcuffs one more time. They were the same covered trucks and the same handcuffs as before, but this time we felt happy. This transfer was entirely different from our transfers to the North.

Everyone had started to realize that if the communists had spared us the death sentence, they had given us life sentences and forced us to witness our families living in abject poverty. We had listened to their nonsensical logic without the right to refute it. We had suffered so much, we had become animals. We had tasted communism and lost everything. However, we still survived so that one day we might witness a new chapter in Vietnam's history, and this raised our spirits. Hanoi was stuck in the mire, abandoned by its masters, even becoming an enemy of China. Finally, Hanoi was pleading with its putative archenemy—the American imperialists—to come to its rescue. It was obvious that only the American imperialists could help it get out of its quagmire.

When evening came, the convoy stopped in a new camp. There was nothing worth observing because one camp looked just like another. Each camp was surrounded by a solid wall with a barbed wire fence on the outside. In addition, People's Security Guards wearing yellow uniforms would act as yet another, more secure fence on the inside.

Camp Hàm Tân was supervised by Major Nguyễn Văn Nhu. He was famous for torturing and tormenting prisoners and for exploiting prison labor to make the camp bigger and more beautiful. At this camp we had to labor seven days a week, rain or shine. Sometimes we even had to work at night. He went beyond the Party's stated goals, and he wanted to achieve even more to impress his superiors. Whenever he wanted men, a team of prisoners had to be ready with their hoes right away. Iron discipline was always applied. There was only one way to survive: labor enthusiastically. No one could express any opposition because the guards were always ready to use force to coerce us. We erected more buildings in the camp, and the communists exploited our labor.

Almost all camp members received adequate supplies from their relatives by this point, therefore our health had improved. We also gossiped that the time had come for the communists to release all of us. That explained why they were trying to take advantage of our labor during the last days of our imprisonment. After we were released, they would have no one else to work for them. Spending over twelve years in communist prisons, we had been living in a separate world, the most horrendous world on this planet.

We had been able to survive until now, and with this knowledge, we continued to live with hope.

~

We hadn't been in this new camp for more than a week when we heard the news that General Vessey was in Hanoi. During this trip, not only did he demand that Hanoi release all political prisoners but, after their release, he wanted the Vietnamese government to allow the former army officers to be sponsored and resettled in the United States. He announced a new program created by the U.S. government, later known as the Humanitarian Operation (HO) program. Newspapers in Hanoi printed this news, but they protested the American demands, claiming that they violated the principles of sovereignty and interfered in the internal affairs of Vietnam. The fact that the communists opposed Vessey's proposal gave us more faith. We had learned from experience that if something was untrue, the communists would say it was true. Black was white, and white was black. We kept hearing positive news, and we were so excited. It was only a matter of time. We began to see light at the end of the tunnel.

I had spent twelve Tết in prison. My body and my spirit were exhausted. I no longer dared to think about the future. I was over the age of fifty; even though I was not yet old, I was no longer young. In addition, my life force had been depleted. It would be difficult to start my life afresh. However, news about being able to go to the United States strengthened my faith. I still had three small children. I had a responsibility to work for their future. The United States was not unknown to me. If we went to the United States, I would be able to help my children during the first stages of resettlement in a new land. Laboring hard for a while longer was no longer so burdensome, even though every day in prison meant one more day for the communists to torture me. I had coped with everything and had survived for over twelve years, so a few more would not mean much to me.

CHAPTER SEVENTEEN

The Day I Left Prison

It was February 13, 1988, and labor teams lined up in the camp just as on any other day. But on this day, instead of the usual routine in which the cadre read out the name of each team, the camp chief came out into the yard with his entourage. He had a long list in his hand. Seeing this unusual sight, the camp members began to whisper to one another, "It's time. It's time"; but we were still only guessing. No one knew what was going to occur, yet everybody hoped that it was good news. The camp chief stood in front of everyone and announced that we would be released from the camp that very day.

"For many years, we have supervised you, reeducated you, and led you through the training process," he began. "We have noticed your progress, and therefore we have proposed your release. Our supervisors have approved. All of you have witnessed the Revolution's clemency and generosity. We have reeducated you, so you can become good, honest citizens and rebuild the fatherland."

Once again, we waited in excitement. During earlier releases, the lists had been short, only three or five people at most. In those cases, no one could hope to hear his name read aloud, but this time, it was different. The camp chief was holding a long list.

More than five hundred political prisoners were held in this camp, and almost all of us were released that day. Only a few dozen were left behind, and they had generally been intelligence officers or special police officers, classified by the communists as criminals or as having blood debts. In fact, the VC released thousands of people that day from Camp Nam Hà, Camp Vĩnh Phú, and other camps as well. Pressure from the outside had finally stopped the Vietnamese communists' policy of revenge. Obviously, the United States had intervened.

The cadre read each name out loud. Before him were the somber faces of those who had suffered thirteen years of imprisonment. Upon hearing their names read aloud, these men stood up gravely and then silently returned to their rooms, packed up their belongings, and handed over their remaining food and provisions to those unlucky camp members who stayed behind.

I waited calmly, not knowing whether my name would be called. After they read over two hundred names, they called mine. Like everyone else, I stood up in a daze, silently, stepping out of line, and going back to my room. Staring at my bag of belongings, I contemplated my fate. All I owned was a tattered bag, which I had patched up myself using nylon thread. This bag had been my companion throughout the previous thirteen years. Inside were some ragged work clothes. I had only one set of clothing that was not torn, and I wore it when my relatives came to visit. I put it on. Nothing of any value remained for me to hold on to. Not even a *đồng* to buy food with. A few camp members shared their spare change with me, so I could buy some food and cigarettes on the way home.

We had been predicting our release for some time, and we weren't really surprised by the news. Even so, no scene could have been brighter, more brilliant, or more magnificent than the scene of our being released from prison. Yet, apart from that, we felt quite nervous. We did not know how we would deal with reality when we got back to our old homes. Some former camp members who had been released earlier had written to us and confided that they found that they were nostalgic for the days when they had lived with everyone in the camp. Even though they had suffered deprivations and lived in filth, these men felt that people had loved and protected one another in the camp. They had experienced camaraderie. After they returned to their families, they had felt lonely and lost, as if there was a deep chasm between them and their loved ones. They spoke about how those of us who had been cast away by the communist regime should have been greeted and consoled by their relatives. Instead, these very relatives had collaborated with the regime and cast them out. These men claimed that if they had continued to live in a prison camp, they would have been happier than they were with their families. It was such a bitter irony. We waited nervously, not knowing what would happen when we returned.

An hour after hearing the release order, we were loaded onto trucks to go back home. Each of us was given a release document to bring with us. Inside the trucks, we were no longer handcuffed, as we had been during all the other camp transfers. Nonetheless, everyone understood that the communists had released us, but they had not yet freed us. Releasing us and freeing us were two different concepts. They released us because they had to. However, they hadn't freed us or forgiven us. The regime was still in place, and they had hundreds of thousands of ways to arrest us again any time they wanted. No law existed to protect human beings who lived under the communists, particularly for former RVN officers. We still had to be cautious over the coming months.

The trucks left the camp and traveled on the national highway in the direction of Saigon. Since we were no longer trapped inside covered trucks, I was able to look outside at the countryside. The scenery looked familiar, but it seemed that the people had vanished. The roads seemed to have become narrower and dirtier, and the lights that had shone brightly on the Biên Hòa Highway before were dark, because most of the bulbs had been taken out of the lamps. Houses on both sides of the street looked dilapidated, and green moss covered their walls. The traffic was sparse, and bicycles were the dominant means of transportation. The sky looked gloomy. Before my eyes was the truth. The communists had ruled over the South for thirteen years already, and I did not see any new construction. Instead, I only saw everything crumbling around me. Even the light poles along the street were gone. Darkness covered the life of the people in the South.

Hồ Chí Minh had said that the communists would build up the country and make it five or ten times more beautiful than before, but I did not see it. Back in 1954, when I first migrated to the South, Saigon had already acquired a new face. Within such a short time, it had become so bright and elegant. The ponds where people had grown water spinach in suburban swamps had been transformed into bustling business districts. Life was fresh and bright, and everyone had access not just to modern conveniences but all the basic necessities. What about now? What had the communists done to improve the life of the people? They had liberated the people, but over those thirteen years, people from all walks of life had all been trying to find a way to escape, to flee the country, with the single purpose of escaping the yoke of communism. Despite the winds and the waves and the rapacious pirates, millions of people had risked their lives on boats made of fragile wooden planks and crossed thousands of leagues on the high seas.

The trucks on the Biên Hòa Highway entered Saigon, weaving along familiar streets and then stopping in front of the Second District police station. We went in to complete the paperwork, and, after that, we were allowed to go home on our own.

Climbing onto a cyclo to return home, I felt excited and nervous. Having been away for so many years, I stood in front of my gate for a long time, looking around at the scenery. The wall surrounding the front yard was covered with moss. Inside the yard, weeds had grown haphazardly; the beautiful and cozy house of old had become cold and desolate. The electric bell on the gate was no longer there. In its place was a chicken wire connected to a bell. My wife and children were still living here. I pulled on the chicken wire, and after a long while, my son came out to open the gate. He gazed at his father, speechless. No one had known that I would be released.

On the same day that I had left the camp, my oldest daughter had gotten on a bus in order to visit me and give me supplies. Our paths had crossed without our being aware of it. But just a few minutes after I arrived at home, my daughter also returned from the camp. Instead of presenting me with some wrapped packages inside the camp, she gave them to me in our own home.

I stepped into the house and hugged my wife and children. I was overwhelmed. There we were: father and mother and children all hugging one another, with our tears streaming down our faces. We were choked up. No one was able to say a thing. The silence and the tears alone expressed the meaning of our reunion. It took us a long while to recover. My wife appeared exhausted. She had been through so much. Even though the sky and the sea had calmed down, she still seemed like someone who was seasick and unable to recover.

My wife had faced so much misery in protecting our old home. When the RVN officers were imprisoned, the communists had forced their wives and children to go to the New Economic Zones. They had confiscated our houses and fields and gardens. The communists had caused all kinds of difficulties and burdens for our relatives, so that they would no longer be able to bear life in Saigon. Many of these women were forced to abandon their houses and go to the New Economic Zones, and the communists took away their property.

My wife, like thousands of other women, had become extraordinary Vietnamese women. With her husband in prison, she had managed to protect our house and our children despite the communists' many treacherous traps. My wife had been a woman who had everything, and then suddenly she lost it all. She had struggled all by herself. But in the end, she was able to bring up our children. Her motherly devotion to our children was like endless water flowing from its source.

On the day we were separated, I had held my children in my arms. Now they were all grown up. I left my youngest daughter when she was only ten months old. I had not been able to witness her take her first steps or speak her first words. Now she was quite a talker, pretty, and cute. She was the mirror image of her mother in her youth.

I had finally achieved my purpose. I silently thanked Jesus. I had been praying for many years from the bottom of my heart and with my supreme faith. Jesus had responded. Even though for many years Jesus had tested me with much hardship and struggle, I had overcome them all. For many years, I thought that I had lost my family. Now, I had returned and could hold in my arms all that I thought I had lost.

After I was released, life went on, with many meaningless days. I was fighting for my place in society, but it was not easy. I had become powerless, a good-for-nothing without a job. I survived these first months thanks to supplies sent to us from our relatives living abroad. My wife's younger siblings lived in America and

Australia, and they had been helping us out regularly. The former army officers without any outside support had to accept lowly jobs and lived hand to mouth. All they could find was menial work, such as patching up bicycle inner tubes or selling lottery tickets on the sidewalk or going back to the countryside to plant potatoes.

Life was difficult. The communists still ruled Vietnam, and they used force to keep us down. If we continued to live in this country, our children would never be able to lift their heads. Their future was covered up with a black curtain.

I had to find a way to leave the country. I began to contact a few people who had been organizing escape plans. They knew about my experience at sea, and therefore they had connected me with some intermediaries in the hope that I could pilot a boat to escape Vietnam. Whenever I wanted to go, they would be ready. But I still wanted to rest for a while. I had just been released from prison, and I had to think it through and do some careful research before I accepted their proposal.

Almost a year after my release, the HO program came into being. This program was established for RVN government officials and army officers who had spent over three years in a reeducation camp. It would permit them to resettle in the United States. The U.S. government sponsored this program as part of an agreement with the communist government of Vietnam. Those who qualified could go to a police station in their district, sign up, and complete the paperwork in order to leave the country legally. And so I gave up the idea of escaping from Vietnam surreptitiously. Instead, I applied for the HO program and waited for the day of our departure to arrive.

Once again, I had to wait. All my life, I had been waiting. In 1975, I had set foot in part of the United States, Guam, but I had to wait for the day I could return to Vietnam. Upon arriving in my own country, I had been imprisoned and spent many years waiting for the day I would be released. Now, after I had been released, I would have to wait for the day I could leave Vietnam. And once I had left Vietnam, I did not know whether I would have to wait for whatever would come next. Living, hoping, waiting. Even after I had achieved my goal, I still felt unsatisfied and had to keep on waiting.

The communists created many obstacles for those of us who wished to leave under the HO program. They had imprisoned us for many years, but that was not enough. They continued to exact their revenge against us, so that if we left Vietnam, we would have to leave empty-handed. The HO application was long and cumbersome. We had to navigate multiple levels of bureaucracy, including the subdistrict public security office and the Municipal Department of Foreign Affairs.

After each stage, we had to know what to do for our file to be passed on quickly. Some people even went to Hanoi to bribe the right officials so that their files would go through faster. The communists paid particular attention to those who had the rank of major up to colonel; they had to turn their houses over to the state before they could board the plane. The communists said their houses had been built out of the blood, sweat, and tears of the people, therefore, if the owners wanted to go, they had to return their houses to the people. The VC's word was law, so no one could argue with it. Before this act of blatant robbery, we had no choice but to carry our loathing within ourselves and leave. As long as the communists stayed in power, everyone would want to leave, even though it meant that they would lose all their property. We would do it with no regrets. My wife and I had worked and saved for years before we were able to buy our house. We had a permit and the proper deeds, but the communists still said that our house belonged to the people. We didn't understand who "the people" were. Where were they from? Where did they live? We saw only the communists.

$\sim$

On December 13, 1991, I left my house to go to Tân Sơn Nhứt Airport. Workers from the Municipal Department of Land and Housing came to my house to confiscate my property. It was a truly shameful act of robbery. The VC employees were so enthusiastic that they arrived a few hours before the scheduled time. They made an inventory of the lightbulbs and the door locks and verified that the house had no damage. They inspected it very carefully before they gave me a receipt to certify that I, the owner of the house, had agreed to transfer the house to the state. Once the paperwork was completed, they provided me with an exit permit. The procedures were so strange that I was certain that they could happen only under a communist government.

I looked back at the house. I couldn't help feeling nostalgic. Just as when I was on Guam, I had had no choice other than to go back to Vietnam. Now, I didn't want to leave my home, but there was no other way. I had lived the most beautiful years of my life in that house. It held so many memories for us. My children were born here, and they had lived many carefree, innocent years at home. It was also in this house that they had witnessed the painful events that had separated us ever since the country had fallen into the hands of the communists.

$\sim$

It was so difficult to leave my beloved home, but after so many years of struggling, we reeducation prisoners were worn out and bitter. The communists had taken away all our skills, all our energy, and all our hope. We finally had some solace in our lives: we were able to resettle in the United States.

We left not for ourselves, but so that our wives and children could look toward the future. After many years in prison camps, we had all become elderly. Our health had declined, and we no longer had the ability to adjust to a society as civilized as that in the United States. By ourselves, we would have to find a way to build a new life. It would not be easy.

The past was filled with sorrow, and the present was laden with bitterness. As for the future, we did not know where it would take us.

Acknowledgments

I thank Kim-Ngan Nguyen and Tan Pham for their invaluable help in arranging our (the translators') first meeting with Mr. Trần Đình Trụ in Texas in 2012. I also thank my sister Mai and her husband, Terry Salmans, for allowing us to meet with Mr. Trụ in their home in Southern California in 2015, thus giving the three of us the priceless opportunity to sit down together one more time to tie up some loose ends and put the finishing touches on the manuscript. Last but not least, I thank my wife, Thu Thi Phuong, for her enthusiastic support for my various book projects and, specifically, for my engagement in the long and arduous process of translating this important memoir into English with Jana.

—*Bac Hoai Tran*

This book is the product of a great deal of time, energy, and support from many people. Among them, I thank Greg Eveline, Edward Ladd, Elisabeth McMahon, Marguerite Nguyen, Marline Otte, Naomi Paik, Allison Truitt, and Mark Van Landingham for their advice and support at various points throughout this project. I also thank the U.S. Army Military History Institute for offering me its General and Mrs. Matthew B. Ridgway Research Grant in support of my earlier work, which led to my research on the Vietnamese repatriates on Guam. I also must note the special interest Lionel Rosenblatt has had in this project for many years, and my gratitude to Harriet McGuire, who put us in touch and made one of her many wonderful small world connections. Thank you.

Finally, I thank Eli Feinstein for his patience, support, and, yes, tolerance of this project over many years. On many late Sunday evenings, he was forced to listen to my long Skype conversations with Bac as we worked on this manuscript for months on end. Thank you for all your love and support, and I promise no more late Sunday-night Skype meetings.

—*Jana K. Lipman*

ABOUT THE AUTHOR

TRẦN ĐÌNH TRỤ is a former naval commander in the South Vietnamese Navy. He has lived in Texas since 1991.

About the Translators

BAC HOAI TRAN is the Vietnamese Language Coordinator of the Southeast Asian Studies Summer Institute (SEASSI) at the University of Wisconsin–Madison and was, for more than twenty years, a lecturer in Vietnamese at the University of California, Berkeley. He is the cotranslator of the collection of short stories titled *The Stars, The Earth, The River* (1997), as well as several other short stories in the anthologies *The Other Side of Heaven* (1995), *Vietnam: A Traveler's Literary Companion* (1996), *Night, Again* (1996), *Virtual Lotus: Modern Fiction of Southeast Asia* (2002), and *Crossing the River* (2003).

JANA K. LIPMAN is an associate professor of history at Tulane University. She currently teaches classes on the U.S. war in Vietnam and U.S. foreign relations. Her book, *Guantánamo: A Working-Class History between Empire and Revolution*, was the Co-Winner of the 2009 Taft Prize in Labor History. She has published articles in *American Quarterly*, the *Journal of Asian American Studies*, the *Journal of Military History*, the *Journal of American Ethnic History*, and *Radical History Review*.

INTERSECTIONS

Asian and Pacific American Transcultural Studies

RUSSELL C. LEONG AND DAVID K. YOO
Series Editors

Bulletproof Buddhists and Other Essays
FRANK CHIN

A Ricepaper Airplane
GARY PAK

New Spiritual Homes: Religion and Asian Americans
DAVID K. YOO, ED.

Words Matter: Conversations with Asian American Writers
KING-KOK CHEUNG, ED.

Music through the Dark: A Tale of Survival in Cambodia
BREE LAFRENIERE

Blues and Greens: A Produce Worker's Journal
ALAN CHONG LAU

Tomorrow's Memories: A Diary, 1924–1928
ANGELES MONRAYO
RIZALINE R. RAYMUNDO, ED.

Fighting Tradition: A Marine's Journey to Justice
CAPTAIN BRUCE I. YAMASHITA, USMCR

The 1.5 Generation: Becoming Korean American in Hawai'i
MARY YU DANICO

This Isn't a Picture I'm Holding: Kuan Yin
KATHY J. PHILLIPS
JOSEPH SINGER, PHOTOGRAPHER

Sparrows, Bedbugs, and Body Shadows: A Memoir
SHELDON LOU

Entrys
PETER BACHO